Ernest Renan

History of the People of Israel

Vol. 4

Ernest Renan

History of the People of Israel
Vol. 4

ISBN/EAN: 9783743347991

Manufactured in Europe, USA, Canada, Australia, Japa

Cover: Foto ©ninafisch / pixelio.de

Manufactured and distributed by brebook publishing software (www.brebook.com)

Ernest Renan

History of the People of Israel

OF THE

PEOPLE OF ISRAEL

FROM THE RULE OF THE PERSIANS TO THAT OF THE GREEKS

BY

ERNEST RENAN

AUTHOR OF THE "LIFE OF JESUS," "THE FUTURE OF SCIENCE," ETC.

BOSTON
ROBERTS BROTHERS
1895

Copyright, 1895,
BY ROBERTS BROTHERS.

University Press:
JOHN WILSON AND SON, CAMBRIDGE, U.S.A.

CONTENTS.

BOOK VII.

JUDEA UNDER PERSIAN RULE.

CHAPTER I.

The Arrival of the Caravans at Jerusalem after the Return from Babylon 1

CHAPTER II.

Re-establishment of Divine Worship at Jerusalem. — New Laws of Ritual 8

CHAPTER III.

Levites. — Nethinim 23

CHAPTER IV.

The End of the House of David. — The Triumph of the High-Priest over the Nasi 30

CHAPTER V.

Levitical Additions to the Torah. — Elaboration of the Rites of Worship 45

CHAPTER VI.
Nehemiah and the Walls of Jerusalem 56

CHAPTER VII.
The Administration of Nehemiah 73

CHAPTER VIII.
Legendary Story of Ezra 84

CHAPTER IX.
The Final Consolidation of the Torah 93

CHAPTER X.
Promulgation of the Law 103

CHAPTER XI.
Bigotry 115

CHAPTER XII.
The Last Gleams of Prophecy 123

CHAPTER XIII.
The Samaritans 130

CHAPTER XIV.
What the Jews borrowed from Persia.— Angelology 136

CHAPTER XV.
The Decadence of Jewish Literature 149

CHAPTER XVI.
The Deep Sleep of Israel 161

BOOK VIII.

THE JEWS UNDER GREEK DOMINION.

CHAPTER I.
ALEXANDER. — ALEXANDRIA 171

CHAPTER II.
THE RULE OF THE PTOLEMIES 182

CHAPTER III.
PROSEUCHÆ. — SYNAGOGUES 190

CHAPTER IV.
THE GREEK TRANSLATION OF THE PENTATEUCH . . 198

CHAPTER V.
LITERATURE OF THE ALEXANDRINE JEWS 208

CHAPTER VI.
COMMENCEMENT OF PROSELYTISM. — PIOUS FRAUDS . 220

CHAPTER VII.
THE RULE OF THE SELEUCIDÆ IN PALESTINE. — FIRST APPEARANCE OF ROME IN THE EAST 229

CHAPTER VIII.
MIDDLE CLASS. — SACERDOTAL NOBILITY 237

CHAPTER IX.
JESUS, SON OF SIRACH 246

CHAPTER X.

THE STRUGGLE FOR HELLENISM IN PALESTINE. — ANTIOCHUS EPIPHANES 259

CHAPTER XI.

THE PERSECUTION OF ANTIOCHUS. — THE ABOMINATION OF DESOLATION 266

CHAPTER XII.

THE EVIDENT NECESSITY OF REWARDS IN A FUTURE LIFE 277

CHAPTER XIII.

THE NATIONAL UPRISING 289

CHAPTER XIV.

THE BOOK OF DANIEL 297

CHAPTER XV.

VICTORIES OF JUDAS MACCABEUS. — THE JEWISH WORSHIP RESTORED 314

CHAPTER XVI.

PRINCELY RULE OF JUDAS MACCABEUS 321

CHAPTER XVII.

THE HELLENIST REACTION. — LIBERTY OF CONSCIENCE . 327

CHAPTER XVIII.

THE ASMONEAN FAMILY: JONATHAN 343

HISTORY OF
THE PEOPLE OF ISRAEL.

BOOK VII.
JUDEA UNDER PERSIAN RULE.

CHAPTER I.

THE ARRIVAL OF THE CARAVANS AT JERUSALEM AFTER THE RETURN FROM BABYLON.

THE numerous caravans which brought Israel back to its ruined acropolis must undoubtedly have reached Jerusalem by way of the north, over the *Via dolorosa* travelled sixty-five years before by the unhappy captives urged forward by the lash of Nebuzaradan. The joy and the grief of these pious emigrants when they beheld the desolated city of their dreams made doubtless one of those impressions on the nation which a people never forgets, more especially when there is no rhetorical narrator to spoil them. Nothing remained of the ancient city but the foundations of its buildings, beside which lay great stones detached from the walls, the Temple, and the palaces.*

* Isaiah lviii. 12; lx. 15.

Half a century is but a short time in which to complete the ruin of buildings formed of strong materials; and there can be little doubt that the chiefs who led the return from Babylon found Jerusalem in the state in which it had been left by the Assyrians. A ruined city never wholly disappears until it is rebuilt, or at least until another city has been built near it. Only the slight structures that had once been private houses had been totally destroyed. The very ruins seem to have been left entirely deserted.* But the country around it was still inhabited. The little towns of Judah and of Benjamin still offered means of subsistence. The emigrants for the most part endeavoured to take up their quarters in the belt surrounding these ruined walls, where, since the murder of Gedaliah, some little order had been established.†

---

* See Isaiah, before quoted.

† The documents relating to the Return from the Captivity are contained in the six first chapters of the book of Ezra. These six first chapters are composed from two documents. The first (A) is of great historical value, extending from chap. ii. 1 to iv. 5, then afterwards from vi. 14 to vi. 22. The other (B) is full of apocryphal passages. It comprises chap. i., then extends from chap. iv. 6 to vi. 13. The writer who compiled (B) had before him the prophecies of Haggai and Zechariah, and has borrowed their chronology. The author of the Memoirs of Nehemiah (chap. vii.) has copied from (A) his list of those who returned from Babylon, with some changes. Again, the passage in Nehemiah, from xii. 1 to xiii. 3, incorporated into that book, repeats the list with some further alterations. The change from Hebrew to Aramaic (iv. 8) and the return to Hebrew (vi. 19) is of no critical importance. Like the Aramaic verse in Jeremiah, and the Aramaic portion of the book of Daniel, it was due to carelessness on the part of the copyist. After the books of Ezra and Nehemiah had been arranged, as we have them now, by the author of the Chronicles, some

The new-comers, it appears, were received with little welcome. The day after their arrival they found themselves surrounded by enemies.* The villagers whose worship Josiah had destroyed had probably relapsed into being Iahvists of the ancient kind, — that is to say, they offered sacrifices on high places, and they had no objection to practising the rites of Moloch, Astarte, and Adonis, whose efficacy everybody else in Syria firmly believed in. The faithful, therefore, whose ideas had been much advanced during the Captivity, found themselves confronted by their old co-religionists, who had made no progress, and must have felt as if they were hardly of the same religion. They succeeded, however, in establishing their ascendency; and soon there rose around Jerusalem a number of Jewish villages. Later, the colony of Ezra experienced the advantage of these settlements. By degrees these successive strata of returning colonists formed strong Jewish centres at Jericho, at Gibeon, at Mizpah, at Zanoah, at Beth-haccerem, at Beth-zur, and at Keilah.† At Tekoa the Jewish community was numerous, and seems to have always entertained some fears

---

copyist after iv. 8 has followed the Targum instead of the original; misled by the word אֲרָמִית, he preferred to insert what he considered the original Aramaic to the Hebrew text (compare Daniel ii. 4). In other words, neither in Jeremiah nor in Ezra nor in Daniel are the changes into Aramaic, and back again to Hebrew, preceded by such marks as would prove a difference of documents. It was mere chance that gave us in these passages the Targum instead of the original.

* Ezra iv. 1. Compare Psalms cxx., cxxi., cxxiv., &c.
† Nehemiah iii.

touching the preponderance of Jerusalem. Southern Judea had been acquired by the Edomites.* The city of Hebron, however, never seems to have been entirely outside the circle of Israel. †

The destitution among the people after their return must have been terrible. They had no houses, and no lands to raise crops upon. The supplies they had brought from Babylon grew less and less every day. Their political situation too, with a Persian *pekah* for their governor, must have been extremely humble. It does not appear that Zerubbabel had any well-defined local jurisdiction. He was simply the head of a religious family, a *millat-pasch*, as such men are still called in the Ottoman Empire. The land was by no means restored to its former owners. The enemies of Israel had taken possession of nearly all of it. There was no trade, no purveying for luxury. Those who had not strong faith must often have envied their brethren who stayed behind in Mesopotamia.

Besides all this, the means of attaining moral and intellectual culture were very deficient. The writings of Haggai and Zechariah (of which we shall presently speak) give us the impression that those who first returned from Babylon brought few books with them. A man without much original talent, fairly well read in the ancient writings of his people, might have composed something less feeble than

---

* Ezekiel xxxv. 10; 1 Esdras iv. 50.
† 1 Maccabees v. 65.

these two scrolls of Haggai and Zechariah, which we may regard as the last sighs of the expiring Hebrew genius. Writings addressed to the multitude, such as these two prophetic books, are rude, rough, and illiterate, while on the other hand the elegiac poems of the time show all the literary skill that distinguished Hebrew poets during the Captivity. Some of the most beautiful of the Psalms seem to belong to this period.*

> When Iahveh turned again the captivity of Zion †
> We were like unto them that dream.
>
> Then was our mouth filled with laughter
> And our tongue with singing.
>
> Then said they among the nations,
> Iahveh hath done great things for them.
>
> Iahveh hath done great things for us,
> Whereof we are glad.
>
> Turn again our captivity, O Iahveh !
> As the streams from the South.
>
> They that sow in tears
> Shall reap in joy.
>
> Though he goeth on his way weeping, bearing forth the seed,
> He shall come again with joy, bringing his sheaves with him.

And again : —

> They that trust in Iahveh are as Mount Zion ; ‡
> They who dwell in Jerusalem stand fast forever. §

---

* For instance, Psalms xxxiii., xcv., xcvi., xcviii., cxxiv., cxxvi., and several others.

† Psalm cxxvi. (The English is from the Revised Version of the Old Testament. — Tr.)

‡ Psalm cxxv.

§ The author says this reading from the ancient versions is preferable; ירשלם being twice repeated.

As the mountains are round about Jerusalem,
So is Iahveh round about his people
From this time forth and forevermore:
For the sceptre of wickedness shall not rest upon the lot of the righteous,
That the righteous put not forth their hands unto iniquity.

Do good, O Iahveh, unto those that be good,
And to them that are upright in their hearts.

But as for such as turn aside unto their crooked ways
Iahveh shall lead them forth with workers of iniquity.
Peace be upon Israel.*

Sometimes Jerusalem and the psalmist relate to each other their anguish, their anxieties, and their sorrows.

JERUSALEM.

I will lift up my eyes unto the mountains;†
From whence shall my help come?
My help cometh from Iahveh,
Which made heaven and earth.

THE CHOIR.

He will not suffer thy foot to be moved;
He that keepeth thee will not slumber.

THE PSALMIST.

Behold, he that keepeth Israel
Shall neither slumber nor sleep.

THE CHOIR.

Iahveh is thy keeper,
Iahveh is thy shade upon thy right hand. ‡

The sun shall not smite thee by day, §
Nor the moon by night.

---

* Words perhaps added for liturgical purposes.
† Psalm cxxi. ‡ Read צילך.
§ With his malign influences.

Iahveh shall keep thee from all evil;
He shall keep thy soul.

Iahveh shall keep thy going out and thy coming in
From this time forth, and forevermore.*

A mighty deed had been accomplished. This wonderful return from captivity, carried out through frightful difficulties, is compared to the exodus and the passage through the Red Sea.

The psalmist saw in it a miracle, a fresh manifestation of the favour of the Almighty towards his people Israel.† The heathen are supposed to be struck with amazement at such a prodigy.‡ A God who exercises such care over his little ones demands in return piety and submission. To renew the rebellions of their fathers in the Wilderness would have been madness. There is no sign now of former daring. Absolute docility and a fervent ritualism § have replaced the bolder, ruder faith of ancient times. The era of piety was about to begin. Jewish piety was to be the origin of piety throughout the world. By piety Israel was to accomplish its marvellous destiny, and without dogma or theology or abstract speculations create the religion of mankind.

* Compare Psalms cxxiii., cxxiv.
† Psalms xcv. to c., cxxvi. Compare Isaiah lii. 14 and what follows; lvii. 2; lxvi. 19 and what follows.
‡ Psalm xxiv. 2, 3.
§ The analogy with the ritualism of the Church of England is striking.

CHAPTER II.

RE-ESTABLISHMENT OF DIVINE WORSHIP AT JERUSALEM. — NEW LAWS OF RITUAL.

This first restoration of the captives to their own land was nevertheless but a feeble enterprise, and we may well doubt, if nothing had followed up the action of Zerubbabel and Joshua, whether Judaism would have had a future. It was like a palm-tree planted in a flower-pot. The seed sown for the future was vigourous, but the soil provided for its development was insufficient. Judaism, such as the Prophets had pictured it, needed the freer air it found in the dispersion. Its national existence was now ended. But what of that? What is under the protection of Iahveh is not a petty kingdom subject to the vicissitudes of human things; it is a mighty work, a principle of life for all mankind. The mission appointed to Israel is that of a religious society. The end of its political life, the destruction of its national framework, far from entailing spiritual ruin upon Israel, will be the means of developing its destiny. While Persia, Greece, and Rome occupy the foreground of the world's history, little Israel, like the white ant of Africa, works its way silently through the structure of ancient society, and will bring the subsoil to the surface. The Prophets and the Law (*Torah*) fulfil their slow task of working as the leaven of coming ages. Above the ruins of the Oriental, Greek, and Roman civilisations spring two mighty trees, Christianity and Islam, each an offshoot of Judaism. For a thousand years at least it is all over with the principle of nationality.

The host that returned to Jerusalem from Babylon under the leadership of Zerubbabel was mainly composed of priests and levites. These men, consecrated to God's service, proposed as their first object the restoration of divine worship. The levites, who "lived by the altar," had an especial interest in the speedy re-establishment of the rites of sacrifice. The rebuilding of the Temple was therefore decided upon from the first. Immediately after the arrival at Jerusalem certain heads of families began to accumulate treasure for this purpose, by making free-will offerings.* They caused, besides, a hundred priestly garments to be made at their own expense; and from that moment the things that most engaged the attention of all Israel were the due performance of public worship and the regulation of its liturgy.

The place where the altar had stood was still visible; perhaps the stones of its base had been scarcely overthrown. Joshua (son of Josedeck) and Zerubbabel caused it again to be set up. Thus this altar

* Ezra iii. 1 and what follows.

bore some analogy to the little altars built in haste out of the remains of heathen temples by the inhabitants of Lebanon at the close of the fourth century, as circumstances favoured them.*

At Jerusalem it soon became possible to restore the system of sacrifices, appointed, as was believed, by Moses, while in addition great changes were made to the ancient ritual. The moment had come to carry out all the liturgical dreams in which priests had indulged themselves since the days of Ezekiel.† A morning and an evening service was established, and sacrifices were offered at each of them. At the new moons and other feasts, especially at the Feast of Tabernacles, the worship was more complicated, and the number of the victims was increased. Besides these public sacrifices, there were those of individuals.‡ The levites and the singers were thus provided for. The money brought by Zerubbabel from Babylonia was freely employed to purchase victims for the daily sacrifices. The people had no bread, but the altar of Iahveh smoked upon the spot that he himself had chosen. The future at least was secure.

A few months after the restoration of the altar the rebuilding of the Temple was begun under the superintendence of Zerubbabel and Joshua, while the task of overseeing the workmen was committed to the levites and their sons. The new Temple no doubt

---

* *Mission de Phénicie*, p. 219 and what follows.

† See vol. iii. p. 365.

‡ Ezra iii. 2 and what follows; Numbers xxix. 13 and what follows; Exodus xxix. 12.

was of the proportions of the old, but it was far inferior in grandeur and magnificence.* The porches, or *liskoth*, were an essential part of the structure, and were rebuilt like the *naos* itself.† The Saitic style must have been the rule in all the details of ornamentation.

Workmen, as in the days of Solomon, had been brought from Tyre and Sidon; their materials came from Tyre by way of Joppa. No doubt the funds needed for these purchases were at first contributed by rich men who had stayed in Babylonia.

The laying the foundation of the sacred edifice was the occasion of pious ceremonies, at which the priests assisted in costume with trumpets, the levites sounding cymbals, and all singing to Jehovah the hymns of praise in which the words "Hallelu-jah," "Praise to Iahveh," were continually repeated. The refrain was, "Praise Iahveh, for he is good;" the people replying in their turn, "For his mercy endureth forever." ‡ In this they believed themselves to be following the example of David,§ to whom they no doubt by this time attributed the many Psalms of the *hallel* which form the last portion of the Psalter, and which have been the model for Christian liturgies throughout the world. The younger generations danced round the walls of the Temple, which

---

* Josephus, *Antiquities*, xv. xi. 1.

† Ezra viii. 29. In Nehemiah viii. 1, the Water Gate is evidently within the limits of the Temple.

‡ Ezra iii. 11; 2 Chronicles v. 13; vii. 3; xx. 1.

§ Ezra iii. 10; 1 Chron. v. 16; 2 Chron. xxiii. 18; xxix. 27.

were beginning to be built, with cries of joy; but those who remembered the old Temple wept, so inferior did this new edifice seem to that which it was intended to replace.

The work of reconstruction, made easier by what remained of the foundations and the great stones of the old Temple, might have been completed in three or four years, but it took twenty. One is tempted to suspect that the ultra-idealists, who held that God has no other temple but the universe, may have opposed the work, alleging that Iahveh had respect only to the piety and contrition of the poor.* Orders and counter-orders from an Oriental central government are like daily bread to officers in charge of its provincial affairs. The worshipper of Iahveh who had not adopted the reforms of Josiah, and above all the inhabitants of Ephraim and of the former kingdom of Israel, raised difficulties, which impeded the work of Zerubbabel and Joshua. If things passed as is related in the document that has come down to us,† we must own that at first the new builders of the Temple seem to have met good treatment from the old Iahvists. They came to Zerubbabel and Joshua and the heads of Jewish families, to explain that they too were worshippers of Iahveh; they asked leave to take part in the construction of the Temple,

---

* Isaiah lxvi. 1-4, — a passage which cannot be by the unknown hand of the author of the second portion of Isaiah. It sometimes happens that a book of the Bible will contain passages for and against the same opinion. Compare Jonah, the 2d Zechariah, &c.

† Document A. See page 2, note.

that there they also might have a right to offer sacrifice.* But Zerubbabel answered them, "Ye have nothing to do with us to build a house for our God."† Iahveh is now the God only of Judah and of Benjamin. The appeal for unity which resounds through the Prophets will be heard no longer. The schism between the two parties in Israel was made perpetual, and Samaritanism in consequence became a separate religion. This was directly contrary to the ideas, or at least the hopes, of Jeremiah, Ezekiel, and their disciples. But we must remember that those who conducted the return from Babylon were for the most part animated by the sacerdotal spirit. It was priests who first hindered the realisation of the unity dreamed of by the Prophets; and their opposition was but natural. The successive purgings Judah had imposed upon itself excluded other Israelites. The ancient Iahveh of the Israelites, and Iahveh as developed by the Prophets, were hardly the same God. Every reform in the Church throughout its history has produced a schism. The straiter the way the closer are the ranks; and the closer the ranks the more are excluded.

Whatever may have been the causes of the antipathy between the ancient worshippers of Iahveh and the new arrivals, this hostility was thenceforward an important factor in the history of Judaism. The

---

* For examples of temples raised by joint assistance, *Corpus inscr. Semit.* vol. i. p. 100 and what follows.

† A similar reply may be found in Nehemiah ii. 20.

opposing party attempted to arrest the reconstruction of the Temple by all sorts of intrigues with the Persian governor and his officials. Zerubbabel, though he had received his authority from the King of Persia, was only a subordinate officer in the army of administration. Events that took place at the centre of the Empire were felt, though feebly, in its remotest provinces. Cyrus, who appears to have been personally favourable to the Jews, died in 529 B. C. The end of the reign of Cambyses saw the beginning of revolutions, which did not end until Darius, son of Hystaspes, was established on the throne. In the second year of the reign of Darius,* 520 B. C., work on the Temple was resumed, still under the authority of Zerubbabel and Joshua. The hostility of the Samaritans for a time was powerless.

These bitter quarrels left their deep trace upon the Psalter. The faithful servant of Iahveh is surrounded by enemies eager to devour him. All stratagems, all falsehoods, are employed to ruin him. He is in the midst of hostile savages who seek his hurt. He is himself a man of peace, but others all around him are for battle.† The contempt of the profane — designated as the mighty, the proud, the hinderers of the work (in contrast to the meekness and humility of true believers) — burns to the heart‡ those who have had much to

---

* Ezra iv. 24; date taken from Haggai i. 1, and from Zechariah i. 1.
† Psalm cxx.   ‡ Psalm cxxiii.

endure. Patience was not the virtue of the ancient Israelites.

> Many a time have they afflicted me from my youth up *
> Now may Israel say.
>
> Many a time have they afflicted me from my youth up:
> But they have not prevailed against me.
>
> The ploughers ploughed upon my back;
> They made long their furrows.
>
> Iahveh is righteous;
> He hath cut asunder the cords of the wicked.
>
> Let them be ashamed and turned backward,
> All they that hate Zion.
>
> Let them be as the grass upon the housetops,
> Which withereth afore it groweth up:
>
> Wherewith the reaper filleth not his hand,
> Nor he that bindeth sheaves his bosom.
>
> Neither do they that go by say, The blessing of Iahveh be upon you;
> We bless you in the name of Iahveh.

Or again: —

> If it had not been Iahveh who was on our side
> Let Israel now say;
>
> If it had not been Iahveh who was on our side
> When men rose up against us:
>
> Then they had swallowed us up alive,
> When their wrath was kindled against us;
>
> Then the waters had overwhelmed us,
> The stream had gone over our soul;
>
> Then the proud waters had gone over our soul.†

---

* Psalm cxxix.

† Aquila, ὡς τὰ ὕδατα οἱ ὑπερήφανοι. Compare ר״מ, and later on, page 120, note.

Blessed be Iahveh
Who hath not given us over a prey to their teeth.

Our soul is escaped as a bird out of the snare of the fowlers;
The snare is broken, and we are escaped.

Our help is in the name of Iahveh
Who made heaven and earth.*

The thing that even more than difficulties of administration seems to have retarded the building of the second Temple † was the extreme poverty of the colonists. Bad harvests and disastrous droughts impoverished the community. Work on the Temple was resumed feebly and slowly. Zerubbabel and Joshua thought they must have recourse to the prophetic spirit, and stirred up one Haggai to influence the people.‡ Prophets were beginning to be dimly discerned as men of the past, — a phenomenon that hereafter might never be seen. Since the death of Jeremiah and Ezekiel — that is, for more than forty years — no man had arisen to assume that post of danger. The great Anonymous Prophet of Babylon desired to remain in obscurity: probably he was as little known to his contemporaries as he is to us. The restoration of the Temple led to a revival of prophecy. The *nebiim* (the prophets) appear to have been held superior to the *cohanim* § (the priests). There were several contemporary prophets whom we might call prophets of the reconstruction of the Temple.‖

---

* Psalm cxxiv.
† Neither Haggai nor Zechariah mentions these difficulties.
‡ Haggai i. 11.
§ Zechariah vii. 5-7. ‖ Zechariah viii. 9.

Four times in the year 520 Haggai lifted up his voice to reprove the colonists for their slackness. Their poverty and all the ills that they endured proceeded, he told them, from their lack of zeal. The people he addressed showed great indulgence in receiving him as one from whose lips they heard the voice of Iahveh. If we read his brief prophecy written sixteen years after the *Surge illuminare* of the great Unknown Prophet, and even perhaps while he was still living, we shall be surprised to observe how literary art had become debased in Jerusalem by the rabbinical subtleties and casuistic distinctions that were then in vogue. The breadth, the resonance, of the ancient poets have been lost by their successors. Theirs is the prose of a second-class journalist, pleading for his party. And yet Haggai stirs our hearts, when, speaking to the few among them who could have seen the former Temple, he owns that the new building must appear to them very poor, but predicts its future splendour. He tells them that the gold which it now lacks shall be brought to it by converted heathen. He says that the glory of this latter house shall be greater than the glory of the former. Does not all gold belong to Iahveh, Lord of Sabaoth? Peace is worth more than gold. Peace is Iahveh's special gift, and in this place he will give peace.

Another prophet who in those days arose in Jerusalem was hardly superior in talent to Haggai, but he had higher political aims in view. He was Zechariah, son of Berechiah, of whose prophecy we possess a short *megilla*;* in which we can perceive the decadence of Jewish taste and of the Jewish language, though his ideas frequently remind us of those of the great Anonymous Prophet.† Zechariah is inferior to Ezekiel, who was himself so inferior to Isaiah and to Isaiah's imitators. He sets his ideas in a framework of symbolic visions. Apocalyptic visions of things that are to come to pass, beginning in Ezekiel, are completed by Zechariah. Unfortunately, his visions often degenerate into enigmas, and several passages are unintelligible,‡ as it was apparently the intention of the writer that they should be.

Zechariah rose to greater heights than Haggai, but we feel that the days of the *nabis*, the ancient seers, are passed. For though in Zechariah's eyes the greatest crime of the people of old was that they had not obeyed the voice of their prophets, and the chief duty of the men whom he addressed was to hearken to the new ones,§ it is clear that the office of an inspired teacher is not of the importance it was once, and will before long give place to a system of permanent prophecy called the Torah. Prophecies

---

* Chapters i.–viii. We have several times explained (vol. ii. pp. 391, 392, and vol. iii. p. 274, note 1) how very ancient writings came to be added to the close of the prophecy of Zechariah, by those who collected and put together the prophetical books.

† Zechariah evidently must have known his prophecies, but attributes them to Isaiah (vii. 7 and what follows).

‡ Zechariah vi. 1–8, shows a strong resemblance to the sibylline oracles.

§ Zechariah i. 1–6.

delivered verbally — and such delivery was the very soul of ancient prophecy — were no longer in fashion. After Ezekiel, the prophet became a writer. Apocalyptic visions were an easy form of fiction in which to convey revelations intended to be read, in which completeness of each composition was a necessity.

The visions of Zechariah all relate to the events passing in his time, — to efforts made to stimulate religious revival; to the rebuilding of the Temple; to aspirations towards a better future; and to the certainty of final triumph. Horsemen clad like Persian light-horsemen (*angares*) have overrun the world; all is tranquil; yet the day of Iahveh's vengeance has not yet arrived. An angel asks when he will have pity upon Judah? The answer is that the angel must have patience.* Another vision is an earnest appeal to the Jews who are still in Babylonia or elsewhere, to come and join the colony at Jerusalem. Iahveh is about to strike the world with terrible blows. The safest place must be Jerusalem.† Iahveh will establish his throne in Zion. Many nations will flock to worship him there, and will become his people.

An event had happened that had aroused these feelings, and had given Zechariah occasion to write one passage as beautiful as anything to be found in the pages of the Anonymous Prophet of Babylon.‡

---

* 1st vision, chap. i. 7-17.   † 3d vision, chap. ii.

‡ Zechariah vii. 1 and what follows. In verse 2, בי-כאל, there is an evident error. I propose: בדבל-שראצר, or כבבל. Be this as it may, the names of the two Jewish envoys are of heathen origin.

In the year 518 the Jews in Babylonia, having heard that the Temple was nearly completed, sent a deputation to do homage to Iahveh. The envoys were greatly comforted by what they saw, and asked the *cohanim* of the Temple and the *nebiim* if it was necessary, now that the restoration was complete, to observe the fasts that had been instituted in memory of the misfortunes of 588, the year of the Captivity. The Temple had been rebuilt after seventy years of desolation : why need they still mourn for its destruction? Zechariah replied by referring to the authority of the Prophets of old. As he considers the second part of Isaiah the work of Isaiah, he quotes its pages as such ;* but not having the text before his eyes he gives the passage with some shaping of his own. There is no more occasion to fast. All that has made way for spiritual religion.

Execute true judgment, and show mercy and peace every man to his brother, and oppress not the widow nor the fatherless, the stranger nor the poor. And let none of you imagine evil against his brother in your hearts.

Like the great Anonymous Prophet, Zechariah has boundless hope in the future of the restored Jerusalem.†

I am jealous for Zion with great jealousy, and I am jealous for her with great fury, saith Iahveh-Sabaoth. I am returned unto Zion, and will dwell in the midst of

---

* Compare Zechariah vii. and Isaiah lviii.
† Zechariah viii. 1 and what follows.

Jerusalem; and Jerusalem shall be called the City of Truth and the Mountain of Iahveh-Sabaoth the Holy Mountain. There shall yet old men and old women dwell in the streets of Jerusalem; every man with his staff in his hand for very age. And the streets of the city shall be full of boys and girls playing in the streets thereof.*

This era of happiness seems about to begin. Iahveh will bring back his people from all corners of the earth. Before the Temple was rebuilt "men received not the reward of their labours, neither did the beasts." There was no safety from their enemies, for Iahveh set men one against another. Henceforth all shall be changed. As Iahveh had set himself to bring evil on his people who of old had angered him, so since his Temple is rebuilt will he turn and do them good.† Judah has now only to observe one law.

Speak ye every man the truth with his neighbour; execute the judgment of peace and truth in your gates, and let none of you imagine evil in his heart against his neighbour, and love no false oath, for these things do I hate, saith Iahveh. There shall come peoples and the inhabitants of many cities, and the inhabitants of one city shall go to another, saying: Let us go speedily to entreat the favour of Iahveh, and to seek Iahveh-Sabaoth; saying, I will go also. Yea, many peoples and strong nations shall come to seek Iahveh-Sabaoth in Jerusalem, and to entreat the favour of Iahveh. Thus saith Iahveh: In those days it shall come to pass that two men shall take hold out of

---

* That is, every one shall live to be old. See vol. iii. p. 397. The plays of the children shall not be interrupted.
† Zechariah viii. 14, 15.

all the languages of the nations of the skirt of him that is a Jew, saying: We will go with you, for we have heard that God is with you.

In this passage occurs for the first time the employment of the word "Iehoudi" as a name designating a religion. The word "Jew" from that day forth made its entrance into the world. Zechariah was right. The religion of the Jew was to become the religion of mankind. Yet a little while, and all the people of the earth should be Judaised.

CHAPTER III.

LEVITES. — NETHINIM.

The completion and final dedication of the second Temple took place 516 B. C. Several passages in the Psalms probably refer to this solemn occasion. Though the general poverty of the people was extreme, great pomp was displayed; for the levites were numerous. The *hasidim,* as they were called, appear occasionally to have been counted as priests;* what we read of them reminds us of the crowd of inferior clergy who clustered round cathedrals in the Middle Ages. The priestly vestments had been in use ever since the first days of the restored worship.† Music, in the unoccupied hours of a leisure life, had made great progress.‡ The musicians were organised into bands, under banners bearing mythical names taken from the writings of old, as Asaph, Heman, Ethan.§ The different choirs seem to have performed their music in parts in a very scientific way. The musical

* Psalm cxxxii. 9, 16.
† See p. 91.
‡ 1 Chronicles ix., xv., xxv. It is hard to be exact on this difficult subject; for the imagination is apt to refer much that belonged only to the service of the second Temple to the first.
§ Jeduthan is an error for Ethan, the *aleph* sometimes being softened in י.

terms invented at this period have come down to us,* but they are little more than enigmas, in which one can only conjecture the parts assigned to tenor, barytone, and soprano. The orchestra consisted of stringed instruments (*cinnor, nebel*), and wind instruments, as the hautboy, flute, and sundry kinds of trumpets, which were accompanied by tambourines, cymbals, shawms, triangles, and castanets. Antiphone and response were one of the most favourite forms of melody. The people took part in the service by joining in refrains, and by words of assent, like *Amen*.

This was the origin of that splendid worship which grew up around the Temple at Jerusalem to a marvellous degree of solemnity, and which all Christian liturgies took for their model from the fourth century through the Middle Ages. This form of worship was not, as is generally supposed, that of the first Temple, but the worship of the second. The Psalms of praise used in the liturgy which the Christian Church has so nobly incorporated into its services, almost all date from this period. They were the poetry of the levites. Those poor *hasidim*, frequently half starved, were great artists; they created the liturgy, — that fruitful mother of many arts in the religious ages. The habit of composing hymns trained these poor people to a certain facility in verse; so that a large part of the book of Psalms was the work of men little better than beggars, who lived

---

* Titles of the Psalms; Habakkuk iii.; 1 Chronicles xv., xvi.

upon what charity might give them from the offerings in the Temple, and were frequently in the depths of destitution.* The Catholic clergy later took delight in this melancholy literature, in which they found their own secret feelings of sadness and resignation expressed.

The singers (*mesorerim*) had in this family of the servitors of the public worship a somewhat superior position. After them came the porters (*sourim*), hadjibs, who kept the gates of the Temple; last of all were the *netinim* (devoted from their birth to the service of the sanctuary), the " serfs of Solomon." They were, in fact, serfs of the Church, slaves of the levites,† hewers of wood and drawers of water, mostly of foreign origin,‡ first given to God for the harder labours of his services, when his cause was victorious, but grown happy in a servitude which

---

* See Psalms vii., ix., xiii., xxi., xxvi., xxvii., xxviii., xxxv., xl., xliii., lii., lvii., lix., lxiii., lxix., lxxi., lxxiii., lxxv., xcv.-c., cix., cxxxviii. Note the expressions, —

תמימי דרך,
ישרי לב.
קרי יהוה, חסיבו,
ידאי אלהים.
אהבי שטי,
דרשי אלהיך,
מקשי אלהיך,
רנעי אוע,
ישרים, צדיקים,
חסידים.

It is impossible to make a strict distinction between Psalms written during the first century after the building of the second Temple, and those composed in the days of Josiah.

† Ezra viii. 20. ‡ See vol. iii. p. 422.

gave them ample leisure. All these made up a world curiously mixed, active and powerful by reason of its numbers and its poverty, which further increased the band of ancient *anavim*.* These men — God's poor — believed that the reign of Iahveh would be their day of triumph. The poverty of Israel was fruitful; a whole world of poetry has grown out of it.† Love for God's house, delight in his worship, the happiness of dwelling in his courts, of being fed from his hand, of looking upon themselves, poor as they were, as superior to the rest of mankind, — all these things began to show themselves faintly in the days of Hezekiah,‡ and were developed in the poor levites after the return from Babylon. The clerical spirit strikes always deep. He who has once said *Dominus pars hæreditatis meæ* is no longer like other men. Let laymen beware!

The inferior clergy, having no employment outside the Temple service, found often reasons of complaint against the priests of the house of Zadok, who frequently oppressed their servitors, and withheld what was due to them.§ The martyr wail that so frequently arises in the Psalms, the indignation of the *hasid*, who is compelled to remain poor while the proud Sadducean priest enjoys prosperity and riches, may have been the expression of bitter cleri-

---

* See vol. iii. p. 31 and what follows.

† Psalms xxiii., xxv., xxvii., xlii., xlvii, lxxi., lxxiv., cxii., cxlvii.

‡ See vol. iii. p. 29.

§ 2 Chronicles xxxi. (retrospective); Nehemiah x. 2d part, xii., xiii.

cal hatreds. Let us imagine the singers and the servitors forming a party against the priests. With us such an alliance would end in scenes like those in the Lutrin of Boileau. In Israel it concerned great social questions. Of all democracies the most dangerous is a democracy of saints more pious than their priests, despised by the official clergy and by the middle classes, but avenging themselves upon the former by their superior sanctity. The assertion that God is the defender of the poor; that he loves the poor best of all his creatures; that poverty is a title of honour in his sight; that when God helps the poor he glorifies his name,* — involves a mute attack upon the established order of things. The cause of the poor being thus identified with that of God, the door is opened for recriminations of the boldest kind among a people who do not hold that the compensations of divine justice are carried over to another life.

What made the situation particularly serious was that the levites were united in close brotherhood,† and formed a powerful community, a sort of church among themselves.‡ The *anavim* were brothers§ living together, bound by ties of affection and familiarity. Iahveh nourished them in the courts of his house, out of the superfluities of his feasts.‖ It was among such in after years that Jesus would dwell.

---

* Psalms xi., cix.   † Psalm xxii.

‡ See Psalm xiv. (liii.), רוד דרשי יהוה, דור צדיק, ישרים, צדת צדיקים, xxiv.

§ Psalm xxii. 27 and what follows.   ‖ Psalm cxxxiii.

The poor love each other. Among them through all centuries are those who have sung cheerfully the verse of the canticle, —

> Ecce quam bonum et quam jucundum
> Habitare fratres in unum.

Thus in Jerusalem was formed in the latter years of the sixth century B. C. a whole people of priests, very different from the religious orders of the Middle Ages; since a rigorous rule, and a hierarchy upheld by the secular arm, did not coerce them. The singers in particular grew more numerous than were needed for the Temple service; and as residence in Jerusalem * was not thought particularly desirable, they frequently found quarters for themselves outside the city, — at Netophah near Bethlehem, at Beth-Gilgal, and in the country round Geba and Azmabeth. There they built *hacerim* or *villæ*, humble hamlets where they lived apart, no doubt cultivating the land around them. Hymns could not but be born in so singular a situation. The necessity of making pilgrimages to Jerusalem gave occasion to pleasant periodical journeys. The *Sire ham-maaloth*[†] were probably composed at this period. These "songs of degrees" are little poems perfect in form, delightful as poetry, having a religious charm which has made them the delight of all ages. They were sung either in chorus or in alternate verses, which

---

* Nehemiah xii. 28, 29.
† *Cantica graduum.* The origin of this name is unknown.

accounts for their repetitions,* the employment of the same words, the crossing and recrossing of certain passages, the apparent transpositions of parts of phrases which have been observed in them. The poverty-stricken artists who created such gems of language and of feeling were assuredly the equals of those world-famous poets who, at about the same period, were composing the lyric treasures of Dorian verse, — the masterpieces of Greek genius in poetry.†

* For instance, Psalm cxxiv. 1, 2. Besides which, copyists have omitted much.
† See especially Psalms cxx. to cxxx , all exquisite little poems.

CHAPTER IV.

THE END OF THE HOUSE OF DAVID. — THE TRIUMPH OF THE HIGH-PRIEST OVER THE NASI.

For fifteen or twenty years Zerubbabel appears to have exercised the authority of a *nasi** over Israel, and at the same time the power of a *pekah*, or Persian governor, in Jerusalem, without much difficulty or opposition. Haggai, in 520, puts him always on a par with Joshua the high-priest, the son of Josedeck, and indeed always names him first. In his last utterances he announces that in the midst of the overthrow of empires which is at hand Zerubbabel will pass in safety through the flood.† God has taken him under his protection. He has put his signet-ring upon his finger, — that is to say, the thing most personal and precious to himself. Zerubbabel is the elect servant of God, chosen by him to rule his people.

Another poem has preserved for us a true expression of the feelings of the legitimists of that day, the Hierosolymites, whose hopes were fixed upon the restoration of the House of David: ‡ —

---

* For the conception of the *nasi* of Israel at this period see Ezekiel xii., xlv., xlvi.

† Haggai ii. 20-23. Cf. Ecclesiasticus xlix. 11 and what follows.

‡ Psalm cxxxii. Cf. 1 Kings xi. 34 and what follows. It is very singular that Psalm cxxxi., which immediately precedes cxxxii., is

Iahveh, remember for David
  All his affliction,*
How he sware unto Iahveh
  And vowed unto the Mighty One of Jacob:
Surely, I will not come into the tabernacle of my house
  Nor go up into my bed;
I will not give sleep to my eyes,
  Or slumber to mine eyelids,
Until I find out a place for Iahveh,
  A tabernacle for the mighty God of Jacob.
Lo, we heard of the same in Ephraim, †
  We found it in the field of the wood. ‡
We will go into his tabernacles,
  We will worship at his footstool.
Arise, O Iahveh, into thy resting-place,
  Thou and the ark of thy strength.
Let thy priests be clothed with righteousness,
  And let thy saints shout for joy.
For thy servant David's sake
  Turn not away the face of thine Anointed.§

And the answer is: —

Iahveh hath sworn unto David in truth,
  He will not turn from it:
Of the fruit of thy body will I set upon thy throne.
  If thy children will keep my covenant,
  And my testimony that I shall teach them,
    Their children also shall sit upon thy throne forevermore.

attributed in the Syriac version to Joshua the son of Josedeck. The Syriac version was made from a Hebrew manuscript, which contained valuable passages that are omitted in the received text (Ecclesiasticus). Cf. 2 Chronicles vi. 41, 42. In general, all that relates to the second Temple is told as if relating to the first. Parallelism of צדק and ישע (v. 9, 16) is characteristic of the Deutero-Isaiah.

* עָנְוּתוֹ. Read "piety."
† At Shiloh. Read אפרים.
‡ At Kirjath-Jearim (or Jaar: see 1 Chronicles xiii. 5).
§ Zerubbabel, — the last representative of the kingly power of David.

> For Iahveh hath chosen Zion,
>> He hath desired it for his habitation.
> This is my resting-place forever,
>> Here will I dwell: for I have desired it.
> I will abundantly bless her provision,
>> I will satisfy her poor with bread.
> Her priests also will I clothe with salvation
>> And her *hasidim* shall shout aloud for joy.
> There will I make the horn of David to bud,*
>> I have ordained a lamp for my Anointed.†
> His enemies will I clothe with shame,
>> But upon himself shall his crown flourish.

Old prophecies, misinterpreted, increased the illusion, and augmented the agitation of the people. As always happens in a time of great calamity, chimeras took shape. The nation dreamed of an ideal Saviour, a perfected David, who would restore to it the glory of its former years. At the moment of the overthrow of Jehoiakim (598) Jeremiah found comfort in the thought that a Branch ‡ should grow out of the root of David, — a king, wise and just, who would restore prosperity to Israel. § Under Zedekiah, towards the end of the siege (588), he uses almost the same words to repeat his confidence in these invincible illusions. ‖ These passages, like all that belongs to Jeremiah, keenly touched the fancy. Men talked mysteriously in those days ¶

---

* אצמיח, an allusion to צמח of Jeremiah and Zechariah. See subsequently pp. 37, 40, &c.

† An allusion to 1 Kings xi. 36; xv. 1; 2 Kings viii. 19; 2 Chronicles xxi. 7.

‡ צמח. § Jeremiah xxiii. 5.

‖ Jeremiah xxxiii. 15. See vol. iii. p. 315.

¶ Zechariah. See subsequently p. 35 and what follows.

of a *Semakh,* or Branch, who would appear as the Saviour of Israel. Zerubbabel for a time seemed to fulfil these expectations. With shades of difference that we cannot now appreciate, he was at the close of the sixth century B.C. to the faithful in Israel what the Comte de Chambord has been to Legitimists in our own day. His death or disappearance is a matter of mystery. We know absolutely nothing of his end. The overthrow of the hopes built upon him by his nation was no doubt due to the Persian authorities, who had no wish to encourage local semi-royalties in the Persian empire; and we cannot but own that the anomalous position of the heir of a long line of Jewish kings reduced to the position of a sub-prefect* could not last long. Besides, we have seen ten times already in the course of this history that the destiny of Israel was not to found a temporal kingdom. The sacerdotal party, when it had secured its triumph, apparently made haste to efface all traces of its expulsion of the ancient dynasty. The princes of the House of David, who up to this time had been both rich and honoured in the land, sink out of sight, and apparently have passed into neglect and poverty. Zerubbabel, after having played so prominent a part in the history of his people, passes suddenly into oblivion, we know not how. He had no successor. He was, so far as we know, the sole *nasi*. After him the high-priest takes the first place among his people,

---

* The Persian *pekah* was a sort of under-satrap.

and becomes more powerful than ever. He is the real Governor of Jerusalem. We have lists of the high-priests* thenceforth, as we have lists of kings preserved elsewhere. The sacerdotal nobility jealously guarded its privileges; and like every other nobility its claims gave rise to many frauds. Consequently a sort of genealogical register was kept in Jerusalem for the purpose of rectifying errors.†

How did so important a revolution take place? Its details we would gladly know. Certain things make us suspect that it was not accomplished without violence. The way in which Haggai clings with passionate ardour to Zerubbabel would seem to indicate that the power of the *nasi* was in his time being threatened. With Zechariah it is different. His fourth vision ‡ is certainly a very strange one. Joshua the son of Josedeck stands before Iahveh clad in filthy garments; Satan § stands beside him to accuse him. Iahveh will not hear his accusations, not because Joshua is innocent, but because Jerusalem has been sufficiently stricken, has suffered from conflagration. Joshua is a brand snatched from the burning. Iahveh makes him change his filthy garments ‖ for priestly robes. A clean *sanif* is placed upon his head; he is solemnly clothed (i. e. he re-

---

* הַכֹּהֵן הָרֹאשׁ or הַכֹּהֵן הַגָּדוֹל. This function was introduced retrospectively in the legislation attributed to Moses, and in writings in the times of the Kings.

† Josephus, *Against Apion*, i. 7.   ‡ Chapter iii.

§ Compare this with Satan's part in the book of Job.

‖ כַּחֲלָצוֹת = خَلَصَ

ceives investiture) before the angel of Iahveh, and is then told: "If thou wilt walk in my ways, and if thou wilt keep my charge, then thou also shalt judge my house and shalt keep my courts, and I will give thee a place among those that stand by.* Hear now, O Joshua the high-priest, thou and thy men which sit before thee (for they are men that are a sign), for behold I will bring forth my servant the Branch.† For behold the stone that I have set before Joshua, upon one stone are seven eyes.‡ Behold I will engrave the engraving thereof, saith Iahveh-Sabaoth, and I will remove the iniquity of thy land in one day..."

It is very difficult for us to comprehend what the Prophet evidently wished not to reveal clearly to his contemporaries. Another vision is a little less unintelligible.§ Zechariah sees a candlestick having seven branches, with a bowl on the top of it communicating by pipes to the seven lamps. On the right side and on the left are two olive-trees. These two olive-trees are the two Anointed Ones ‖ who stand beside the Lord of the whole earth." They are Zerubbabel and Joshua. The oil proceeds from them, they transfer it into the bowl upon the candlestick, and thence it is distributed into all branches of the family of Israel.

* The angels.
† The allusion is to Jeremiah. xxiii. 5: xxxiii. 15.
‡ I think that this must mean seven times the letter *ain*.
§ Fifth vision. Chapter iv.
‖ בני יצהר.

his is the word of Iahveh unto Zerubbabel, saying: Not by might nor by power, but by my spirit,* saith Iahveh-Sabaoth. Who art thou, O great mountain? Before Zerubbabel thou shalt become a plain; and he shall bring forth the head-stone † with shoutings, crying, Grace, grace, unto it.

The same voice adds, —

The hands of Zerubbabel have laid the foundations of this house; his hands shall also finish it. . . . For who hath despised the day of small things? For they shall rejoice and see the plummet in the hands of Zerubbabel, even these seven which are the eyes of Iahveh; they run to and fro through the whole earth.

Then comes a clearer vision. ‡ Three rich Jews from Babylon have arrived at the house of an Hierosolymite: —

And the word of Iahveh came unto me saying: Go thou into the house of Josiah the son of Zephaniah. There thou wilt find those of the Captivity, Heldai, Tobijah, and Jediah, who have come from Babylon. Take of them silver and gold, and make crowns and set them upon the head of Joshua the son of Jehozadak the high-priest; and speak unto him, saying, Behold the man whose name is the Branch, and he shall grow up out of his place, and he shall build the Temple of Iahveh, even he shall build the Temple of Iahveh, and he shall bear the glory, and shall sit and rule upon his throne; and he shall be a priest upon his throne, and the counsel of peace shall be between them both. And the crowns shall be to Heldai and to Tobijah and to Jediah and to Hen the son of Zephaniah, for a memorial in the Temple of Iahveh. And

---

* The spirit of God, symbolized by the oil.

† The stone that crowns the edifice; perhaps it has a figurative meaning.

‡ Zechariah, vi. 9 and following verses.

they that are afar off shall come and build in the Temple of Iahveh, and ye shall know that Iahveh-Sabaoth hath sent me unto you.

If this passage has come down to us as Zechariah wrote it,* it is certainly very strange. Zerubbabel is not mentioned at all as taking part in rebuilding the Temple. The whole glory of the work — at least of its completion — is assigned to Joshua, who now seems to unite royalty and priesthood. He is *cohen*, or priest, upon his throne, and suddenly assumes the rank of *Semakh*, or Branch. It has been conjectured that the cause of this change was some revolution, possibly effected by gold brought from Babylon. To this supposed revolution some have attributed the well-known Psalm,† written evidently on the accession of a sovereign not yet honoured by the title of *melek*, a priest forever after the order of Melchizedek, adopted by Iahveh in his wrath against profane *melakim*, whose power he will break. The Psalm appears to have been sung by two choirs, the second choir speaking in the name of Iahveh: —

FIRST CHOIR.

Iahveh saith unto my lord: Sit thou on my right hand,

SECOND CHOIR.

Until I make thine enemies thy footstool.

* This is very doubtful. בין שניהם in verse 13 is incomprehensible if the name of Zerubbabel be not in what precedes it. In verse 11, עטרות supposes the same thing.

† Psalm cx., the most difficult of all the Psalms by reason of the alterations in its text and the obscurity of its allusions. The fact that it has been placed among the Psalms written after the return from Babylon is our only indication of the circumstances of its composition.

FIRST CHOIR.

Iahveh shall stretch forth the rod of thy strength* out of Zion.

SECOND CHOIR.

Rule thou in the midst of thine enemies.

FIRST CHOIR.

The people will bring thee freewill offerings †
    In the day of thy power,
    In the glory of thy holy place.‡

SECOND CHOIR.

In my womb I have conceived thee.§

FIRST CHOIR.

Iahveh sware and will not repent.

SECOND CHOIR.

Thou art a priest forever, after the order of Melchizedek. ||

FIRST CHOIR.

    The Lord [Adonai] at thy right hand
Shall strike through kings in the day of his wrath.

---

* Thy sceptre.

† The text of verse 3, as understood by the Greek translators, seems better than the Massoretic version.

‡ Cf. Psalm xxix. 2, —
    Thy people offer themselves willingly
        In the day of thy power
        In the beauties of holiness.
                    Revised Version.

§ From the womb of the morning thou hast the dew of thy youth. — *Revised Version* (Trans.).

This verse is imitated from Psalm ii. 7. משחר is a marginal variation for כרהם; the four letters לרטל were wanting in the manuscript of the Greek translators. There seems to be some transposition. The original reading may have been מרחםי ילדתיך.

|| An allusion to Genesis xiv.

SECOND CHOIR.

The Lord [Adonai] shall judge the nations, he shall fill the places with dead bodies,
He shall strike through the head in many countries!

BOTH CHOIRS.

He shall drink of the brook in the way;
Therefore shall he lift up his head.*

Of course, all this does not amount to a certainty. Did Joshua the son of Josedeck inherit all the power of Zerubbabel? After the disappearance of Zerubbabel was the popular idea of the *Semakh*, or Branch, transferred to priests of the house of Zadok? † We are so entirely ignorant of all that was passing in Jerusalem at this period that we hardly dare venture even on conjectures. Jewish historiographers have chosen that this episode should remain dark, and they have succeeded. Two things only are clear: first, that Zerubbabel, by death or in some other way, fell from power shortly after the Temple was completed, or just before; ‡ secondly, that his descendants became obscure private individuals.§ while we have a list of the descendants of Joshua as a line of hereditary sovereigns.‖ Joshua was succeeded by his son Joiakim, he by his son Eliashib,

---

* An allusion we do not understand.

† The passage in Zechariah, given on p. 21, would lead us to suppose so; but the text is strongly suspected of alteration.

‡ According to some Jewish traditions Zerubbabel returned to Babylonia. Derenbourg, *Palestine*, p. 18 and what follows.

§ 1 Chronicles iii. 19 and what follows (to say nothing of the two genealogies of Christ, in some places possibly fictitious).

‖ Nehemiah xii. 10 and what follows. This list is defective.

whom we shall find to have been contemporary with Nehemiah.* The priesthood was more and more held to be the appanage of the mythical brother of Moses. The office of high-priest was hereditary by right divine. All priests were sons of Aaron; the high-priest descends from him in direct line by order of birth. This feeling was kept up by the circulation of writings in which theocratic authority was far more strongly insisted on than in the ancient scriptures. Old versions were retouched to conform to the sacerdotal reorganisation of the nation, and a constitutional theocratic authority was centralised in the house of Aaron.

A sort of second legitimacy was thus formed in place of that of the now displaced House of David. The high-priest became the leader of the nation. His power, transmitted from father to son, from first-born to first-born, ennobled the whole family, and gave to the brother of the high-priest the right even to ascend the steps of the high altar.† The record of the genealogy of the high-priests is preserved in official documents, which come down to the destruction of Jerusalem by Titus. Tithes gave wealth and strength to the new power. Israel had ceased to be a nation; it became an ecclesiastical community. Jerusalem gives the first example of the materializing of a spiritual power. The Rome

---

* Nehemiah iii. 1; xiii. 1.
† Josephus, *Antiquities*, xi. viii. 2.

of the Papacy there found a model which in lordly fashion it imitated in after years.

It is certainly very strange that the official record of the descendants of David should have broken off thus suddenly and silently, and that not one word of complaint or of regret should have come down to us. Some critics have thought that such feelings are embodied in certain Psalms in which they fancy they can detect covert reproaches to Iahveh for having abandoned the family of the man after his own heart, whom he had chosen to be king. Such is Psalm lxxxix., whose author seems to have himself belonged to the House of David, and sadly recalls to the mind of Iahveh the forlorn situation of his faithful ones, while he looks forward to their restoration. This Psalm has been attributed to Zerubbabel, or to one of his descendants. It is certain that the Psalms written at this period contain many personal allusions. We have already spoken of the touching Psalm "Lord, remember David," * and how strange it is to find next to it in the Psalter † a little prayer attributed to Joshua the son of Josedeck, which seems like a protest on his part against accusations made against him of inordinate ambition.

The oblivion into which the House of David so suddenly fell need not take us by surprise. Except four or five good kings, the dynasty, according to the pietists, had contained nothing but wicked

---

* Psalm cxxxii. See p. 31.
† Psalm cxxxi. Note the Syriac title.

ones. The latter kings of Jerusalem, those who came after Josiah, were anathematised by Jeremiah and his school. Ezekiel in his visions rarely mentions legitimacy, or the House of David. In short, the Prophets seem to have thought little about the dynasty of David or the Temple. In their ideal pictures of Messiah's reign they never predict that a descendant of David shall bear rule in Jerusalem when the whole world flocks thither to do homage to Iahveh. Many Jewish puritans would have willingly left the Temple in its ruins, believing that God dwelleth in the heavens, and that all the beasts of the earth are his, before any are offered to him in sacrifice. That view it was not, however, possible to accept. The second Temple rose. Feeble efforts to restore the prestige of David availed little. It was not until the last days of the Maccabees, or rather in the times of the Herods, that the idea is seen to spring up that the Messiah was to be a son of David, and pains were then taken to reconstruct genealogies of that line, and to discover those lineal descendants of David who (it was said) for centuries had lived forgotten and unknown. The Asmoneans, it is well known, were noway descended from David, and made no attempt to usurp a title upon that ground.

The power of the high-priest seems not to have been considered political in any way by the Persian government. There were always in Jerusalem, besides the high-priest, who exercised authority over the Jews, a Persian *pekah* * appointed by the court at Susa.† It is probable that Jerusalem was a sort of secondary sub-prefecture, forming part of the whole government of the Trans-Euphrates. The residence of the *pekah* at Jerusalem was near the corner-gate, on the spot where the Tower of Hippicus was afterwards built, now the *Kalaa*. The high-priest lived in the Temple. The palaces of the ancient kings, which were south of the Temple, lay in ruins. To have restored them and inhabited them would assuredly have been considered an act of rebellion by the Persian government.

Jerusalem in the days of Darius and Xerxes must have been a strange little city, — a city of priests, prophets, and levites, of everything except real citizens. In Greece, the period of which we treat was that of the three hundred Spartans, and of Marathon, Miltiades, and Cimon. There were but few prophets after Haggai and Zechariah. There was nothing left but a temple with its priests and its underlings, not very unlike the heathen temples of that age at Gebel, Tyre, and Cyprus.‡ From that time forth there was no attempt to combat an invading idolatry; monotheism reigned undisputed in Jerusalem.§ A secular civilisation was destroyed there

---

* The *pekah* of Jerusalem exercised authority under a satrap, who had a fixed residence elsewhere.

† Malachi i. 8. The case of Nehemiah differed only in that he was a Jew.

‡ See *Corpus inscr. semit.*, 1st Part, Nos. 1, 10 and the following, 86, 87.

§ Ezra ix. and what follows.

forever. The second Temple, like the first, was built by Phœnician workmen. They settled afterwards in the city, where they carried on trade and commerce, especially in provisions.* The grand aspirations of the Prophets seemed forgotten. Ritualism, or rather casuistry, had absorbed all things into itself. The Torah triumphed. The laws regulating religious observances became stricter every day. It is easy to perceive what fate was in store for Israel.

* Nehemiah xiii. and what follows.

CHAPTER V.

LEVITICAL ADDITIONS TO THE TORAH. — ELABORATION OF THE RITES OF WORSHIP.

THE TORAH, during these years whose history is so dark to us, grew by many additions. We have seen* that ever since a period prior to the Captivity there had existed in writing certain laws of ritual, certain Temple customs. More than one arrangement of the liturgy may have been drawn up at the time of the return from Babylon.† Many ancient practices had fallen into disuse, many disputed points needed to be authoritatively adjusted. Priests, about the time of Ezekiel, had one after another exerted themselves to invent a Temple service as brilliant as they had seen it in their visions or their dreams. Such conceptions must have exercised great influence on the restoring of the Temple worship. The people made — and above all they imagined — all sorts of splendours, on such a scale as their poverty would allow. All difficulties were disposed of by insisting that the scale of this magnificence had been ordained

---

* See vol. iii. pp. 52, 53, 159.
† Haggai ii. alludes to levitical laws, especially Leviticus vi. 20.

by Moses in his lifetime in the journey through the Wilderness.*

The period of Zerubbabel and Joshua the son of Josedeck was poor in every way. The writings of Haggai and Zechariah show such lack of skill that at first view it hardly seems probable that at such a moment the great code of levitical law could have been composed. But in the literary work of those days there were various degrees of skill required. Indeed, we may, if we please, suppose Joshua the high-priest engaged in it, and we may not be wrong in the conjecture. It is as likely to be true as any other.

Conjectures founded on probabilities are as legitimate as conjectures without such foundation are intolerable. Those descriptions of the sacerdotal garments, for example, so carefully elaborated, so minutely detailed, — are they the work of dreamers of the school of Ezekiel, to whom it cost nothing to manufacture them sparkling with jewels? Or are they due to the first colonists who accompanied Zerubbabel, and comforted themselves in their poverty by imagining costly vestments made splendid by all that was rich and rare? Or perhaps should we rather refer them to the days of the grand religious ceremonies brought about by the active persuasions of Nehemiah? Who can tell? The levitical laws concerning vows,† those relating to sacrifices,‡ the

---

* Exodus xxv. and what follows.
† Leviticus xxvii.; Numbers xxx.   ‡ Leviticus i.–vii.

commands respecting sexual relations,* laws concerning what was clean and what unclean,† — we cannot be sure as to their date. All we can say is that they appear to belong to a time when an anxious casuistry had become dominant in Israel.

It however seems as if the lawgivers of the Restoration had altered very little as to important things. They drew up a code of costumes; they gathered together scattered laws that had remained unwritten.‡ But while they copied ancient texts they not unfrequently added to them.§ Perhaps it is to them we owe the strange manner in which death was made the punishment of mere infringements of ritual, though such passages may have proceeded from the pen of some believer in a religious utopia, who scattered his penalties here, there, and everywhere.

These years after the return may also have been the time when regulations were made concerning feasts and pilgrimages to Jerusalem,‖ the system of which is more complicated in the levitical code than it is in the book of Deuteronomy or even in Ezekiel. Sacrifices were also duly regulated. They received technical names; ritualistic observances were affixed

---

* Leviticus xii., xv., xviii. The law concerning leprosy was most certainly in writing in the days of the first Temple. See vol. iii. p. 52, note.
† Leviticus xi., xii., xiii., xiv., xv., xviii., xxi., xxii.
‡ See vol. iii. p. 52, note 1.
§ As, lists of beasts clean and unclean. See vol. iii. p. 52, note 2.
‖ Leviticus xxiii.

to the smallest details of existence. The sacrifices were no longer family feasts. The victims belonged almost entirely to the priests, who alone seemed to profit by them. The gift of prophecy became limited to the priesthood, and indeed became almost the prerogative of the high-priest. Purity of heart, so much insisted on in Deuteronomy, became only legal purity of an outward kind. Isaiah and the prophets of the classic period, who were so hostile to sacrifices, were set aside. The money expended to provide victims was the first consideration. Pharisaism, against which Jesus directed his sharpest darts, already existed in all its essentials. There was never a more striking example of how the mere ceremonial development of religion leads to materialism rather than to progress.

The new feasts had all an expiatory character, which put them far below their old character of festivals devoted to thanksgiving and joy. The *Iom kippurim* * (the *Kippour* of the present day) and the penitential fasts † took an exaggerated place. The idea of expiation (a very false one, for the only way in which men can expiate what has been evil on their part is to do better in future) always opens the door to abuse. The rite concerning the ashes of the red heifer ‡ had most likely provoked the ridicule of the Prophets; but now it was taken up, consecrated,

---

* Exodus xxix. 36; xxx. 10, 16; Leviticus xxiii. 27; xxv. 9.
† Leviticus xvi. 1–34; xxiii. 26–32; Numbers xxix. 7–12.
‡ Numbers xix.

and made a dogma. It was the same with the law of purification. A belief in Azâzel* was almost the sole pagan superstition which clung to the Jews. Is it not wonderful that a people which had spent its strength in expelling superstition in all its forms should have written whole pages on the manner in which the wretched scape-goat was to be chased into the wilderness? Religion is on the decline when it is given up to masters of ceremony and sacristans.

Fasts took deep root in the old religion of Israel, and in that of all peoples of the Semitic race.† All that was now done was to regulate them. But the system strengthened in the popular mind one of the saddest errors of Iahvism; namely, that God is jealous of man, and is glad to see him humbled. The important part of the Semitic *som*, or fast, is not abstinence from food, but humiliation, sackcloth and ashes, the dishevelled hair, the disfigured face.

About this time the observance of the Sabbath and the rite of circumcision became the very basis of Jewish life. In scrupulous observance of these things men forgot the fundamental conditions of true piety. They did as the peasant does, who eats no meat on Fridays, and goes scrupulously on Sundays to mass, but continues nevertheless in his evil ways. The Passover‡ was becoming the great feast of the Jews. The rites of this grand public cele-

---

* Leviticus xvi.
† See vol. i. p. 47; vol. iii. p. 161.
‡ 2 Chronicles xxx.; 2 Esdras i.

bration took an especial character of national solemnity, not unmixed with mysticism.

The laws of health and cleanliness were rightly a matter of chief attention among ancient lawgivers.* The laws that forbade certain unwholesome or filthy meats to be eaten were an essential part of the old codes.† The swine, which almost always transmits disorders in the East, deserved the strict exclusion which the law required, at a time when the only safe remedy against sickness was a rigid system of precautions. The additions made by levitical law to the list of other proscribed animals ‡ are naïve. The ideas concerning clean and unclean were founded at first on what is really clean or foul; § they responded to man's inbred feelings of refinement, to those disgusts which very often we ourselves are unable to account for.‖ Almost all nations in the East exaggerate these distinctions, and make of them burthens grievous to be borne.

The levitical code was in the daily life of the Jews the cause of many evils.¶ Questions about clean or unclean became the source of endless scruples and the

---

* See vol. i. pp. 103, 104 ; vol. ii. p. 311, note 5.

† Compare the laws of other nations on such matters, — the codes of Manou, of the Zend-Avesta. Herodotus i. 140, ii. 07.

‡ Leviticus xi. Compare Deuteronomy xiv. Cf. vol. iii. p. 52, note 2; p. 53, note 1, &c.

§ It is so to this day in the higher castes in India.

‖ Strange mixtures, contacts that make us fancy we may catch cutaneous maladies or sores, or fermentations generally held to be disgusting.

¶ Leviticus, from chapter xi. to xxii.

most minute inquiries, which, especially when they had relation to women, were extremely inconvenient. The life of a Jew was singularly hedged about with restrictions. It is true that sometimes the saving strength of a religion is afforded by the uncomfortable obligations it may impose. The more onerous they are the more men cling to them. The religions of the East are fenced round by material regulations and prohibitions, till they become the business of men's lives. On the other hand. they are ruined in the end by such restrictions, men being isolated by them from the great stream of human progress. These fatal distinctions between clean and unclean have made society impossible in the East. Society assumes the free contact of individuals; the rules of which we speak raise barriers of separation between them. The Asiatic world accepts these puerile distinctions of religion or of caste; but Europe will have nothing to do with them. As soon as the Jews were dispersed throughout Europe, their levitical law prevented their free contact with other individuals of the human race. Judaism will never conquer the world till it renounces them, — that is, till it becomes Christianity, such as Saint Paul conceived it, without circumcision. without distinctions of separation either in board or bed.

The Torah thus, as it were, remained incomplete during the later years of the sixth century B. C. Those who accept the narratives in Ezra as authority make the end of the labour spent upon its revision

come down to about 450 B. C. And, indeed, half a
century is no long time in which to suppose so great
a task, attended with many hesitations and inter-
ruptions, could have been accomplished. It would
appear, however, that the additions made in the
time of Ezra, if indeed there were any, were not
considerable, and that no essential part of the Torah
is of later date than the year 500 B. C. No attempt
was made to give unity to what resulted from this
revision. The additions seem to have principally
affected the levitical code, reduced to writing during
the Captivity * and generally believed to have been
given on Mount Sinai.† Creative energy had died
out in Israel. The fount of prophecy had run dry.
Meditation on the Torah, not the making of it, was
thenceforward to absorb the religious activity of the
nation. The second Isaiah, the latest and most inspired of the ancient Prophets, was perhaps still living when some pious Israelite composed Psalm cxix.,
that mass of repetitions, which rings its changes on
the same thoughts through twenty-two times eight
verses, the octaves corresponding to the twenty-
two letters of the Hebrew alphabet, each verse
containing in every variety of synonym praises,
one hundred and seventy-six times repeated, of the
law of Iahveh.

All the legal part of the Torah, which is relatively
modern, though far inferior in moral breadth to the
Book of the Covenants, to the Decalogue, or to

---

* See vol. iii. p. 340. † Exodus xxiv. 16.

Deuteronomy, had in one way an importance not belonging to the older books. It forged the chain that Judaism could never break, which on the contrary it has used its best efforts to make heavier and heavier. The first founders of Christianity threw it off, and went back to the life-giving record of Israel, — that which contains the spirit of the Prophets. Christianity was the teaching of the second Isaiah springing to life after an interval of six hundred years, and reacting against the routine of centuries. But routine was not conquered. The fanaticism engendered by the Torah survived all attempts to kill it. The best energies of the race were engaged in mad squabbles of mere casuistry. The Talmud, that bad book which to this day is the evil genius of Judaism, took life from the Torah, and then in great part filled its place, becoming the new law of Judaism. It has been said that Israel, in lack of other superstition, created a new superstition out of the Torah. The desire of the writer of Deuteronomy has been accomplished. The Law has become the absolute rule of life to Israel. Each Jew has it for a frontlet between his eyes, — a hypnotic plaster. Ask a learned Jew at what hour it is permitted to study Greek, he will allow none to be lawful but when it is neither day nor night; "for is it not written of the Law, Thou shalt meditate thereon day and night"?

Worship became every day more and more strangely complicated. The Sabbath was no longer merely a day of rest: it became a sort of Sunday, a weekly religious festival, having its especial services.* The daily sacrifice (*tamid*) was regulated.† The three prayers a day, and the custom of kneeling to pray, date possibly from this period.‡ When adopted by the Moslems this custom became like rhythm in Oriental life, scanned as it were by the cry of the muezzin.

Another Jewish custom which was adopted into Mahometanism and became a matter of great importance was the practice, when out of Jerusalem, of turning towards the Holy City in the act of prayer.§ Worshippers thought to invite a sort of electric current that could be set up, as they imagined, if they should open their windows in the desired direction. The Samaritans had the same habit of turning towards Mount Gerizim. ‖ The practice was much in favour among Judaising Christians, ¶ and no doubt it was from them that Mahomet adopted it. Mahomet looked upon the *Kibla* — that is, the act of turning towards a sacred spot in prayer — as essential to any reli-

---

* Leviticus xxiv. 8; Numbers xxviii. 9. Cf. 1 Chronicles ix. 32; 2 Chronicles xxxi. 3; Nehemiah x. 33 (Ezekiel xlvi. 4).

† Numbers xxviii.; Daniel viii. 11–13; xi. 31.

‡ 2 Chronicles vi. 13; Ezra ix. 5; Daniel vi. 11; Acts ii. 15; iii. 1; ix. 40; x. 9; Luke xxii. 41. Cf. 1 Kings viii. 54.

§ 2 Chronicles vii. 34; Daniel *l. c.*; 2 Esdras iv. 58. Mischna, *Berakoth*, iv. 5, 6, Tertullian, Clement of Alexandria, Origen, — all speak of it as no longer the custom.

‖ *Epist. Sichem.* ed. Bruns. p. 14 (Eichhorn, *Repert.*, ix. 9).

¶ *Orig. du Christ.*, vol. v. pp. 52, 53, 461; vol. vi. pp. 279, 280, 286.

gion. He hesitated some time as to his choice, and at one period in his prophetic career adopted Jerusalem, like the Judaising Christians his masters.* But at last the Kaaba decided him; and Mecca, five times in each day, became the central spot to which the whole Mussulman world turns in prayer.

The Sabbath, which was legally sanctioned by the penalty of death,† and circumcision, which was obligatory, ‡ became at last terrible burthens because of the scruples of conscience to which they gave rise. § Before the Captivity, no correct man neglected these duties; but afterwards their observance became an exaction which engendered a thousand inconveniences and a thousand perils. Judaism became a powerful vise, which threatened to crush all within its grasp, had not Jesus and Saint Paul by more than human effort succeeded in loosening its grip, returning, as the elder Prophets had aspired, to the worship of God in spirit and in truth.

---

* Sprenger, *Das Leben Mohammed*, vol. iii. pp. 46, 47.

† Exodus xxxi. 14 and what follows; xxxv. 2; Numbers xv. 32 and what follows. Mischna, *Sanhedrim*, vii. 8.

‡ Leviticus xii. 3.

§ Exodus xxxv. 3 (the Jews forbidden to light fire on the Sabbath). Later the observance of the Sabbath gave rise to the wildest casuistic reasoning (The Gospels; Josephus; Talmud).

CHAPTER VI.

NEHEMIAH AND THE WALLS OF JERUSALEM.

WHILE this labour of revision silently went on in Judea, the Jews who still remained in the East went their different ways, according to their degrees of piety. Some fell away from day to day, until their religion was little more than a kind of deism.* Others scrupulously guarded the shrine of Iahveh, and took great interest in what was passing at Jerusalem. It was decided that those who stayed behind should one day rejoin the pious multitude who were already singing praises to Iahveh upon the hill of Zion. In 518 B.C., as we have seen, certain Jews of consequence, residents in Babylonia, bearing fine Chaldean names, had come as envoys to perform their devotions at Jerusalem, and to inquire of the elders whether now, after all that had been accomplished, it was still necessary to keep the Fast by which they mourned for the destruction of the Temple.† About the same time rich Babylonians brought much gold to Jerusalem,‡ and may very

---

* The Book of Jonah possibly proceeded from some one of these persons. They may have been few, but they certainly existed. See vol. iii. p. 420, &c.

† See what came before p. 20.

‡ Zechariah vi. 9 and what follows.

probably have played a part in the overthrow or banishment of Zerubbabel.

In some respects it seems that the Jewish families who had remained in Babylonia were richer and more cultivated than those who had decided to return. The study of the ancient Scriptures, especially those relating to the Law, was in these orderly retired families, living apart from the surrounding population, certainly carried on with as much interest as in Jerusalem. In Babylon they possessed more pages of the ancient writings than at Jerusalem, and these were commented upon with ardour. The *soferim* were numerous. Associated with the Priest there now begins to appear the Doctor, or Teacher, called in Hebrew *mebin*,—that is, "he who expounds" the Law. It was a sort of official title.* The name of *sofer-mahir* † ("scribe," or "ready writer"), given in allusion to a verse in one of the ancient poems, ‡ implied the constant habit of holding the pen, which the poverty-stricken life led at Jerusalem would hardly have permitted. Time facilitated this state of things. Nearly a hundred years passed before the Eastern Jews ceased to send fresh reinforcements to the colony at Jerusalem, composed of men often more enterprising than the older immigrants. Great intellectual and moral changes took place during this interval. The peace of the Orient during the long and prosperous reigns of Darius, Xerxes, and Arta-

---

* 1 Chronicles xxvii. 32 ; Ezra viii. 16.
† Ezra vii. 6.   ‡ Psalm xlv. 1.

xerxes Longimanus, gave opportunity for steady sedentary development. There was not much intercourse between the Jews and Persia. The great evolutions of the Iranian religion took place at a later period. One single rite was borrowed from Persian custom,* and one non-religious festival, that of the New Year.† Israel, as it had done during the days of its Captivity, shut itself up in its own literature, in its own past.

The proximity of the central power under the Achæmenian kings was of great advantage to the Jews of the East. Susa and other ancient capitals were fountains of favour and of wealth, of which the Jew did not fail to take advantage. To be head of a great feudal house, the channel by which everything came in and everything went out, was a position greatly coveted. High posts in the state were open only to men of the conquering race; but government had many employments to dispose of in which the Jewish *raia*, and especially the *sofer*, well skilled in the Aramaic script, ‡ found lucrative employment for his industry. It was thus that towards the middle of the fourth century a certain Nehemiah, son of Hachaliah, a very pious Jew, found a career in one of the sub-prefectures. In the year 445 B. C. he arrived in Judea, from the Persian court, with the

---

* See what follows p. 140.

† The names of the angels, Asmodeus, &c., were borrowed at a later period. The demonology of Psalm xci. is doubtful.

‡ Clermont-Ganneau, *Revue archéol.*, August, 1878, pp. 93–107. Compare *Corpus inscr. semit.*, 2d part, Nos. 144 and the following.

title of *pekah* of Jerusalem, and very extended powers committed to him, as he said, by the sovereign at Susa.* His arrival was very welcome to the stricter party among the Jews; for Nehemiah, like all pious men bred in the East, belonged to the party of strictest observance, and brought with him a plan for very conservative reforms, on which he had already determined.

Nehemiah, who was possibly a eunuch,† had made his little fortune in the household service of the court in the reign of Artaxerxes Longimanus. According to the recital, which seems written by himself, — throughout which one feels his desire to make himself appreciated according to the ideas of his own people at that period, — he had been the king's cup-bearer, and while exercising the functions of

---

* There exist memoirs of Nehemiah, in which Nehemiah speaks in the first person, besides what, in the hands of the author of Chronicles, has come down to us as the Book of Nehemiah, sometimes called the 2d Book of Ezra. To obtain the original text, we must cut out chapters viii., ix., x., which formed part of the Memoirs of Ezra (see on that subject p. 85, note 1; 94, note), and some additions by the writer of Chronicles, in chapter xii. 1-26 and 44-47; in chapter xiii. 1-3. The style of Nehemiah's Memoirs has its own peculiarities; for example, he never uses the word "Iahveh." The authenticity of this narrative, though many parts of it seem romantic, is not so doubtful as that of the memoirs of Ezra. See especially chapters iii., vi. If there has been any imitation between the memoirs of Ezra and the memoirs of Nehemiah, it is the writer of Ezra who has imitated Nehemiah, not Nehemiah who has borrowed from Ezra. In after years the Jews strangely added to the power and importance of Nehemiah. He and Ezra were both made leaders of the first return to Jerusalem (2 Maccabees i. 18. Cf. Ecclesiasticus xlix. 13. Greek).

† See later, p. 89, note 1.

that office found means to serve his race. Domestic service was in the Persian empire, as it has always been in the Ottoman empire, a very common way of attaining administrative employment. On the other hand, this custom of arriving at some high position by first serving in a menial one is too often found in Jewish stories of the same period* to let us accept it very confidently. The cringing nature of Orientals made domestic service come easy enough to them. There are persons in our own day willing to claim close relations with a king or with the President of the Republic because they have obtained a letter from some subordinate official. The Jews were proud of anything which apparently brought them into connection with the head of the government; they boasted of it to make others fancy they were powerful, and not seldom have they employed their favour to injure or annoy their enemies.

Among the official powers that Nehemiah derived, as he asserted, from the King of Kings, he had one that his countrymen must have deemed inestimable: he was authorized to rebuild the walls of Jerusalem. Jerusalem for ninety years had remained a defenceless city, and its condition often led to jeers from neighbouring nations very irritating to patriotic Jews. The outline of the former walls was still traceable by a long line of great detached stones. There were places, particularly near Siloam, where the ruins of the walls blocked up the public way, but

---

* Daniel, Zerubbabel (Josephus, *Antiquities*, xi. iii. 1).

others where there was little need of doing more than to repair the breaches. Nehemiah tells us himself, if his memoirs are authentic, of his first night-visit to this scene of ruin :*—

So I came to Jerusalem, and I was there three days. And I arose in the night, I and some few men with me; neither told I any man what my God had put into my heart to do for Jerusalem; neither was there any beast with me save the beast that I rode upon. And I went out by night through the valley gate,† even toward the dragon's well, and to the dung gate,‡ and viewed the walls of Jerusalem which were broken down, and the gates thereof were consumed with fire. Then I went on to the fountain gate and to the king's pool ;§ but there was no place for the beast that was under me to pass. Then went I up in the night by the brook, and viewed the wall; and I turned back and entered by the valley gate, and so returned.

And no one knew whither I went, nor what I did; nor had I yet told it to the Jews, nor to the priests, nor to the nobles, nor to the rulers, nor to the rest that did the work. Then said I unto them : Ye see the evil case that we are in, how Jerusalem lieth waste, and the walls thereof are burned with fire; come and let us build up the walls of Jerusalem, that we be no more a reproach. And I told them of the hand of my God which was good upon me, as also of the king's words that he had spoken to me ; and they said, Let us rise up and build. So they strengthened their hands for the good work.

Nehemiah's enterprise could not be otherwise than disagreeable to the inhabitants of Samaria. The

---

* Nehemiah ii. 11 and following verses.
† The present Gate of Jaffa.
‡ At the southwest corner of the Eastern Hill.
§ The Pool of Siloah.

relations between this people and the Jews continued to be strained. The wealthy, the chief-priests, and those who were about them would willingly have assented to a reconciliation of the two branches of the worshippers of Iahveh, which would have led to intermarriage. Notwithstanding the harsh answer which the Samaritans are said to have received from Zerubbabel,* the entire nation was not by any means converted to intolerance. There were, amongst the Judean nobles,† large-hearted men, who did not think that their fidelity to Iahveh demanded hatred and religious exclusiveness. Among the principal persons in Samaria was a certain Tobiah, whose son was called Johanan, and surnamed "officer of the Ammonites," probably because he came originally out of the country of Ammon. The names of these two persons indicate that they were worshippers of Iahveh, but assuredly they had not conformed to the pious reforms of Josiah. Now, Tobiah was connected with the high-priest Eliashib; ‡ he had married the daughter of Zechaniah, son of Arach, one of the leading men in Jerusalem, and his son Johanan married the daughter of Mesullum, the son of Berechiah. These Hierosolymite Jews [men who loved the rule of the ancient kings better than that of the high-priest] spoke of Tobiah in high terms, and sometimes took rather a malicious pleasure in enlarging upon his good qualities before the other party,

---

* See above, p. 12.   † Nehemiah vi. 17. חרי יהודה.
‡ Nehemiah xiii. 4.

who considered him an enemy of God. Associated with Tobiah we find Sanballat, the Horonite,* a rich man,† who seems to have been at one time governor of Samaria. One of his daughters afterwards married Joïada, son of Eliashib, who was high-priest after his father. A certain Arabian Sheik, Geshem or Gashmu,‡ appears to have joined with Tobiah and Sanballat in plans for retarding the new work of the Jews. One can see that the priestly aristocracy of Jerusalem, attracted by the prospect of rich marriages, had become very tolerant towards the Samaritans. It is not uncommon to find fanaticism more fierce among lay zealots than among the clergy.

At first, when Sanballat and his friends were informed of the intentions of Nehemiah, they affected to treat the matter as a joke. Sanballat mocked at the idea of raising those mighty stones into their place, and Tobiah said that the spring of a jackal would bring down their stone wall. By a manœuvre that might have been dangerous to themselves, they affected to think the enterprise denoted an intention to revolt against the Persian government. Nehemiah took no notice of all this, but divided the circumference of the city into sections, and distributed the work to the principal groups of the population of Jerusalem and its environs.§

---

* Either he came from Horonaim (which would make him a Moabite), or from Beth-Horon, near Jerusalem.
† Josephus, *Antiquities*, xl. viii. 2.
‡ Geshem, in the English Bible. — *Trans.*
§ Nehemiah xiii. 28.

The sections were about forty. All persons in easy circumstances, all rich corporations, merchants, jewellers, and sellers of perfumes, took charge of that part of the wall which was nearest to their bazaars or houses. The priests, from the high-priest Eliashib downwards, showed much zeal on the occasion, and built long portions of the wall. The levites and the *nethinim* were not less industrious. Besides this, the towns and districts near Jerusalem, under the conduct of their elders, contributed their share largely to the work, — Jericho, Gibeon, Mizpah, Zanoah, Beth-haccherem, Beth-zur, and Keilah. The men who lived in villages around Jerusalem worked during the day, and returned home at night. The only people who showed slackness were the men of Tekoa, at least their leaders.

The walls seem to have been rebuilt entirely on the line marked out by the ruins of the former ones. Workmen dug the old stones from piles of rubbish, and from under the soil that had been covering them, little by little, for a hundred years. And this work was very hard.* The city of that day nearly corresponded with the present one, excepting some parts towards the south and a broad belt towards the north. The numerous gates and towers were rebuilt with exceeding care. The somewhat complicated erections which surrounded the Pool of Siloam, the reservoirs of the king's gardens, the steps that were on that spot, and the tombs of the family

---

* Nehemiah iii.; iv. 2.

of King David, were restored to their original state. Nehemiah does not seem to have thought of rebuilding the palaces and the great buildings which had been erected south of the Temple. A fortress near the Temple* seemed, however, necessary. This citadel, or *bira* (*baris* in the time of the Maccabees), was a large construction, occupying the spot where Herod afterwards built the tower of Antonia (which is now the seraglio).†

When the wall in its different sections had reached nearly half its height, the animosity of the surrounding nations broke suddenly into violence and opposition. Sanballat, Tobiah, the Arabs, the Ammonites, and the Ashdodites joined together to go up to Jerusalem and lay it waste. The Persian empire was a feudal one; private wars could be carried on between towns, nations, and powerful chiefs. The men of Jerusalem were informed, by other Jews living on the plains, of these evil designs against them. The dwellers in neighbouring villages tried to persuade their friends in Jerusalem to come home, and so escape the danger that threatened the capital. Nehemiah took open precautionary measures which prevented an attack. From that moment every man was on his guard. They worked, as Nehemiah's memoir metaphorically tells us, with one hand, while

---

* Nehemiah ii. 8; vii. 2.

† It is singular that no mention is made of this in the division of labour among the sections. Perhaps שר הבירה does not imply a real *bira*.

they fought with the other.* They had their swords girded to their sides while they built, or while they carried burthens. Nehemiah commanded them, having a trumpeter beside him to give, if necessary, instant signal of combat, and half the population was kept under arms from morning until starlight. At night the men who had been accustomed to return home stayed in the city, and helped to keep watch. Nehemiah and his men never put off their clothes, and kept their weapons within reach of their hands.†

The financial condition of the city during this time was extremely perplexing. Before the arrival of Nehemiah the population of Jerusalem and its outlying villages had become deeply in debt. In order to pay tribute to the King of kings the chief part of them had mortgaged their houses and their lands, nay, even had had to sell their sons and daughters, and to hypothecate all they possessed so deeply that they were in danger of in a short time becoming slaves. The rebuilding of the wall brought matters to a crisis. If there was not absolute usury in these proceedings, money was lent on conditions very shocking to religious feeling, for it was by reason of their piety that these people were going to be robbed. By previous mortgage the crops became the property of the money-lender, and the poor were destitute of food. Such behaviour of Jews to Jews

---

* Several Psalms may be referred to this really poetic moment in the history of Israel, — Psalm cxxvii., for example, which is supposed to have been written by Nehemiah.

† Nehemiah iv. 17. Instead of שלחו המים, read שלחהו כירו.

was most abominable! Nehemiah, his relations and his officers, had lent money on these terms. Nehemiah was the first to release his debtors, and his eloquence on behalf of the poor was so persuasive that all other creditors followed his example.

When the work was almost finished, the breaches repaired, and nothing wanting but to set up the doors to the gates, Sanballat, Tobiah, and other creditors of the Jews renewed their opposition. Four several times Sanballat and Geshem invited Nehemiah to a conference in one of the villages on the plain of Ono, near Lydda. Their intentions were treacherous. Nehemiah made a reply that ought to be in the heart of every one who has a duty to fulfil: "I am doing a great work, and I cannot come down."* Sanballat returned to the charge. He sent an open letter to Nehemiah, which ran thus: "It is reported among the nations, and Geshem saith it, that thou and the Jews think to rebel; for which cause thou buildest the wall. And thou wouldest be their king, according to these words. And thou hast also appointed prophets to preach of thee at Jerusalem, saying, There is a King in Judah. And now shall it be reported to the king according to these words. Come now, therefore, and let us take counsel together." Sanballat's design was, by alarming Nehemiah, to hinder the completion of the work and the placing of the doors of the gates.

---

* Magnum opus facio, et non possum descendere.

Nehemiah was careful not to fall into the snare. There were still in truth *nebiim* in Jerusalem, but all were not favourable to Nehemiah. One of them, Shemaiah, son of Delaiah,* allowed himself to be won over by Sanballat, and strove to ruin Nehemiah by a plot, with most complicated details; but the wise *pekah*, who well knew his countrymen, skilfully frustrated his design.

It is singular that Nehemiah should have encountered, even among the class considered eminently pious men, an active opposition. A little poem which possibly belongs to this period seems to contain allusions unfavourable to him. His activity and human skill seemed to denote self-confidence and a proud heart, a sin unpardonable in any Jew.

> Except Iahveh build the house,†
> They labour in vain that build it;
> Except Iahveh keep the city,
> The watchman waketh but in vain.
>
> It is vain for you that ye rise up early
> And so late take rest,
> And eat the bread of toil;
> For so he giveth unto his beloved sleep.‡
>
> Lo! children are an heritage of Iahveh,
> And the fruit of the womb is his reward.

---

* Nehemiah vi. 10 and what follows. In the 11th verse read ליתר וגם לשמיעה הנביא בם. Noadiah should be stricken from the list of the Prophets.

† Psalm cxxvii. We have already observed that the Bible often gives side by side arguments for and against matters of which it treats. The same thing may be observed in the great collection of fragments put forth by the Greeks under the names of Plato, Aristotle, and Hippocrates.

‡ Or "sleeping." Read לידידו שנים, by the rule ם׳ = א.

> As arrows in the hand of a mighty man,
> So are the children of youth.*
>
> Happy is the man who hath his quiver full of them!
> They shall not be ashamed when they speak with their enemies in the gate.†

The wall was at last finished on the 25th day of the month Elul (the autumn equinox), after a labour which, according to the Hebrew text we have, lasted fifty-two days, but according to Josephus two years and four months. It was, as it were, the personal work of Nehemiah. In the city itself there was a party that hindered and thwarted him in every way, and carried on a regular correspondence with Tobiah. This personage, as we have seen, was connected by marriage with some of the leading men [of Jerusalem], who consequently were his sworn friends and allies. They kept him informed of all the words of Nehemiah. Tobiah, on his part, wrote them letters intended to be shown to Nehemiah with a view of intimidating him.‡

The months that followed the completion of the wall were full of cares and anxieties for Nehemiah. Tobiah watched him, and set spies on all his doings. The Shecaniahs and Meshullams wounded deeply the sensitive heart of Nehemiah by making in his presence pompous eulogies of Tobiah. § As soon as

---

* If this Psalm refers to Nehemiah, and if, as some suppose, because he had been a member of the household of the Persian king he was a eunuch, these latter verses may contain a contemptuous allusion.

† Read ירב.

‡ Nehemiah vi. 17–19.

§ טובתיו, a play on the word.

the doors of the gates were hung, and gate-keepers
put in office,* Nehemiah appointed his own brother
Hanani commandant of Jerusalem, and put the *bira*,
or citadel, in charge of a certain Hananiah, a man
much trusted by the ultra-religious party. The gate-
keepers were instructed to take the most severe
precautions. They were to open late in the morning,
and all night those who inhabited each section were
to set a watch on that part of the wall opposite to
their houses.

The inauguration of the walls† took place with
great ceremony. Levites were gathered together
from all directions, to make a great *hanukka* with
psalms of thanksgiving and praise, with an accom-
paniment of cymbals, nebels (psalteries), and kinnors
(harps). The singers living in the villages they
had built in the neighbourhood of Jerusalem flocked
into the city. They proceeded first to perform great
purifications on their own persons; then they purified, by sprinkling, the people, the gates, and the wall.
Nehemiah caused the Princes of Judah to stand upon
it, besides two great choral bands, which starting,
preceded by music, from the corner-gate (now Jaffa
Gate), marched in opposite directions, — one south,
the other east, — and were to come together at the
Temple. The two processions consisted first of the
singers, then of the Princes of Judah, and the priests

---

* Nehemiah vii. 1. Leave out the words והלוים והמשררים added by
the compiler of Chronicles.

† Nehemiah xii. 27–43. A fragment of the Memoirs.

with their trumpets,* Nehemiah himself closing the line of march in one of them.† One of these processions marched on the top of the wall southward till it reached the Pool of Siloam, where it left the wall, and mounted the steps which led along Ophel to the City of David, — that is to say, to Zion. The second procession, of which Nehemiah formed part, followed the line of the ramparts on the north through all its curves, until it reached the gate nearest to the Temple. There the two choirs met, and doubtless a solemn *toda* was sung by all of them. They imagined that the shade of David presided over these ceremonies; the songs and the musical instruments they used they believed had come down from him. The festival ended by sacrifices and feasting and songs of joy.

Never had the foundation of a city on the pure basis of religion without the aid of warriors been so openly avowed. Ancient cities seldom survived the overthrow of their country. If the Acropolis at Athens had been taken by the Persians, we should never have seen an assemblage of priests returning there and restoring the stated Panathenaic festivals, while Athens was still enslaved. Now, Nehemiah does not seem to have once dreamed

---

* Compare Psalm lxviii. But this Psalm is ancient; the processional hymn imitated the Psalm.

† According to our present text Ezra marched at the head of the first procession; but this must be an insertion on the part of the compiler of the Chronicles, who makes Nehemiah figure in the demonstration of Ezra, and Ezra in that of Nehemiah.

that anything of importance was lacking to his city, or that this city of priests and musicians wore the yoke of servitude. The priests who sounded their trumpets upon walls built by permission of a despot did not consider themselves slaves. So true is it that a church was founded that day in Jerusalem, and not a city. A crowd of people amused with *fêtes*, nobles flattered by honourable places being accorded to them in a procession, are not the elements that form a nation: a warlike aristocracy is also needed. The Jew will never be a citizen; he will simply live in the cities of others. But let us say at once that there is something else in this world besides even one's own country. Socrates at the moment of which we write was laying the foundation of philosophy, while Anytus and Melitus were about to contend that he was sapping the basis of the State. Liberty is distinctly a creation of modern times. It is the outcome of an idea which antiquity had not: that the State protects impartially the most opposite elements of men's activity, while remaining neutral in matters of conscience, sentiment, and taste.

CHAPTER VII.

THE ADMINISTRATION OF NEHEMIAH.

Not uncommonly devout men — even bigots — make excellent administrators; for the spirit of strict exactness which is dangerous in religion is a useful thing in government. Nehemiah appears to have made an admirable prefect in Judea, according to the ideas which, since the days of Ezekiel and the editors of the laws in Leviticus, represented constitutional rights in the Jewish nation. The singular growth of Jerusalem gave rise to many especial difficulties. The new city was enclosed in precisely the same space as the former one; but as the population was much smaller, there were many vacant spaces within the walls. Very few new houses had been built. The methods by which Judea was now governed, exclusively by men of ultra-religious views, made life in Jerusalem uncomfortable. The tribute due to Persia was heavy. Forced labour and requisitions were frequently called for.* A crowd of people who lived in Jerusalem were absolutely without the means of meeting the demand.

* Nehemiah v. 4; ix. 36, 37.

Nehemiah, to remedy this evil, made some singular regulations.* Jerusalem was to be looked upon as an aristocratic city in which it was a privilege to dwell. The heads of the people — laymen, priests, or levites — alone had a right to live there; as for the rest of the population, they must draw lots. Every tenth Jew was admitted to become an inhabitant of the Holy City; the other nine were to live in the suburbs. Those who were chosen were congratulated on their good fortune. The poems composed at this time are full of ardent devotion to Jerusalem. To dwell there was happiness; the favour of Iahveh was for those who abode therein. And then it was so beautiful a place! It was builded as a city that is "compact together" and can defend itself.†

> I was glad when they said unto me,
> Let us go into the house of Iahveh.
>
> Our feet are standing
> Within thy gates, O Jerusalem!
>
> Jerusalem, thou art builded
> As a city that is compact together, ‡
>
> Whither the tribes go up,
> Even the tribes of Iahveh,
>
> For a testimony unto Israel,
> To give thanks unto the name of Iahveh.

---

* Nehemiah xi., which should come immediately after chap. vii.

† Psalm cxxii. Many things would lead us to think that this Psalm was written in the reign of Josiah; but its style is later than the Captivity, and the whole Psalm exactly corresponds to the situation. Nehemiah xi. 1, 2.

‡ Ibn-Batoutah says the same thing of Mecca (vol. i. p. 303).

> For there are set thrones for judgment,
> The thrones of the house of David.*
>
> Pray for the peace of Jerusalem: saying,
> "They shall prosper that love thee.
>
> Peace be within thy walls,
> And prosperity within thy palaces."
>
> For my brethren and companions' sakes
> I will now say, Peace be within thee.
>
> For the sake of the house of Iahveh our God
> I will seek to do thee good.

Nehemiah then proceeded to take a census, the authentic text of which has come down to us.† The tribes of Judah and Benjamin were still mentioned separately, although they had become mixed as to residence. The priests were the aristocracy of the city. The levites, their subordinates in the hierarchy, the gate-keepers, and all employed in the Temple service had duties which must have given them wealth. We do not however know what were their duties outside of the Temple.‡ The singers of the choir of Asaph and of Ethan, whose duty it was to sing psalms of praise beginning by *Hodou*, were well off;§ they had their daily support assured to

---

* Possibly retrospective.

† This text is copied in 1 Chronicles ix. The variations are so great, and the numbers are subject to so many reserves, that it is very difficult to make much out of them. The fragment, xii. 1–26, is another list which the editor of the Chronicles did not wish to lose. Verses 10, 11 are an addition to the list of high-priests given us in Chronicles.

‡ המלאכת החיצנה.

§ Nehemiah xi. 17; xii. 9, &c. Note בקבקיה, the baqbouq of Jahve, — the Arab bakbouk.

them by a royal decree.* Other Israelites, priests and levites, lived in the hamlets of Judea. The *nethinim* lived at Ophel. Mezezabel was the king's commissioner to look after things in general. One cannot say exactly what was the nature of his employment.

The greater part of the men of Judah and of Benjamin continued to live in the country, each one on his own land. Chief among those places which the Jews had recovered, were Kirjath-arba, or Hebron, and its dependencies; Dibon (not the city of the Moabites) and its villages; Jekabzeel and its villages; Jeshua, Moladah, Beth-pelet, Hazar-shual, Beer-sheba and its dependencies; Ziklag, Meconah, En-rimmon, Zorah, Jarmuth, Zanoah, Adullam, Lachish, Azekah, and their dependencies. Jews were thus resettled in ancient Judea "from Beer-sheba even unto the Valley of Hinnom." The Benjamite villages also, Geba, Michmash, Aija, Bethel and its dependencies, Anathoth, Nob, Ananiah, Hazor, Rama, Gittaim, Hadid, Zeboim, Neballat, Lod, Ono, and Gehaharashim recovered a population more numerous than they had before the exile. In a hundred years the little nation had thus almost reconquered its former frontiers. The power of birth is strong.† The loss of population created by war and transportation to another land was rapidly remedied.

---

* Nehemiah xi. 23. Cf. Ezra vi. 8 and what follows; vii. 20 and what follows.
† Psalm cxxvii. 3–5.

Nehemiah, after being twelve years ruler in Jerusalem, all that time under Artaxerxes, made a journey in the year 433 B. C. to the seat of the Persian government.* As might have been expected, the liberal and tolerant party took advantage of his absence to relapse in many ways. Tobiah, his personal enemy, having come up to Jerusalem, was well received there by the best society. The high-priest Eliashib, his near connection, who had superintendence over the *liskoth* of the Temple, set apart for his lodging a large *liska*, used in general to store the offerings, the incense, the furniture and utensils needed in the Temple service, the tithes of money, wine, and oil, — all that was due, in short, to the levites, singers, and porters, and all that was set apart from the offerings for the priests. Many persons, it would seem, hoped that now Nehemiah had departed Tobiah might be appointed governor of Jerusalem, and they welcomed the prospect. These sentiments were to be found even among the priests, who were far from being, all of them, persons of exalted piety.

Nehemiah's stay at the Persian court appears not to have been long. He probably felt that his authority might be undermined if he were absent. On his return to Jerusalem he was extremely dissatisfied. The mere fact of Tobiah being lodged in the courts of the Temple shocked him exceedingly. He caused all Tobiah's furniture and effects to be flung out of the *liska*, had all the rooms he had occudied purified,

---

* Nehemiah xiii. 6.

and had the Temple offerings and the incense, which had been removed for his accommodation, put back into their place.

Nehemiah soon found that during his journey other abuses had crept into his jurisdiction. The dues of the levites had not been regularly paid; the levites and singers who should have officiated in the Temple, finding that they had not means of subsistence in Jerusalem, had gone back to their own lands that they might cultivate them. Nehemiah addressed sharp reproaches to the magistrates who should have looked to this; then he recalled the levites, and reinstalled them in their posts. He also organised a board, composed of a priest, a scribe, a levite, and a layman, who were all considered faithful men, to keep a watch over the stores. The members of the board were charged to make proper distributions to their brethren, and for a while abuses disappeared.

The observance of the Sabbath was becoming more and more the central principle of Judaism. Nehemiah, in one of his walks, saw men pressing out their grapes, while others brought into Jerusalem on asses wheat, wine, grapes, figs, and all sorts of other provisions on the Sabbath day. He sharply remonstrated. There were men of Tyre established in the city, who on the Sabbath sold fish and other articles; rich and influential people did not hesitate to buy of them. Nehemiah reproached them vehemently, and to put an end to the abuse employed a very decisive measure. He ordered that the marketplace should be closed at nightfall of the day before the Sabbath, and kept closed all the next day. During this time agents of the governor, posted at the gates of Jerusalem, prevented any loaded beast from entering the city. Men who had merchandise to sell had to pass the night outside the walls. When that had happened once or twice, the order was followed up by reprimands, then by threats, and after that the Sabbath was rigidly observed. The levites, ceremonially purified, were commissioned to watch over the observance of the holy rest.

Amongst Nehemiah's reforms nothing is said of circumcision, because probably of this there was no need. Every Jew in the fifth century B. C. was circumcised as a thing of course; and as the practice of circumcision was more and more discontinued through the East it became a simple sign, a mark in the flesh, of the covenant made with Iahveh.

Purity of race was the chief aim of these ancient zealots. Nehemiah objected above all to mixed marriages. These mixed marriages, forbidden in Deuteronomy,* had become very common in Judea. It was one of the consequences of the immigration. When people emigrate, men are always more numerous than women. The lists of those who returned to Palestine with Zerubbabel and Ezra contain only the names of men. The returned Jews therefore,

---

* Deuteronomy vii. 3, &c.; xi. 8; xxiii. 7; Nehemiah i. 7, &c. Cf. Ezra ix. 11, &c.

the rich especially, were thus forced to make marriages with the neighbouring people, — Moabites, Edomites, and Ammonites.

It would appear that those exiles who had been transported to Babylonia had been more strict on this point than those who stayed behind. Horror of the heathen was intense among the faithful in the far East; all nations except their own — the Children of Israel — were abominable in their sight.*
One day Nehemiah met some Jews who had married women of Ashdod, Ammon, and Moab, half of whose children spoke the speech of Ashdod or some other dialect, and did not know how to speak the language of the Jews.† Nehemiah reviled them vigorously, cursed them, smote some of them, and plucked out their hair, adjuring them in the name of God to make no alliances in the families of those who were not Jews.‡ The example of Solomon, led into sin by the influence of strange women, was held up to them as a salutary warning against such unions.

One of the sons of the high-priest Eliashib, named Joiadah, who afterwards succeeded his father, raised the scandal to its height; he married his son Manasseh to a daughter of Sanballat the Horonite,§

---

* Ezra ix. 14 ; see on the other hand Zechariah viii. 14, &c.

† יהודית.

‡ Nehemiah xiii. 23, &c. The same thing is attributed to Ezra.

§ Nehemiah xiii., 28, 29 ; Josephus, *Antiquities*, xi. vii., viii. Josephus has confounded ידוע and ידוע, and has consequently erred in the dates. See p. 134, notes.

called Nicaso. Nehemiah drove him from the city. Manasseh seems subsequently to have played a considerable part in the Samaritan schism. The feud between Nehemiah and Eliashib was increased by these things day by day. "Remember them, O God," he cried, "because they have defiled the priesthood and the covenant of the priesthood and of the levites." * The zealous reformer and the chief priests became more and more sharply opposed to each other, and the mutual antipathy which separated Nehemiah from Eliashib grew every day more bitter. It opened the gulf which five hundred years later lay between Jesus and Caiaphas. Caiaphas compassed the death of Jesus; but Jesus rose again.

The priesthood, busied exclusively with the sacrifices, gave little time to the reading of the Torah. Reading the Torah on the contrary was the great lever by which Nehemiah hoped to raise his people. Men left the gatherings [where the Torah had been read to them] with feelings of pride and frenzied national jealousy.† One day while reading the Law they heard how Moabites and Ammonites were to be excluded forever from the household of God, because they had refused bread and water to the Israelites, and had hired Balaam to curse them.‡ When they heard this they put out from among themselves such persons with zeal still more severe. How far was

---

* Nehemiah xiii. 21.

† Nehemiah xiii. 1, 2, 3, — an addition by the writer of Chronicles to prepare the way for the episode that follows.

‡ Deuteronomy xxiii. 3 and what follows.

all this from the spirit of the great Anonymous Prophet of the Captivity! The *odium generis humani* had its root in those far-off days. But the faults of Israel have always been the faults of a noble minority, which has in the eyes of history absorbed the rest of the race, and been accepted as its representative.

Nehemiah appears to have died at a good old age, and to have seen the first years of the reign of Darius Nothus.* He was a conscientious fanatic, perfecting his plans with care and a strong will. In the latter part of his life he wrote his autobiography; and this curious document, one of the most precious relics of Hebrew literature, has come down to us with only slight alterations, proceeding probably from the writer of Chronicles.† Few writings bear more strongly the impress of personality than these memoirs, though we may suspect fable in the anecdotes of childhood.‡ The pious ejaculatory prayers, full of piety and self-complacency, and of rancour against Sanballat and Tobiah, give a most true idea of the piety of these times. Nehemiah looks only to Iahveh for his reward; but yet the opinion of men is by no means indifferent to him. He has self-complacency, nay, even vanity. He wants every one to know what he has done, the gratitude his people owe him, and the disinterested-

---

* Josephus, *Antiquities*, xi. v. 8; *Chron. Alex.*, p. 381; Ol. lxxxi.

† See previous page 59, note.

‡ Nehemiah ii. Compare the story of the youths of Darius's guard, 1 Esdras iii., iv. Esther and Daniel begin in a similar way.

ness with which he has conducted all his enterprises. He wishes to pass for a model *pekah,* governing his co-religionists.* Prefects in those days were paid (that is to say, supported) by those they ruled over. Nehemiah during the twelve years of his administration refused to receive such maintenance. He and his family cost his people nothing. He says: —

> From the time that I was appointed to be governor in the land of Judea, from the twentieth even to the two and thirtieth year of Artaxerxes the king, I and my brethren have not eaten the bread of the governor. But the former governors were chargeable unto the people, and took from them bread and wine, yea, besides forty shekels of silver; even their servants bore rule over the people. But so did not I, because of the fear of God. Yea, also, continued I in the work of this wall, neither bought we any land, and all my servants were gathered thither unto the work. Moreover, there were at my table of the Jews and the rulers an hundred and fifty men, besides those that came unto us from among the heathen that dwelt round about us. Now, that that was prepared for one day was one ox and six choice sheep, also fowls were prepared for me, and once in ten days store of all sorts of wine; yet for all this I demanded not the bread of the governor, because the bondage was heavy upon this people. Remember unto me, O God, for good all that I have done for this people.

This is very fine, no doubt; but how much grander does the bleeding heart of Jeremiah appear to us with its sombre and despairing self-devotion!

* Nehemiah v. 14-19.

CHAPTER VIII.

LEGENDARY STORY OF EZRA.

THOSE who were personally cognisant of the manner in which reforms were effected in the fifth century B. C. no doubt attributed all the success of this great movement to Nehemiah.* That reform, effected by a governor appointed by the King of Persia, must certainly have created a deep impression on the Jewish mind. The reading of the Memoirs of Nehemiah, a scroll circulated shortly before or after his death, must have increased the effect, and seems to have provoked among the priests, the levites, and the pharisaic class in general a somewhat violent reaction. It seemed to these personages dangerous that a mere lay functionary should have played so prominent a part. They would have preferred that a scribe, a man of priestly birth, should at least have contributed an equal share to the great restoration, and should have given the last touch to the Torah.

Hence came the creation of the part of Ezra, a part parallel to that of Nehemiah. The Memoirs of Nehemiah served as a pattern for those of Ezra.

---

* Ecclesiasticus xlix. 13, and the letter at the beginning of 2 Maccabees i. 10, &c.

Memoirs for the scribe were composed on the same lines as those of the governor.* Then the author of Chronicles soldered both together, in such a way as to convey an impression that both scribe and governor acted in concert, both being concerned in the same reforms and presiding over the same ceremonies.†

A branch of the family of Seraiah, which did not go back to Jerusalem like Joshua the son of Josedeck, is thought to have kept the old family tradition. Sometime in the reign of Artaxerxes Longimanus, a great-grandson, or rather the son of a great-grandson, of Seraiah, named Ezra, is supposed to have formed a resolution to go up to Jerusalem, and settle there, taking with him a considerable treasure contributed by the Jews still living in Babylonia. Is this pure fiction, or is it some reminiscence of how a real personage, a member of the house of Seraiah, played an important part in Jerusalem in the fifth century? It is hard to say. All we know is that

* Chapters vii.-x. of what we know as the Book of Ezra and viii.-x. of Nehemiah, have been made out of the so-called Memoirs of Ezra, in which Ezra is supposed to speak in the first person. Such compositions in autobiographical form were the taste of that period. Compare Nehemiah and Tobit. We shall then see on what a weak foundation the history of Ezra as an historical personage rests. The son of Sirach (author of Ecclesiasticus), xlix. 11-13, mentions only Zerubbabel, Joshua the son of Josedeck, and Nehemiah. See 2 Maccabees i.

† Everything leads us to think that Ezra, if really an historical personage, died before the arrival of Nehemiah, notwithstanding Nehemiah viii. 9 and xii. 36. Compare Josephus, *Antiquities*, xi. v. 5. The circumstances of the assembly held by Ezra, whether real or imaginary, presume Nehemiah's wall not to have been built.

the story of Ezra has several contradictory facts at its foundation. According to some he came to strengthen the Hierosolymite feeling in the colony, a hundred years after its resurrection. According to others the book that records the return of Ezra is a νόστος, a poem of return like many others. These νόστοι had become a kind of literature which took for its theme some touching episode. Ezra is made to organise the return, as though Sheshbazzar and Zerubbabel had never existed. The Temple, the town, the Law, the walls, — all date from him. He shines under Artaxerxes as the great reorganiser of the Jewish nation.

In this narrative the author dwells with great complacency on grand pictures of scenes in religious story, such as were in conformity with the manners of the time. The caravan of Ezra, we are given to understand, left Babylonia in the year 458 B.C.* It was composed of about fifteen hundred men.† There were among them many priests of the house of Aaron, and at least one member of the family of David, — Hattush, grandson of Shechaniah.‡ Ezra

---

* The autobiographical chapters are more vague. See viii. 1. It was desirable to bring the dates of Zerubbabel and Ezra nearer together. Josephus felt this. The desire to make Ezra the contemporary and equal of Nehemiah may have led to lowering the dates of Ezra thirty or forty years.

† Even if we look upon the Memoirs of Ezra as fictitious, we may permit ourselves to perceive in them many true facts which the writer may have got from some other narrative, or general facts in the history of the time.

‡ Cf. 1 Chronicles iii. 22.

appointed a gathering on the bank of the Canal of Ahava near Babylon; they encamped there for three days, and their leader held a sort of review and took a census of his band. All were priests (*cohanim*) or laymen (the *mebinim*, or doctors of the law, must have been counted as such). It was found that there were neither levites to serve the priests, nor *nethinim*, serfs of Solomon (or, as they were then called, "servants of David and the princes"), to minister to the levites. Ezra sent heads of families and some of the *mebinim* to a certain Iddo, chief of the *nethinim*, who lived at a place called Kasifia,* in order to provide servants for the House of God.† Thirty-eight levites and two hundred and twenty *nethinim* joined the band of emigrants.

Before setting out, the caravan united in a solemn fast on the bank of the Ahava, to humble themselves before Iahveh and to obtain his blessing on their journey. Ezra, a man who loved order, had an inventory taken of all the vessels of gold, silver, and copper-gilt‡ which he was carrying up to Jerusalem for the service of the Temple, and gave them in charge to certain priests and levites, who were to remit them in safety to the chief rulers of the Temple. These weighed them in their turn in the *liskoth* of the Temple, to see if their weight was correct, before giving a discharge to their bearers.

---

* Ezra viii. 17. The text is certainly faulty. I would substitute ואחי לאל. In verse 18 א׳ששבל is also undoubtedly a proper name.

† It appears he did not know that there were already levites at Jerusalem.

‡ No mention is made of coined money.

The journey was fortunate. It lasted four months, lacking eleven days, — from April to July. On arriving, the caravan rested three days. The fourth day Ezra gave in his accounts, which were found correct; the gifts were committed to two priests, Meremoth the son of Uriah, and Eleazar the son of Phineas, assisted by two levites. The accounts were compared and duly ratified. The new arrivals offered magnificent sacrifices, and the poor feasted for many days.

We repeat, it is doubtful if such things took place simply on the arrival at Jerusalem of a priest called Ezra in the days of Artaxerxes Longimanus; but the facts related were undoubtedly true when any companies of consequence from the East arrived to reinforce the Hierosolymite idea of the restoration of the kingdom of Israel, — a hope so bold yet so little understood. As always happens when two currents of ideas which start from the same point meet after parallel developments, the two branches of the family of Israel found that their views were different. At the date assigned to Ezra they had lived apart seventy-eight years; those who came out of Chaldea were richer than their brethren in Palestine, more cultivated, and more scrupulous in religious observances. There could not but be disagreements. The most orthodox party always gets the better of the less orthodox in the history of Israel. The new arrivals soon proved severe censors of the resident population. The carelessness that seemed to them prevailing in Jerusalem appeared backsliding. One thing especially made them indignant,— the very little care the population at Jerusalem took to keep itself apart, in the choice of wives, from the surrounding populations.

Here Ezra is at one with Nehemiah. To combat abuses that he considered enormous, he employed, we are told, means that were not unsuited to the customs of the time, giving out that he was acting under the authority of the King of Persia. According to the canonical account he had come to Jerusalem bringing a letter from King Artaxerxes, which, amongst other extraordinary powers, conferred on him the right to appoint magistrates to administer justice according to the Jewish Law, and to teach that Law to those who did not know it. The law of God and the law of the Persian king are thus in some sort identified. Ezra had received power to enforce the Law, "by death, by exile, by fines, or by imprisonment."

We can hardly believe that Artaxerxes ever could have written such a letter.* We doubt that Ezra ever grounded his authority on such a document; we would rather believe it an invention of his biographer.† What may be true is, that, having

---

* Compare the so-called edict of Cyrus with Ezra vii. 27. The man who wrote the memoirs of Ezra must have had in his hands that other document. Ezra i.; iv. 6; vi. 13. Examine also chap. x. All are literally fragments, pious romances.

† The letter has its echo in Ezra viii. 22, 25, 36; ix. 9. It is part of the so-called Memoirs.

come from the East, he may have uttered threats giving his people to understand that he had lived on terms of intimacy with the king and with his officers, whom undoubtedly he never met personally.* It is an old device practised by the Jews, always to bring forward a plea that they have an official mission from government. The Roman Catholic Church, and sects in general which pretend to despise force, fall into the same error. The man of peace is very apt to plume himself on the favour of the man of war. He looks towards what is strong, — that is, to active power wherever it may chance to be. Thus the Jews have persecuted with the power of Persian kings; nay, even with the might of Rome itself. No man is more domineering than a priest when he can make use of the secular arm; no man more insolent than the Jew when a functionary not of his faith is placed under his orders, or a regiment is at his command. Fanatics are always servile towards those in power, in order to induce them to show rigour to those who are the objects of their aversion. We have spoken elsewhere † of the weakness of mind that supposes Iahveh to obtain for his people the protection of the mighty. By favour of the Persian king he caused his Temple to be rebuilt. This seems to us rather a small thing for the Almighty. But in all this development of the Jewish mind we need not look for a motive in reason.

* Ezra viii. 22, 25.
† See vol. iii. p 384 and what follows.

Whether Ezra was or was not acting under Persian authority, he employed, if we believe the documents concerning him, the roughness of a fanatical gendarme to carry out his work of reform. Seconded by a certain man named Shechaniah son of Jehiel, he organised what we might call a league against mixed marriages. Not only did the members of this league engage never to contract such alliances in future, but they promised to send away the poor women whom they had lawfully espoused, and also their children. Nearly all the nobles, especially the members of the sacerdotal aristocracy, drew down on themselves the anathemas of the ultra-pious. Several resisted; others had recourse to deceptions; some sent away their wives, but retained their children. But the greater part committed the monstrous act required of them by Ezra. Almost all the members of the high-priest's family submitted, and offered a sacrifice of expiation. A very dangerous fanaticism had now taken root in Israel,—not such as the State may exert, but what zealots may accomplish when they claim to be backed by official power.

The mass of the people, however, did not willingly submit. The debate lasted three months before it was settled. A sort of grand assemblage of all the inhabitants of Judea, called together on the open space before the Temple, proved very tumultuous; they demanded time to send each case before a court, on pretext that a heavy rain was falling. But finally, as was always the case, the party of the zealots won the victory.

One thing which shows a decided step made by the Jews of those days in the history of Judaism, was that Ezra, though certainly a descendant of Aaron, never seems to have exercised the functions of a priest. Still less was he a prophet. He was a doctor learned in the Law (*sofer mebin*). This is decisive. From that time forward it is easy to foresee that it is not the *cohen* who will lead in the affairs of Judaism, but the doctor. To obey the Torah being the chief end of a man's life, he who interprets the Torah has the most power. And who should nominate this interpreter of the Torah? Not the body of the priests; not the Church as a whole (that idea would not prevail before the second century of the Christian era). The doctor will be appointed for his knowledge, his merit, his ease of address, and his audacity. The *sofer mahir* will be spiritual king in Israel. The most insignificant doctor rising in the synagogue, if he has a good memory and confidence in himself, will be able to put down the man who holds authority.

The Talmud was the destined outcome of the idea started by Ezra. One feels that Judaism will have no organised sacerdotal body, no papacy, no œcumenical councils. It will be something like Protestantism in the sixteenth century, — a struggle between learned leaders, each founding his opinions upon certain written texts, which he will hold to be of paramount value.

CHAPTER IX.

THE FINAL CONSOLIDATION OF THE TORAH.

A VERY common belief, and one that has been put forth to answer many purposes and in different ways, is that Ezra had an important share in the re-editing of the Pentateuch.* Some think he rewrote from memory the contents of the books lost in the sack of Jerusalem, and thus restored them to their place. But that is a mere childish hypothesis, which has its origin in the apocryphal books of Esdras, written, it is supposed, in the latter years of the first century of our era, for which, notwithstanding, Saint Jerome and other fathers of the Church have shown singular complaisance. According to others, Ezra was the author of the sacerdotal parts of the Pentateuch, which at present envelop and complete the ancient Iahvist portions. Nothing can be more unlikely than that a work of such importance should be intrusted to a mere scribe of no especial ability. What is possible, nay, even probable, is that Ezra may have had a hand in putting the last touches to the ritualistic portions of the levitical law. As the

* See vol. iii. p. 362, note 1.

covenant made in the days of Josiah led to the creation of new texts concerning the Law, so we may suppose that the covenant of Nehemiah, which differs little from that of Ezra, left its trace upon the Torah.* A great number of special regulations had never been written down, or had been added in a sporadic manner, as separate laws.

And even when the Torah of Iahveh had absorbed almost the whole religious consciousness of Israel, the unity of the book was not yet firmly established. Copies of it were extremely scarce; no two of them were exactly alike. Many Jews considered that Deuteronomy alone comprised the Torah; others that the Torah contained all the accumulation of religious writings both before and after the days of Hezekiah, having absorbed, under Josiah, both Deuteronomy and many supplementary levitical customs. Others thought it consisted only of a small collection of the laws supposed to comprise the revelations given to Moses on Mount Sinai.†

The fusion of all this into one code seems to have been after the restoration of public worship; the first restoration of which was made by Zerubbabel and Joshua the son of Josedeck, when literary ability was very feeble. The *sofer*, or scribe, appears to have had little to do with it. The restoration of Nehemiah

---

* Observe the similarity of the things ordained by Ezra, and those by Nehemiah (Nehemiah x., xii., also p. 107, &c.), with the levitical code.

† See vol. iii. p. 44 and what follows, and pp. 207, 243.

(or Ezra), on the contrary, was mainly the work of *soferim,* or *mebinim.* As far as we can judge of the documents in the possession of Nehemiah or Ezra, they do not seem to have been at first acquainted with the Pentateuch as we have it now. But during their abode in Jerusalem they were not idle. It is quite probable that the different portions of the Hexateuch were at this time put together in definitive form. The collection formed, as we think, under Hezekiah, and enlarged by Deuteronomy under Josiah, was nearly doubled by the insertion of a crowd of laws, enacted at various periods, and proceeding from divers sources. On these the theoretical essays of Ezekiel and his school were founded. And thence comes the important fact that the priestly and levitical code has not the unity that we find in Deuteronomy, — except, indeed, the brief code of the school of Ezekiel;* and this seems like a rounded pebble which no after changes have decomposed.

In what concerns the laws, the work of insertion and compilation was easy, for in those days men were not particular as to method and order; but in all that concerned the life of Moses the matter was more delicate.† They had to proceed as their predecessors had done under Hezekiah, when they fused

---

* Leviticus xviii.-xxvi.

† Many episodes of levitical origin in Exodus and Numbers might be explained either by supposing a life of Moses written about the year 500 B. C., from a priestly or levitical point of view, or by levitical and sacerdotal interpolations made by the old Elohist. In general, the work of the levitical interpolator is strikingly like that of the Elohist

together two documents, — one Iahvist, the other Elohist. The most remarkable instance of this is the fusion of the rebellion of Dathan and Abiram with the revolt of Korah, which was found only in new lives of Moses. The fusion has been very roughly performed.* As to the episodes of Balaam, and that of the daughters of Zelophahad, they proceeded by way of simple juxtaposition, at the risk of making the narrative contradictory or redundant.

If Ezra was really the author of this work of final compilation and arrangement, we must attribute to him the numerous critical remarks and glosses — written at first on the margin, and afterwards inserted in the text — which are to be found in the most ancient portions of the Hexateuch. These additions are sometimes whole paragraphs explanatory or apologetic.† Often on the margin several texts would be transcribed, giving the look of experiments at reconciliation. These texts were recopied later into the place to which they seemed to belong, which gave rise to strange repetitions. These may be seen particularly in lists containing numbers,

(note in particular what concerns the manna). But then we should have to admit that this fusion of the writings of the Iahvist with those of the ancient Elohist took place in the fifth century: whereas, I maintain that it took place in the days of Hezekiah. After the Captivity there was no more meddling with the patriarchal stories, and it is probable that the additions made to the old text of the history of Moses were made by original insertions, not by incorporating the pages of any other book.

* Numbers xv. 1, &c.

† The most striking example may be found in Numbers xxvi. 9–12, which was certainly inserted later than the last fusion.

in which the sum total has not been changed, even when one or two items have been added.*

Putting aside the personality of Ezra, concerning which we have very little to go upon, we should probably be not far wrong in placing the final arrangement of the Hexateuch about the year 450 B. C. It had become the custom to write after the Hexateuch the books of Judges and of Samuel, as they had been arranged at the time of Hezekiah, and revised with interpolations in Josiah's day. The books of the Kings followed, with many passages cut out, of which the compiler takes care to inform us, so as to increase our regret.

Thus was formed, in about four centuries, by the union of the most diverse materials, that strange conglomeration which contains fragments of epic poetry, scraps of sacred history, bits of the law of custom, ancient popular hymns, the stories of wild tribes, utopias with fictitious religious observances, legends stamped with fanaticism, and morsels of prophecy, — all coated with a slag of piety, which has made of so miscellaneous a collection a sacred book, the very soul and heart of a people. It is not uncommon in Greece to meet with old towns built in the later period, and sometimes in antiquity, out of the ruins of ancient monuments. Blocks of marble of various sorts, cut with skill but ill assorted, form the first layers, with gaps between them filled in with materials of no value. Fragments of statues,

* Genesis xlvii.

fluted shafts of columns, are mixed in with rude rough blocks of stone; breaches have been repaired by the insertion of layers of cement, or else some modern patchwork fills up the place, as rude clamps hold together the edges of disconnected parts. The citadel of the town is but a heap of stones in which modern Greek chiefs have made loop-holes. The whole seems barbarous, but you have inestimable materials stowed away in this shapeless confusion; and if you demolish the masonry you may form a museum. Such is Hebrew history. No artistic sentiment having presided over its construction, disorder and contradiction may be found on every page; and we may be glad of it. If an historical artist had composed the structure, he would have recut the stones, rectified the incongruities, and filled up with more care the chinks which now offend us. But, thanks to the incoherence of the final revision of the ancient Scriptures, we have now the immense advantage of possessing intact authentic Hebrew documents of the ninth or tenth centuries before the birth of Jesus Christ. All that we need do to find them is simply to wash them, and to peel off the plaster that modern renovators have poured into the interstices.

The old Greeks, who did everything with style and art, would in a similar case have worked over these materials until we could no longer have recognised what was original. The Iliad and the Odyssey are, like the body of ancient Hebrew history, the product of the collection of many earlier fragments. But the Greeks showed genius even in compilation; they executed their work with such perfection that the seams and discrepancies unavoidable in it can be perceived in very few places. The Homer of the Hebrews is no way inferior to the Homer of the Greeks; but he has come down to us in fragments, as if the Iliad and the Odyssey were known to us only in the sections preserved in the Library of Apollodorus, or in the Byzantine chronographs.

Meantime the living animal completed itself. It manifested a tendency to get rid of a sort of tail, which according to the ideas of the time injured its unity. The principal object of the Torah was the legislation of Moses; the Jews grew to consider the records that succeeded the death of Moses — that is, the Book of Joshua — as a different work. Joshua was not placed in the same scroll as Moses. The name of Torah was only given to the part which ended by the death of Moses on Mount Nebo.* Here was the divine revelation complete; all the rest was only so far inspired as the words of any religious teacher may claim to be.†

After the days of Nehemiah, or if you will of Ezra, the Torah was more regularly circulated. Before that time it had been a creation of the mind, which all men had heard of but few even of the learned had

---

* The Pentateuch as the Samaritans received it from the Jews, about the year 400 B.C., did not contain the Book of Joshua.

† Josephus, *Against Apion.*, i. 8. Compare Philo, *De mundi incorruptibilitate*, vol. ii. (ed. Mangey) p. 491.

read. They then began to make discoveries which now astonish us. They found books several centuries old. We have often seen how they introduced as novelties into their own writings commands that had appeared long before in older documents. The Torah was not a code of laws promulgated by the State and administered by judges; it was a sacred book, containing ordinances to which the stricter Jews desired to conform, but which till after the days of which we speak had behind it no sanction of authority. Now all will be changed. In a few years the Torah will have the force of law. The doctor of the law will become a jurist; the *bethdin* will be a court of justice. When political independence shall have disappeared, the Torah will become a statute everywhere affecting the Jew. It will follow him whithersoever he may go, and the Talmud will be its authorised commentary.

About the time when the last touches were given to the Torah, the compilation of the prophetic documents took place; a second collection was thus added to the one that now popularly bore the almost superhuman name of Moses. In making the collection precedence was given to length, always so dear to the East. After the three great inspired prophets,—Isaiah, Jeremiah, and Ezekiel, which were written down exactly as they were read,—they placed other shorter writings which bore other names. Haggai and Zechariah, who belonged only to the preceding generation, closed the volume. At the close of Zechariah were inserted some older fragments, which — thanks to the place given them, and perhaps to a certain misleading likeness of name — passed for the writings of Zechariah.*

The little library of the prophetic writings thus formed is far from presenting to us all that Hebrew genius produced in that line. Already perhaps, before the Captivity, a selection had been made especially from the prophets who prophesied before Isaiah. It seems impossible that all the literary activity of such men as Hosea and Amos should have been summed up in a few pages. The volume that was later called that of the Minor Prophets is only an Anthology drawn from a much larger volume, comprehending particularly writings concerning the kingdom of Israel. The principles that guided the authors of this Anthology we can easily perceive. Like almost all the Israelites who have held the *kalam*, they wished for proof. They took by preference, first, the passages which favoured the idea of union between the kingdoms of Judah and Israel; and, secondly, declamations such as proved that even from ancient times the idea of a Messiah had had birth. This was, as we have seen, the inspiring feeling of the great Anonymous Prophet who in Babylon, about 536, constituted himself the continuer of Isaiah, and was so deeply imbued with the spirit of ancient prophecy. The insertion of the curious Book of Jonah into the canon was due, perhaps, to his

* See vol. ii. pp. 391, 392, and vol. iii. p. 274, note 1.

universalist and humanitary character. The volume of the Minor Prophets was a sort of *Selectæ*, a collection of passages considered to have reference to the Messiah. It saved the early Christians in this way much trouble; the choice of prophetic passages had been made ready to their hands.

CHAPTER X.

PROMULGATION OF THE LAW.

Thus, it may be seen, criticism has reduced almost to nothing the share of Ezra in editing the Hexateuch. But can he have been the promulgator of that Torah which he did not draw up, and which from that day forth was to be as it were the sole centre of the life of Israel? The narrative which has come down to us has on this point no greater historical value than all the rest. It may, however, give us a general idea of an event which under one form or another must have left a deep trace on the Jewish mind.

Eloquent discourses in praise of some object, missions such as the Jesuits subsequently set on foot, solemn covenants ending in feasts and sacrifices, were very much to the taste of the Jews. A number of legendary stories coming down from the times of Moses and of Joshua induced an imaginative people to take satisfaction in scenes of *berith*, or of covenant, which seemed like a fresh departure into new eras in the relations of Iahveh with his people. Ezra had contemplated a brilliant occasion of the kind.* The seventh month (Tisri), answering to

---

* Nehemiah viii. The real Book of Ezra consists of four chapters — vii., viii., ix., x. — of the book called the Book of Ezra, and chapters

the autumn equinox, brought the Feast of Tabernacles, when all Israel passed several days in huts of boughs in the open air. The very small extent of country occupied by the colonists who had returned to their own land, made it easy to assemble nearly all the nation at the same place. This circumstance greatly favoured the stroke planned by Ezra. In a year, probably about 450 B. C., almost all Israel, summoned by the great agitator and scribe, assembled at Jerusalem. The stage for the occasion was in the centre of the great open space near that gate of the Temple known as the Watergate. As the wall was not yet built, the crowd spread out towards what is now the seraglio.

Before the assembled people Ezra presented himself, we are told, holding the roll of the Torah in his hand. Here is the scene as it is related to us in the ancient Life of Ezra: —

And Ezra the priest brought the Law before the congregation, both men and women, and all old enough to hear with understanding, upon the first day of the seventh month. And he read therein before the broad place that was before the Water-gate, from early morning until midday, in the presence of the men and the women and those that could understand; and the ears of all the people were

---

viii., ix., and x. of the Book of Nehemiah. The First Book of Esdras speaks of things in this order (Kuenen, *Hist. crit. des livres de l'Anc. Testament*, i. 502). The name of Nehemiah has been erroneously introduced in viii. 9, by the editor of Chronicles. The memoirs of Nehemiah never mention Ezra. If Ezra had been contemporary with the pious governor, what opportunities there would have been to mention him, especially in connection with the rebuilding of the wall!

attentive unto the book of the Law. And Ezra the scribe stood upon a pulpit of wood which they had built for that purpose, and beside him stood Mattithiah and Shema and Anaiah and Uriah and Hilkiah and Maaseiah on his right hand; and on his left hand, Pediah and Mishael and Malchiajah and Hashum, and Hashbaddanah, Zechariah, and Meshullam. And Ezra opened the book in the sight of all the people (for he was above all the people); and when he opened it all the people stood up; and Ezra blessed Iaveh the great God, and all the people answered, Amen! Amen! with the lifting up of their hands; and they bowed their heads, and worshipped the Lord with their faces to the ground. Also Joshua and Bani and Sherebiah, Jamin, Akkub, Shabbethai, Hodiah, Maaseiah, Kelita, Azariah, Jozabad, Hanan, Pelaiah, and the levites caused the people to understand the Law; and the people stood in their place. And they read in the book in the law of God distinctly; and they gave the sense, so that they understood the reading.

The Israelites all wept. Ezra and the levites * comforted them, and exhorted them to rejoice. The next morning they set themselves to understand what Ezra the day before had read. The Torah from which he had read seems to have been a new document to them, unknown until that day. They found an account of how they should observe the Feast of Tabernacles.† The people hastened at once to keep the feast according to the law of Moses, indeed, but a law forgotten and fallen into disuse from time immemorial. The feast was kept seven days in ar-

* Nehemiah viii. 9. The editor of Chronicles has added האךשתא נחמיה הוא.

† Numbers xxix.; Leviticus xxiii.

bours erected with boughs on the roofs of the houses, in the courts, in the open space before the principal door of the Temple, in the square of the Watergate, and in that before the Gate of Ephraim. Each day they listened to reading from the Torah. The eighth day there was a solemn assembly.*

The narrative thus explains by successive and repeated acts what was probably the result of long habit and slow transformation. The feasts furnished occasions for what we call missions, retreats, revivals, when people assemble for mutual edification and endeavour to revive in each other zeal for the law of God, such as the piety of the time conceived it. The reading of the Law made part of all these feasts. They prepared themselves for them by separating themselves from strangers, by fasting, mourning, and humiliation, by the Psalms of penitence, and by confession of sins, their own and their fathers. The levites assembled on a platform, and played an important part on these pious occasions.†

These manifestations gave rise to certain religious compositions, a kind of public confession, — one of which at least we have recorded in the memoirs of Ezra,‡ and several of which found their way into the Book of Psalms. I wish to speak further of these penitential Psalms, which have become of such great importance in the devotions of pious Christians, —

---

* Compare Deuteronomy xvi.
† Nehemiah ix. ‡ Ibid.

especially of the one known as the *Miserere*,* in which the religious sorrow of our entire race has found so perfect an expression from generation to generation. There are also psalms which may be considered holy narratives in verse,† in which the author, recalling the ancient wonders done by God for the protection of his people, seeks to prove that such miracles may occur again, and above all things wishes to establish as a truth that all the sorrows that have fallen upon Israel are because the people have been unfaithful to the Law.

It was natural that these pious efforts crowned with great success should result in a species of new covenant,‡ even as the proclamation of Deuteronomy under Josiah had called to mind the first covenant of Israel with Iahveh on the basis of the Law of Moses. According to some accounts, the covenant was put in writing with all the formalities of a civil contract; then all the nobles, priests, and levites signed it by appending their seals. The rest of the people gave in their adherence, — both those who had returned from exile, and the descendants of those who had never quitted their country, but had kept themselves aloof from any admixture with the surrounding nations. All, except children not old enough to understand, bound themselves by a solemn oath to obey the entire

---

* Psalm li. *Ut œdificentur muri Jerusalem* proves that it was composed before 445 B. C.

† Psalms cv., cvi., cxxxv., cxxxiv., &c. The manner in which the episode of Korah, Dathan, and Abiram is mentioned gives us its date.

‡ Nehemiah x.

Torah; to abstain from mixed marriages; to buy nothing on the Sabbath, nor on any holy day, from strangers who might offer merchandise or provisions for sale; to observe the seventh year of release, — both as to giving the land rest, and the release of all debts that had been made on mortgage. They also bound themselves to give each year the third part of a shekel* for the service of the Temple, for the shew-bread, for the daily sacrifices and offerings, for the Sabbaths, new moons, and feasts, and for the sin-offerings, etc.; and they regulated by lot the offering of wood to be burnt upon the altar. They promised to bring yearly the first fruits of their grain, of their wine, oil, and fruit, to the Temple; also the first-born of their children and their animals, and this without prejudice to a tithe of the products of the soil which was collected by the levites on the spot. The priests acted as overseers of the levites during this work, and the levites were to bring the tenth part of the tithes they collected to the priests in the *liskoth* of the Temple. These *liskoth* were thus converted into store-chambers, in which were laid up corn, wine, and oil for the use of the priests; there also were kept all things necessary for the service of the sanctuary; also in small chambers, such as are still found in the East in connection with mosques, lived the priests during their term of service, the porters, the singers, and such levites as were necessary for the daily service of the Temple:

---

* Matthew xvii. 24, — half a shekel.

the rest could consume their portion of the tithes wherever they pleased.

In all this they believed themselves, especially in what concerned the singers, to be following out the laws laid down by David and Solomon. Asaph was more and more esteemed as the creator of the music of the sanctuary, and they were confirmed in the belief that David was the author of a great number of the *tchillim* and the *todoth*.*

From that time forward the Torah existed as a completed book. A few additions are believed to have been subsequently made to it; but legislation was settled in all its essential parts, and the copies made differ little from each other. The book was too long to be copied on a single scroll; the practice arose of dividing it, uniformly, into portions making five volumes, or *megilloth*.† Writing was much more common than it had been before this time. Public reading had been hitherto the custom; now private reading was about to commence. The *sefer* ceased to be a document to be consulted in time of need, and became a book of which there were many copies all alike.‡ A similar revolution was going on about this time in Greece. The "Muses" of Herodotus mark out the passage from the book intended to be read aloud in the open air, to the book to be read at home.

* Nehemiah xii. 44-47, are additions by the author of Chronicles. Compare Ezra iii. 10; Nehemiah xii. 24, 35, 36.
† This was called " five fifths " of the Torah.
‡ Note Deuteronomy xvii. 18, 19.

Such a revolution almost always coincides with the time when writing-materials are becoming common and cheap. In Greece as well as in the East the papyrus, prepared in Egypt, was largely used. Books of philosophy, which till now in Grecian countries had consisted only of poems of five or six hundred lines, in which each word was duly weighed, then written upon tablets and deposited in a temple, were soon to become charming conversational chats. As soon as paper becomes cheap, people begin to write as they speak; Plato's Dialogues replace the dark sayings of Heraclitus. In Israel at about the same date books began to be multiplied; many men could read, had copies of the Law, and meditated daily upon it. The book was cut up into sections for the convenience of readers in public. The Bible began to exist in the complete sense of the word. At first it was only the Hexateuch; then the volume of the prophetical books was united to the Hexateuch, and gave a new and powerful stimulant to piety.

Thus in the Semitic world was created the first *Qoran*, or book for public reading. With us, we have but one word for what is to be read privately or in public. Among Semitic people the word *qara* (or *kara*) means only for public reading.* *Mikra* was the sacred text laid before the reader on a pulpit or a reading-desk.†

* For private reading the word *haga* was used.
† Nehemiah viii. 8.

One is sometimes surprised that the revision of the Torah was not carried a step further, and that the Jews, whose whole bent at this period was towards the creation of laws and ordinances for the public service of religion, did not break into the historical framework of their Scriptures, and form a code drawn up methodically and unencumbered by startling contradictions. The temptation to do this must have been all the stronger because within a few years Deuteronomy had been put forth as a Torah in itself, intended to replace former documents which contained many contradictions. The scrupulous good faith of the scribes in dealing with their ancient scriptures carried the day against any attempt at change. They preserved all the irregularities and contradictions. It was not until the second century of the Christian era that they attempted any regular classification of their Law, which may be seen in the titles of the Mishna. If we want what is perfectly systematic, we must seek it in the writings of Moses Maimonides, in the Middle Ages. In law as in dogma, Israel never consented to substitute scholastic summaries for ancient documents. They thus avoided the difficulties resulting from a central theological authority, like that of the Church in after times; but casuistic disputes were only the more eager. For several centuries they were the plague-spot in the life of Israel.

To sum up what has been said, it is not the Torah which has transformed the world. The school of Ezra and of the Rabbi Akibah could never have done more than form a strong, intolerant, exclusive sect. What has transformed the world, what has founded the universal religion, is the idealism of the Prophets, the proclamation of a future of justice for mankind. It is the idea of worship without sacrifice, — worship, consisting in hymns of praise and heartfelt homage. This is the doctrine, preached by the Prophets, revived by the Essenes, the Therapeutæ, and the Christians, which has produced in the world the most extraordinary of religious revolutions. The Book of the Covenant, and above all the Decalogue — the first written expression of the old prophetic spirit — and Deuteronomy, so far as it is the echo of more ancient books, have a first place in this revolution. As for the levitical party, the men whose religion consisted in observance of the ceremonial law, Christianity made an end of it, and with good reason. The priestly code never recovered importance until the Church, grown old and clericalised, became by successive downward steps a mere levitical body, not unlike that for which the sacerdotal code had been drawn up towards the close of the sixth century before the Christian era.

Judaism by its seclusion, in part voluntary and in part compulsory, developed in a levitical and sacerdotal direction. After the Bible, it made the Talmud. But the fountain whence the living strength of Israel came was inexhaustible. Whilst writers of the school of Jabneh put forth their subtleties, Christianity, the legitimate offspring of Judaism, was conquering the world. The Bible became the universal book; and, after all, we may well pardon the nation to which we are indebted for the Bible, for having written the Talmud.

Ezra, as we have seen, represents less a man than a spirit,—a spirit in opposition to that of the Prophets. The fate of Israel was in his day decided. In its bosom it cherished two opposite magnetic currents; and as one or the other had the predominance, so its history was determined. The Torah under Ezra's name won a complete victory. Ezra is the incarnation of pharisaism in the original meaning of the word. The true Jew is in his eyes a *nibdal*, —one "separate,"—or, what comes to the same thing, a *pherous*, or (in Chaldean) *pheris*.* The *pheris* thus becomes the perfect Israelite,—the pure man, who turns his back on all corruptions, assured of the favour of Iahveh. A devotee of this kind can be consoled for not possessing power in the world only by an inordinate spiritual pride. Jesus, five hundred years after Ezra, will appear and give the victory to the prophetic spirit. The earliest Christian writings speak of pharisaism as the perversion of the religion of the Jews,† and of their moral sense.

The second Isaiah had hoped far different things.

---

* See Nehemiah xiii. 30.
† See the Synoptical Gospels.

His Jerusalem, whose gates were open day and night to receive all nations, had nothing in common with the closed portals of a Jerusalem into which none could enter without all kinds of formalities. The great idealist seer would have been much astonished had he been told that to worship Iahveh on Mount Zion circumcision was indispensable. By a singular reaction Iahveh became once more the exclusive property of Israel. The old protector of his chosen people reappeared as a god who was selfish, perverse, inimical to the human race, since all mankind were set aside unjustly for the benefit of the chosen race. Iahveh, brother of Chemosh, the Iahveh of the time of David, had no Torah. That made all the difference. The materialistic Torah of Ezra was a study of how to make a bargain with Iahveh, by strict observance of precepts which he exacted from his people, for the good things at his disposal. The people endeavoured in all ways to meet the wishes of this exacting Divinity. By a grand hymnology they satisfied his love for human praise and glory; and in return he was supposed to give all earthly delights through the instrumentality especially of men of war, whose hearts were in his hand, so that he could turn them whatever way he would.

CHAPTER XI.

BIGOTRY.

As it was evident that the heathen world would not take hold of the skirts of a man who was a Jew to worship in a place where the Gentile would meet only with insult and exclusion, it became clear that the triumph of Israel would be due at a future day to one who, like Jesus, would follow in the steps of the great Anonymous Prophet, and be the opposite to Nehemiah. But in the history of a great revolution one must not lose sight of the conservatives. Without them, all would be chaos. The destiny of France is to complete her revolution. Those who have contributed to the formation of France, even when they were of all men the least revolutionary, were contributing to make the revolution.

All the vexatious measures of the extremists in Jerusalem were taken, as we have seen, in the name of the King of Persia; that is, in the name of an authority that at other times was spoken of with aversion and contempt.* This is no uncommon practice amongst the clergy. They are always either

---

* Ezra vii. 25, 26; Nehemiah ix. 36, 37.

rebellious, or else they pose as victims when they allude to the civil power; but they become ultra-loyal and faithful subjects when they want to obtain any edict of intolerance against the liberals. Keeping a watch on others, pious spying, and other bad habits fostered by fanatics afterwards in Christendom, found in Nehemiah the earliest example. He, the contemporary of Pericles, was the first Jesuit, the most dangerous of Jesuits. Plato, who had never heard of him, has drawn his portrait in his " Euthydemus," if indeed that dialogue be Plato's. Euthydemus is not a priest, he is a fanatical layman. Nehemiah is not a priest. Ezra, according to fiction and tradition, was only a scribe. The priests — above all, those of the family of the high-priest — belonged to the aristocracy, and looked out for rich wives; consequently they were more inclined than other Jews to contract friendly alliances with powerful families who worshipped Iahveh after the old forms, and had their centre in Samaria. In Judaism, as afterwards in Protestantism, it was the laymen who were fanatics; rigorous reforms were forced upon the priests, who marched without remonstrance under the ferule of pious laymen. Not a single name is given of any priest who took a prominent part in the reforms of this period. The Israelite *cohen* was never a reformer; but his facile indifference favoured reforms. There is nothing in one way more dangerous than a pleasure-loving, unbelieving priest. He will sanction any fanaticisms, if fanatics will leave him undisturbed. One of the most terrible outbreaks of religious fury took place under Leo X., who was himself a sceptic. The court of Rome when composed of unbelievers has held tapers before the advance of every kind of pious madness, even as the priests of Nehemiah's day sounded trumpets in his processions.

We have frequently had occasion to observe that the various laws ascribed to Moses were no real laws in the ancient kingdoms of Judah and Israel. Under the dominion of the Persian kings these laws were first applied to the Jews by authority of the government. Nehemiah set the example. But the strict observance of these laws was at first intermittent. The Torah was not enforced by help of the civil power till the days of the Asmonean kings, two hundred and fifty years later. Up to that time the strict observance of the ceremonial law — the law of the Torah — was a matter of individual conscience, influenced only by severe public opinion. The situation of the Jews was much like that of the Mahometans in Algeria under French rule. The Persian *pekah* did not lend himself to serve the theocratic law, though all his subordinates considered it binding upon them as a moral law, and in mixed matters followed it as something personally affecting themselves. Many difficulties resulted from this state of things, and sometimes cruel punishments; so that, to avoid them, many Jews went voluntarily into exile.

The thing that most surprises us is the analogy between these ancient Jews and the Mahometans. Both showed the same incapacity to discern between religious and civil association; both were intolerant; both made the same pretensions of austerity, which naturally degenerated into hypocrisy. The Jewish women, like those among the Mussulmans, had no part whatever in the religious movement. Not many returned from Babylon, and the harsh measures enforced by the fanatics must have created bitter feelings amongst the feminine population of Jerusalem. Semitic religions, of the Jewish and Mahometan type, are exclusively men's religions.* In the fifth century women were present at the religious celebrations; † but they did not know how to write, ‡ and very few women are mentioned. Not one female figure in those days comes into prominence. Male genealogies, on the other hand, are most carefully kept, even if not always reliable.§ The family spirit, as understood in the East, was very strong. These Jews, though transformed by all kinds of proselytisms, changes, and selections, were really only patriarchs turned bigots,—as Mahometans in our own day are simply Arabs who adhere to all that was narrow and rigorous in their original national character.

The bigot was at this period coming into the

---

* See vol. iii. p. 105.
† Nehemiah x. 28–30; xii. 13.
‡ Nehemiah x. No woman signed.
§ Chronicles, Ezra, Nehemiah.

world. Iahveh had ever hated presumption: with vindictive joy he cast to the ground the young rider who pranced too proudly. The servant of Iahveh was to be humble, gentle, and submissive. Therefore the worldly man he considered proud and insolent, because he did not affect the same canting humility as himself. The long war between the devotee and the worldling was about to begin. In Greece the class of men who had laid aside all prejudices was increasing without opposition. The influence of riches, luxury, aristocracy, and increasing liberty of thought formed men of elegance, too often parasites of the great, convinced of the vanity of religious beliefs, but incapable of seeing the higher truth in morality. Cyprus, Phœnicia, Lydia, and even Egypt had their Beau Brummels, — men who set the fashions, votaries of pleasure, free from fanaticism, whose society was much liked by kings. Crœsus was surrounded by men of this stamp. Psammeticus, King of Egypt, considered his greatest misfortune that which had befallen his boon-companion.* Aristippus of Cyrene, who affected to believe in nothing but mere enjoyment, was, though he had no religion, a finished man of the world. Pisistratus, Solon, and the Seven Wise Men of Greece represented a far superior type, — love of truth being with them joined to that love for elegance (somewhat superficial) which was being brought into fashion by the rising dandyism of such young men. Israel had indeed

---

* Herodotus iii. 14, 15.

among its *lecim* and *zedim* many unbelievers of this species, who laughed at old devotional practices, with the free and easy grace of men of the world.* Between these and the saints there was war to the death. Women in general took the side of the *lecim*, and made light of the other party. The godly asserted that Iahveh, to punish them for their light-mindedness, would send them no children.† To understand all this one should have witnessed the difference between the Mahometan puritan and the Mahometan man of the world. The idea of there being any absurdity connected with any religious practice, or of consideration for human nature as we understand it now-a-days, is mere nonsense in the eyes of a Mahometan. Religion, far from attracting ridicule, makes the man most exact in its observances the highest in the esteem of the world.

Times of religious rigour and exclusiveness are by no means unwelcome to most pious men. The principal fault of the Jews is a disposition to annoy and vex each other. They spend their lives in quarrelling and then making up their quarrels. A revelation from heaven, about which one feels certain one is right, makes the very best ground of quarrel. The Law, odious to those who aimed at liberty, gave

---

* There is a shade of meaning in this word *zedim* which at this time was frequently employed to designate the enemies of the godly. *homines protervi* (the proud). Psalms lxxxvi. 14; cxix. 21, 51, 69, 78; xix. 14; Malachi iii. 15, 19.

† See the fine touches in the story of Michal, vol. ii. p. 42.

perfect peace to those who laid it to heart. Their joys were infinite; and the greatest of all was that of seeing their desire upon their enemies. At a low stage of moral culture in a society divided into small circles, one social group finds satisfaction in any evil that befalls another. The Jew who was conscious of his own strict observance of the Law could enjoy the pleasure mankind delights in most, — that of cordially disliking the man who holds different opinions from himself. Such an one, though poor, is happy. Nothing gives more happiness than living by rule, under strict discipline.

FIRST CHOIR.

Blessed is every one that feareth Iahveh,
That walketh in his ways.

SECOND CHOIR.

For thou shalt eat the labour of thy hands:
Happy shalt thou be, and it shall be well with thee.

Thy wife shall be as a fruitful vine
In the innermost parts of thy house,

Thy children like olive-plants
Round about thy table.

FIRST CHOIR.

Behold that thus shall the man be blessed that feareth Iahveh.

SECOND CHOIR.

Iahveh shall bless thee out of Zion,
And thou shalt see the good of Jerusalem all the days of thy life.
Yea, thou shalt see thy children's children.
Peace be upon Israel.*

* Psalm cxxviii.

Riches, consideration, and many children (the blessings most desired in those days) are to be the recompense of the righteous. As to the unbeliever, he has hardly any right to live. The ungodly shall have nothing but misfortune, — so that one wonders how in a world governed according to the views of the psalmist any man could be so stupid as to be wicked. A nation so confident that virtue is the best of all investments would, one would suppose, have been virtuous without exception.

CHAPTER XII.

THE LAST GLEAMS OF PROPHECY.

THOUGH greatly weakened from its early vigor, the prophetic spirit still survived. We have, as it were, its last sigh in a brief writing which was certainly contemporary with Nehemiah. The author is mysterious as to his personality, and has not been willing to tell us his name. The abuses he attacks are those that were attacked by Nehemiah, — negligence as to the payment of tithes and other legal dues; mixed marriages between Jews and heathen women; the prevalence of divorce, especially when a Jewish wife was repudiated that her husband might marry a Gentile; the offering in sacrifice by the priests of beasts lame and sick, that they would not have presumed to offer to the *pekah*. Eschatological and messianic ideas occupy this late comer among the Prophets as much as they had done the minds of his forerunners. The day of Iahveh draws near. It will be a day of fire, of extermination. God will prepare his people for it by sending Elijah from the dead to turn the hearts of the estranged Israelites to one another. This wondrous messenger Iahveh will call *maleaki*, — that is, "my messenger;" and the whole prophecy now bears that name. It was first called "The Prophecy of *maleaki*," and the word was afterwards turned into "Malachi," a proper name.*

The melancholy position in which the Israelite with a divided conscience was now placed, is keenly felt by the anonymous writer. Pious men have lost patience, and are saying, —

Let us do evil: every one that doeth evil is good in the sight of Iahveh.† Ye have said it is vain to serve Iahveh, and what profit have we that we have kept his ordinances and that we have walked mournfully before our God? . . . Henceforward we will say, Happy are the *Zedim!* They that work wickedness prosper. They defy God, and are always delivered.

The reply of Iahveh comes at once. A book of remembrance ‡ is opened containing the names of all those who serve the Lord: —

And they shall be mine, saith Iahveh-Sabaoth, in the day that I shall make even my peculiar treasure. And I will spare them even as a man spareth his own son that serveth him. Then shall ye return and discern between the righteous and the wicked, between him that serveth God and him that serveth him not. For behold the day cometh! it burneth as a furnace, and all the *zedim* and all that work wickedness shall be stubble; and the day that cometh shall burn them up, saith Iahveh-Sabaoth, that it shall leave them neither root nor branch. But unto you that fear my name shall the sun of righteousness arise with healing in his wings, and ye shall go forth and gambol as

---

* Malachi i. 1; iii. 1; iv. 1-6.
† Malachi ii. 17.   ‡ Malachi iii. 16.

calves of the stall. And ye shall tread down the wicked; for they shall be ashes before the soles of your feet in the day that I do this, saith Iahveh-Sabaoth. Remember ye the law of Moses which I commanded unto him in Horeb for all Israel, even statutes and judgments. Behold, I will send you Elijah the prophet before the great and terrible day of Iahveh comes. And he shall turn the hearts of the fathers to the children and the hearts of children to their fathers, lest I come and smite the land with *herem* (a curse).

One may see here the transformation taking place in old ideas. Iahveh keeps a book of remembrance for the names of the faithful who have not seen the day of his judgments on the earth. If the Anonymous Prophet had carried his reasoning a little further, he might have created a place of waiting for those who seemed victims of the delay of the Lord's justice, until their day of final triumph should arrive. This conclusion was not reached till the time of the Maccabees; but already in the days of Nehemiah it was admitted that one of the old Prophets might rise from the dead, or that a living man might be the fit representative of the ancient Prophet. We begin to see the dawn of a new eschatology, in which resurrection shall be considered a thing possible, and in which the ancient Prophets are considered as reappearing to play a new part at the end of time. This was in consequence of the general decline that had taken place in the Prophets. Men ceased to expect great ones like Isaiah, Jeremiah, or even Zechariah. Therefore they looked forward to the resuscitation of one of God's great men of former times. Elijah, a giant among Prophets, — great in his history, great in his vision upon Horeb, which resembled that of Moses, and great by his being taken up into Heaven, — seemed marked out to be the precursor of "the great and terrible day."* This will become a leading factor in the Apocalypse of Christians. John the Baptist and Jesus will owe to the Anonymous Prophet of the days of Nehemiah one of the most important mythical features connected with their history.

Sheol now loosens its clutch upon its prey more easily than it did formerly. The idea that a man may descend into Sheol and come forth alive again we see in the story of Jonah, where strangely enough a man is represented as singing a psalm at the bottom of the sea. Formerly the idea was that there was no prayer in Sheol; here, on the contrary, God accepts prayers addressed to him from a fish's belly.† The need of reward beyond the grave seemed to become evident, since the time of waiting for the fulfilment of earthly promises was prolonged. But two hundred and fifty years were yet to pass before these ideas could be formulated. Martyrs were needed. A martyr clearly receives no reward upon earth: a reward must be given him in another world.

Maleaki having become the name of a prophet was added to the collection of prophetic writings that

---

* See Ecclesiasticus xlviii. 10. † Jonah ii. 3, &c.

had already been gathered into one book.* After Malachi nothing more was added. The new growth of prophecy which took place, and which took an apocalyptic form after the days of the Maccabees, remained in the *Ketubim*, or Hagiographic writings. The scroll of prophecy was tied up, — in a sense, bound; it was never untied again even to admit writings held to be of the highest inspiration. These could not pass the barrier. They were only admitted, as something apart, into the last pages of the sacred volume.† The remarkable words about Elijah struck the Hebrew imagination, and it was the custom to write them in capital letters at the end of the prophetic scroll.‡ It was the consecration of the messianic idea, or rather one more step in its materialisation.

The volume of prophecy thus closed was eagerly read by those whose hopes were fixed upon the future. It also served as a sort of sibylline book, — passages of which were used as oracles, foretelling what would take place in the future. The writings of Jeremiah were especially used for this purpose. What was missed was the spirit of those awful early tribunes, full of such passionate indignation against evil, and such an ardent love of justice. The great Anonymous Prophet of 536 B. C., could he have come back to life a hundred years after his death, would

---

* See p. 97.
† The Greek translation places them there.
‡ This is still the custom in printed Hebrew Bibles.

surely have wept over the enfeebled generation which had substituted observances of the ceremonial law for the things that concerned pure religion. The two great events that the great Prophets hoped for — namely, that Judah would be reconciled with Israel, that reconciliation being effected by the influence of Jerusalem, and the recognition of Jerusalem as the religious centre of the whole earth — were ideas of the past. Zerubbabel and Nehemiah had formally excluded Samaria from participation in the work of rebuilding the Temple: the Samaritan schism was complete. As for the Gentile world, had it come up to worship at the Temple of Nehemiah and Ezra, how ignominiously it would have been repulsed! Put out the infidels! Thrust forth the uncircumcised! No entrance for the unclean! The pious Jew is a *nibdal*, — one separate. He will have nothing to do with those who are not clean. *Nibdalism* gives pride its greatest satisfaction; but it stands in the way of making great conversions, and of uttering large thoughts to men.

No man knows of what he may be laying the foundation. Jesus founded as he hoped a spiritual religion, — and, behold! the Christian religion has been as full of superstitions as any other: the Jesuits could call themselves the Society of Jesus. Saint Francis of Assisi thought he could found a Christian system that should be living and permanent, and yet from him came those miserable communities of friars which fell entirely under the control of the official Church, and were without any moral value. How the Prophets of the grand era of Jewish prophecy would have protested, could they have seen their pure and stern ideas resulting in mere ritualism, in disputes about sacrifices and the law concerning clean and unclean!— they, who had maintained that evil is alone impure, and that wrong cannot be atoned for by sacrifice! Things in this world often meet with such reactions; and yet all earnest and all unselfish effort leaves its deposit. The spirit of the old Prophets was to return; while the worship so carefully studied in its least details, and represented by such an immense staff of men employed in its service, was to die out forever.

CHAPTER XIII.

THE SAMARITANS.

For a long time after the return of the exiles from Babylon, the worshippers of Jehovah living on the lands of ancient Ephraim made frequent attempts in good faith to form a real religious union with Jerusalem. Samaria, the ancient city of Shemer, continued to be the centre of what remained (though ill cared for) of the authentic relics of the old kingdom of Israel. The political and social position of those Israelites who had been spared by the Assyrians was better than that of the poor colonists in Judea; but their sacerdotal organisation, which had not come under the influence of Jeremiah, was very imperfect. They had only vague ideas of the Torah; the writings of the Prophets were unknown to them; they do not seem to have possessed any sacred writings. Thanks to the friendly relations that existed between leading men in Samaria, Eliashib the high-priest and other priestly families, this want was supplied. The Torah, as it had received its last touches, was passed on from Jerusalem to Samaria. The Samaritan scribes copied it, making some abridgments. Their writing was of the ancient, bold, archaic character, whilst writing at Jerusalem had become cursive, a running hand, which frequently led to confusion. This was the origin of the Samaritan Pentateuch, of which several ancient copies still remain.

The Book of Joshua was not in the Torah that was lent to the Samaritans. But it would appear that they were not satisfied to be without so important a document. They received it as a book by itself, distinct from the Torah,* and made numbers of additions to it, bearing upon their own history and popular traditions.† As to the Prophets, the Samaritans dispensed with those gems of Hebrew literature. The reason is evident. Israel in the writings of the Prophets is always held to be subordinate to Judah; the reforms that they insisted on made a gulf between Jerusalem and Samaria. It was natural that Samaria should not adopt writings which tended to her condemnation.

Samaria had no Temple of great renown. The old sanctuary at Shiloh and the old altar at Bethel were almost forgotten. The Samaritans would have liked to worship at Jerusalem, recognising it as the living centre of a common faith in Iahveh. All their attempts, however, as we have seen, were met by haughty refusal. The Jews considered them an impure race, with no mixture of Israelitish blood;

---

* See p. 99, note.

† *Chronicon Samaritanum*, ed. Jugnboll. Aboulfath, *Ann. sam.*, pp. **xxxix** and 21-25.

their worship, which had not been reformed by the Prophets, was considered gross paganism at Jerusalem.* They then resolved to build themselves a Temple which might console them for the unjust contempt of the men of Judah.

Shechem seemed better fitted for this purpose than Samaria. This beautiful spot between Mounts Ebal and Gerizim was associated with some of the most precious memories of the patriarchal age.† The tomb of Joseph was said to stand at the entrance of the valley;‡ they liked to remember that Jacob had long led a nomadic life among its pastures;§ in the times of the Judges, Shechem had been often a national centre for the twelve tribes.‖ Mounts Ebal and Gerizim, which overlooked the town, were holy places in the Mosaic legend. The holy books that the Samaritans had borrowed from Jerusalem seemed to give a character of consecration to those two mountains. In a narrative, taken it would seem from the Torah of Josiah,¶ Iahveh had ordered great stones to be set up on Mount Ebal and covered with plaster, on which the Law should be written, and also that an altar of unhewn stones should be built there;** after which a mighty solem-

---

* Book of the Kings. Evidently partial and erroneous.
† Genesis xii. 6, 7; xxviii. 20; Joshua xxiv. 26.
‡ Joshua xxiv. 32; St. John iv. 5, 12.
§ Genesis xxxiii., xxxiv., xxxvii.
‖ Joshua xxiv. 1, 25; Judges ix.; 1 Kings xii. 1, 25.
¶ Deuteronomy xxvii.
** Deuteronomy xxvii. 4. The Samaritan Pentateuch has גריזים instead of עיבל, which is manifestly a falsification.

nity had taken place on the spot. The representatives of the twelve tribes, with their levites, had gone, some to the summit of Mount Ebal, some to the summit of Mount Gerizim. The levites standing upon Ebal had read curses against those guilty of certain crimes, and all the people assembled in the valley after every curse exclaimed *Amen.* The levites on Gerizim were then in like manner to proclaim blessings, to which the people were again to respond *Amen.* Such was undoubtedly the origin of the Samaritan worship on those mountains. For reasons of convenience the Samaritans preferred Gerizim to Ebal, and justified their preference by a slight alteration in the text of their Deuteronomy.* A rivalry with Zion was thus created, which lasted for centuries. It seems that the new Temple was built after the pattern of the one in Jerusalem, and that its erection had also the sanction of a Persian king, Darius Nothus.†

The schism which divided the Jews from the Samaritans was thus made irreparable. It was the work of Sanballat and his son-in-law Manasseh, son of the high-priest Joïadah, and may be said to have been the result of the intolerance of Nehemiah. Manasseh had shared in the sacerdotal functions of his father Joïadah; ‡ but when obliged to make

---

* See the last note.

† Josephus, *Antiquities,* xi. viii. 2; 2 Maccabees vi. 2; St. John iv. 20.

‡ The Jaddous of Josephus must surely be the Joiada of Nehemiah. Manasseh was son, not brother, of the high-priest.

choice of giving up those functions or of repudiating the wife to whom he was attached, he chose exile. Driven thus from Jerusalem,* he became apparently the first high-priest on Gerizim. Who knows if it were not he who brought the Pentateuch to the Samaritans? Some writings tell us that Manasseh induced certain Hierosolymites, whom the severity of Nehemiah on the subject of mixed marriages had alarmed, to emigrate to Samaria from Jerusalem. Sanballat may also have induced them by promises of land and wealth.† This movement of emigrants did not cease apparently for several centuries. The violation of the Sabbath, the use of forbidden meats, and the infringement of the ordinances of religion entailed cruel penalties. To avoid them, people fled from Jerusalem and became Samaritans.‡

Every step on the road to puritanism and scrupulosity was thus a step that led to schism. Reasonable men in both sections of the nation seem to have understood each other, but Jewish fanaticism demanded separation. This schism, fatal to Judaism, was the work of Jerusalem. The history of all religions shows us that schisms have always had their origin in a spirit of seclusion among the orthodox.

Samaritanism, however, never became anything

---

* See p. 81. The details of the narrative in Josephus (*Antiquities*, xi. vii. and viii; cf. xii. v. 5; xiii. iii. 4) are all made false by his erroneous chronology.

† Josephus, *Antiquities*, xi. viii. 2, 1.

‡ Josephus, *Antiquities*, xi. viii. 7.

great; it was, so to speak, a mere plagiarism from Judaism. Nothing sprang out of it. The best thing that happened to it was that Jesus treated it with kindness.* He had tenderness in his heart for the excommunicated, for heretics, and for men who were decried. It was this that led him sometimes to contrast these schismatics with the Pharisees, priests, and levites in Jerusalem. He created the type of the good Samaritan; and it was at the foot of Mount Gerizim that he pronounced the words: "Woman, believe me! the hour cometh when ye neither on this mountain nor yet at Jerusalem shall worship the Father; but the hour cometh when the true worshippers shall worship the Father in spirit and in truth."

* *Vie de Jésus*, p. 239, &c.

CHAPTER XIV.

WHAT THE JEWS BORROWED FROM PERSIA. — ANGELOLOGY.

THE genius of Israel slumbered at this period. In Babylon, at the time it was most vigorous, it had shut itself out, as it were, from all outside influences; and, besides, the religion of Chaldea was too debased, and Chaldean science too much advanced, for the Jews. Yet some customs, some superstitions, of the people among whom they dwelt, could not but affect them. The influence of Persia is the strongest that Judaism has ever known. It lasted even after the downfall of the Persian empire. Greek influence, strong as it might be, did not hinder the continuance of Persian influence, until the third or even second century before the Christian era.*

The symbols in Persian worship were both magnificent and attractive. The *ferouer* — a sort of apotheosis, an ideal figure, a protestation against reality † — was like the disk of Ahuramazda, ‡ in secret harmony with Iahveh. If Iahveh had never

---

* The Book of Daniel is full of Persian ideas and Persian words.
† J. Darmesteter, *Ormazd und Ahriman*, p. 130.
‡ Flandin et Coste, *Perse ancienne*, pl. clxiv.; Dieulafoy, *L'Acropole de Suse*, p. 440.

been truly set forth to us, we might have dimly discerned him under his Persian symbol. The coins on which some satrap of Judea or Samaria had stamped an image intended to be a symbol of Iahveh belong to this period,* and we can see in it the influence of Persia. Jewish worship itself owed something to Persian dominant customs. The altar of the *tamid*, or perpetual sacrifice in the second Temple, closely resembled a fire-altar, and tradition saw in the fire that never was extinguished a symbol of an eternal flame, — a brother flame, as it were, of the flames of naphtha in the region of Baku.†

Persia, in the fourth and fifth centuries B. C., underwent religious revolutions that perhaps were the most important in its history. The Median magi in the sixth century ‡ had great moral and national enlightenment, far superior to their neighbours. Under the successors of Cyrus this enlightenment condensed itself into certain writings, which attribute all truth to revelations made to one Zerdusht, a name the Greeks turned into Zoroaster. § About the time when the records of Moses were receiving their last touches at the hands of the Hebrews, Persia was acquiring a cycle of religious myths which were not dissimilar.‖ These similarities, and

* See vol. i. p. 161, note. † 2 Maccabees, i. 18, &c.
‡ See vol. iii. p. 382, note 1.
§ Plato, *Alcibiades*, i. 17; Aristotle, according to Diogenes Laertes, proem No. 2 and No. 6.
‖ Such Zend books as we possess seem to have been revised in the times of the Sassanides [A. D. 226-642], and to be a Talmud rather than a Bible.

others, formed a link that drew together the Jews and the Persians. It is certain that their long contact ended in reciprocal borrowings from each other; but as the religion of Zoroaster flourished till long after the conquest of Alexander, we must be careful not to attribute all these borrowings to the days of the Achæmenidæ. Persian messianism no doubt owes much to the messianism of the Jews; but then the Persian period in the history of Israel is precisely that in which the messianic idea was least flourishing. However that may be, the expectation of a Messiah, apocalyptism, and the belief in a reign of a thousand years are very like the prevailing ideas in Persia.* If there were no contact between these two lines of development, it is one of the most striking examples of similarity of ideas to be found in history, — where, indeed, many such may be encountered.

Persian manners, too, were far more analogous to Jewish ways and customs than those of Greece, Rome, or Western nations. All persons who play a large part in the pious fictions of this period — Nehemiah, Zerubbabel,† Daniel, and Ezra up to a certain point — have begun by holding offices at court about the king's person.‡ Jewish narrative-

---

* See *Orig. du Christ.*, vol. iv. pp. 470-472; vol. vi. p. 149.

† See the story of Zerubbabel in 1 Esdras iii., iv., and in Josephus.

‡ Remember also Tobit, Esther, Bel and the Dragon *initio*. In general, Jewish chronology in the reigns of the Achæmenidæ is very uncertain. In Daniel, Darius is the son of Xerxes, and succeeds Belshazzar, and his successor is Cyrus. Compare 1 Esdras iii. 1 with

writers drew their ideal from the same manners that afterwards gave us stories of the Caliphs of Bagdad. We see in all these histories men leading cheerful, quiet, honest lives under a kindly despotism, sometimes stupid, sometimes paternal, sometimes ferocious, sometimes genial. Life under the sceptre of the Achæmenidæ seems to have been very pleasant in the East. Many peculiarities of Jewish life were derived from Persia. A great festival ordained to take place throughout all Persia led to a piece of great good fortune for the Jews, and gave rise to a legend which as it stands written in their sacred books seems to us most repulsive.

The Persians had a day of rejoicing, celebrated at the end of the year by feasts, and presents sent by one friend to another. This festival was called *fourdi*. The Jews adopted it, although it was a heathen feast, and celebrated it, as did the Persians, in the twelfth month by rejoicings and banquets, in which drunkenness was not uncommon. They called it in Aramean *Pourdai*, and in Hebrew *Fourdim*, which became through an error, easy paleographically to explain, *Fourim* or *Pourim*.* This feast was not celebrated in the Temple; it was not at first a religious festival. Still, it was desirable it should have its *hagada*, and thereupon was con-

---

the document *B* in the canonical Ezra. In 1 Esdras iv. compare verses 43 and 57.

 * The manuscript of Josephus has φριυραιους, instead of φουρδιους. Syriac ܟܣܘܪܝܐ. The primitive form in Hebrew should have been פרדים, which by two errors not uncommon has become פורים.

structed the story of Esther. Among the Jews every feast was founded upon some event in their national history, and had its own scroll, or *megilla*. They contrived that *Pourim* should be associated with a great triumph of their people and the death of their most powerful enemy. But as the feast was not religious, the name of God was carefully omitted in the history, and in it no religious allusions are to be found.*

Out of this came a narrative strange, cruel, impious, and revolting, which has nevertheless taken its place among works of religion. Israel figures in it as a people deadly to its foes by some secret force, whose neighbourhood is a thing to fear. Never was national egotism more openly avowed. Meanness, love of base employment, lack of moral sentiment, and hatred of the human race are here carried to the extreme. The story gives us an ideal picture of a bad Jew; it displays him at his worst, omitting his fine qualities. Esther and Mordecai seem to us horrible. What stratagems, what lack of dignity, what cruelty we see in them! The death of her enemies is not enough to satisfy this Fury; she demands that their dead bodies may be exposed, among them even those of children.† And the author of the book expresses satisfaction.‡ Xerxes, who had given permission to exterminate the Jews,

---

* See especially Esther iii. 2; iv. 3, 14, 16.

† Possibly there is here some reminiscence of Parisatis and *Statira* (Esther ?).

‡ Esther ix. 5, 17, 18.

permits the Jews instead to massacre seventy-five thousand of his subjects. It is true that these Persians must have suffered themselves to be massacred by a mere handful of men, which is another proof that these wretched tales are purely fictitious. The best comfort we can derive from this odious little book is to believe that nothing in it really happened.

The Feast of Purim, thus of heathen origin, soon became by the assistance of the book a religious festival. In the days of the Maccabees it was the celebration of a great national triumph.* We think that the Book of Esther, such as we have it in Hebrew, dates before this period. If it had been a book intended to be read at a religious feast, it would have contained more piety; and indeed the Greek translator, who wrote after the time when the Feast of Purim was established as a religious festival, has added prayers and pious reflections to the narrative. The Book of Esther we conceive to have been written about the time when the reigns of the Achæmenidæ came to an end; and to this time also seems to belong a fragment inserted in the Book of Ezra (iv. 6 to vi. 13), which bears a striking resemblance to the Book of Esther.† It forms part of an imaginary history of the return from captivity under Zerubbabel, and is full of apocryphal documents in

---

* 2 Maccabees xv. 36.

† Both contain false documents, words, and Persian names that are very strange.

which the chronology of the Kings of Persia is strangely confused.* Through the writings of this period one sees a very high idea of the Median kings, the Jewish author being always proud and delighted when their power is exercised, however cruelly, in favour of his own people.† He rejoices on such occasions to let the world know that a Persian monarch has hanged many of his subjects for the sake of the Jews.

A national spirit combined with religious fervour always leads in the end to some odious result. When every year the Jews read with delight how Haman and his sons were hanged, they are only doing what Christians do when they sing the *Te Deum* on a battle-field, or hold religious services of thanksgiving over the defeat that has befallen their enemies.

The angel-worship of the Persians — their Amshaspands, Izeds, and Ferouers — especially attracted the Jews. Their old Hebrew conception of angels was simple in the extreme. Myriads of sons of God, without individual names, surround the Almighty, as it were the emanation of his thoughts.‡ One is

---

* See the story of the pages, or body-guards of Darius, in the First Book of Esdras. The return under Zerubbabel took place in the reign of Darius (1 Esdras iii., iv.). Note in the same book v. 1 and what follows. In Daniel it is even more so. See p. 301.

† We find the same sentiment in the fragment inserted in **Ezra**. Observe vi. 11.

‡ Michael Angelo on the ceiling of the Sistine Chapel (compartment of the Creation of Man) has wonderfully apprehended this. A sort of divine canopy encloses the Almighty and his happy cherubim, hardly separated from himself, who swarm around him and seem one with him.

his envoy, his messenger (the so-called *maleak Iahveh*, or *maleak elohim*); another is the adversary, the accuser, whose speeches are represented as sometimes exciting a feeling of amusement in the Almighty. He is *Satan* * the critic, the fault-finder in all things. In their close union with the Almighty, these sons of God see nothing but harmony in his works; all are beautiful and good. They believe in the truth; they are true optimists. But now and then Satan disturbs their confidence. He delights in pointing out what seem to him defects in God's creation; above all, he takes pleasure in depreciating the virtue of men of piety, because in them the Almighty delights more than in any other part of his creation. The Almighty refutes him by peremptory arguments, and Satan finds himself always put in the wrong.

In time this simple conception of the court of heaven became more complicated. The parts assigned to the agents of God's will grew more defined. There came to be hierarchies; angels were sent on different errands; and there were *sarim*,† or archangels.‡ There were even distinctions between the *sarim*.§ There were angels for all employments.‖ Everything abstract had its angel, its *ferouer*, its

---

* Satan, διάβολος, κατήγορος, — the same sense.
† Daniel x. 13, 20.
‡ Ἀρχάγγελος, Jude 9; 1 Thess. iv. 16.
§ Daniel x. 13.
‖ See Targum of Jonathan on Genesis xviii. 2. For further details see *Orig. du Christ.*, index, article ANGES.

universal, very like the spirits that savages think inhabit anything composite, as a ship or a house. There was the angel of the waters, the angel of the winds. Every nation and, later, every church had its angel: the angel of Persia, of Greece, of Israel, strive together, making a sort of background to history, and giving us its explanation.*

One particular class of angels were called Holy Ones, Watchers,† those who never slept (in Greek, Ἐγρήγοροι), — a name in which assuredly may be discovered some connection with the Amshaspands.‡ These Holy Ones, these Watchers, formed a sort of council of Amshaspands, in which human affairs were decided.§ They partook of the divine nature, and were apparently emanations from God.

A trait very characteristic of the change that has taken place in the nature of these celestial beings is that now they begin to have personal names. The ancient sons of God were all alike; there was no name to distinguish them. Satan the Accuser is simply a son of God, like the others. The *maleak Iahveh* is Iahveh himself, as it were his *alter ego*.

---

* Daniel x. Cf. Septuagint, Deuteronomy xxxii. 8; Jonathan on Genesis xi. 7; Philo, opp. ii. 212.

† עיר in the singular עיר וקדיש (Chaldean. The corresponding Hebrew expression is not known), Daniel iv. 10, 11, 20. This expression, frequently used in the Book of Enoch even in its oldest parts (xcii. 15), is in this book an imitation of Daniel. In the *Test. of the* 12 *patr.*, Reuben 5, Naphtali 3, it comes from an imitation of Enoch. See Dillmann, *Henoch*, pp. 104, 105.

‡ Reuss, *Daniel*, p. 245, note 1.

§ Daniel iv. 14. The grouping עירין וקדישין which occurs in the Book of Enoch is an imitation of Daniel.

After the Jews had had relations with the Persians, angels received names and especial functions. There was, first, Gabriel, who seems to have had a certain pre-eminence among them;* Michael, the guardian angel of the Jewish people;† later, Raphael‡ and Uriel.§ These names were probably fanciful, and are not to be taken too seriously.‖

The form of an angel in this new conception was that of a winged man. Some have doubted whether wings were not assigned them later; but those who were *ferouers* were born with wings.¶ They were also men. The Book of Daniel is positive on this point; Gabriel calls himself "the man Gabriel."**

The power attributed to these new angels greatly surpassed that of the old. Among them there were some who by intercession with God could render service to men.†† Seven of them stood before the throne of God, and these were the Most Holy Ones.‡‡

---

* Daniel viii. 16; ix. 21; and frequently in Targums.

† Daniel x. and xii.; Jude 9; Revelations xii. 7; Targum of Jonathan on Genesis xxxii. 24; xxxviii. 25.

‡ In Tobit. He is also to be found in Enoch; but that is by imitation.

§ In the Apocalypse of Esdras. In Enoch by imitation. The systematic enumeration of the four angels together is a sure sign that the writing is not older than the Christian era; they are thus in all the first part of Enoch.

‖ See the Book of Enoch, first part.

¶ Daniel ix. 21 (יָעֻף not יָעִיף, a false sense). Cf. Revelations, xiv. 6; xix. 17. Compare the *seraphim* of Isaiah.

** Daniel ix. 21; x. 16.

†† מלאך מליץ of Elihu in Job xxxiii. 23.

‡‡ Tobit xii. 15; Luke i. 19.

Angels bore to God the prayers of men;* they aided his chosen people, like the angel who smote Sennacherib; they fought beside the Maccabees, they spread terror into the army of their enemies;† they worked miracles when saints were in peril.‡ They came at last to be guardian angels, such as Christianity has delightedly developed them.§

As there were good angels, so also there were bad angels, demons who poured out malign influences on nature.‖ These were the Persian *divs*. They inhabited ruins, deserts, and deserted houses.¶ *Æschma-Daeva* (Asmodeus) in particular was adopted as a demon of sensual desire, laying hold upon women, and killing those who sought to approach them lawfully.** Ideas of demoniacal possession, so rife in the days of Jesus, were beginning to show themselves at this early time. However, we hear nothing of any exorcist previous to Jesus.†† The transformation of the ancient Satan into a *diabolos*,‡‡ the genius of evil,§§ not unlike Ahriman,

---

* Tobit xii. 12, &c.; Enoch xlvii. 2.

† 2 Maccabees xv. 23, 24.

‡ Bel and the Dragon, 38; Daniel iii. 23, cf. 25 and 28.

§ Psalm xci. 11, 12; Matthew xviii. 10; Acts xii. 7; Targum of Jonathan on Genesis, xxxiii. 10; xlviii. 16. See *Orig. du Christ.*, index, article ANGES. Tobit is of such uncertain date that it cannot be quoted.

‖ Psalms xci. 6; cxxi. 6.

¶ Baruch iv. 35; Matthew xii. 43.

** Tobit iii. 8; vi. 15; Talm. of Jer., *Gittin*, 68 *a*. See *Orig. du Christ.*, i. 262; vi. 232.

†† Tobit was possibly later than Christianity. See *Orig. du Christ.*, vi. 554, &c.

‡‡ *Sophia Talm.*, ii. 24. Compare it with the Gospels. Διάβολος is the translation of שטן, *katigor*. Compare Ecclesiasticus xxi. 27 (Σατανᾶς).

§§ Ὁ πονηρός, a Sunday oraison, "the wicked one," true God of

was not yet accomplished. Beliar* was probably the name used to designate the genius of evil; however, we find no obvious example of it before the days of Christianity.

Before the age of Christianity there is no certain trace of the myth of the fall of the angels. These ideas hold so large a place in the writings of the early Christians, especially in the Epistle (essentially Jewish) of Saint Jude,† that we are led to think that the Jewish imagination before the coming of Jesus had been driven to explain the origin of evil by a rebellion of the angels, who, cast out upon the earth, had worked its ruin. These apocryphal chimeras in general were attributed to Enoch; but that part of the Book of Enoch which relates to the fall of angels‡ appears to have been written by a Christian hand. If so, it was not the document referred to by Saint Jude. It is, no doubt, one of those Jewish myths of the later period, most directly inspired from Persia. One thing must be said, however, that all these beliefs, common alike to Persians and to Jews, are the natural outcome of a more primitive creed. The line of reasoning was the same both in Persia and in Palestine; and the absurd being once admitted as a point of departure, the rest is perfectly logical.

These roving fancies correspond to a period of

evil; or else ὁ ἐχθρός, "the enemy" always employed in tormenting the righteous.

* For "Belial." † Verse 9. Cf. 2 Peter ii. 4.
‡ The first part.

ignorance and lack of reasoning. The distinctive advantages of Judaism were obscured by such foreign intrusions, which opened the way to superstitions of an inferior order. People of sense (the Sadducees) would not accept these exotic influences; but the bulk of the nation was stronger than they. Christianity at its birth was stained by these beliefs. We may be sorry, but are we sure it could have been developed without them? Weakness is the beginning of strength; things popular never attain their growth without follies and excesses at the beginning.

CHAPTER XV.

THE DECADENCE OF JEWISH LITERATURE.

THE debasement of literature followed that of politics and morals. The genius of Israel seemed extinct. The old Hebrew language became day by day less used, and was replaced by the Aramean as the vulgar tongue, — a speech that was becoming the common language of the East. It was the language commonly used in law papers or in diplomacy under the Achæmenidæ.* Everywhere, except in towns and in Phœnician colonies, it was gradually supplanting the old Semitic speech, so superior to it in strength and literary beauty. At Jerusalem only the scribes still made use of Hebrew; they learned it in their ancient documents as if it had been a classic. But they by no means always understood their ancient writings,† more especially the difficult or disputed passages, of which they often made great nonsense by searching for mysterious meanings where everything was simple and plain. The primitive spelling of Hebrew, without vowels, gave rise

---

* Clermont-Ganneau, *Revue archéol.*, Aug. 1878, pp. 93–107.
† Witness the author of Chronicles.

to many doubtful renderings, and they therefore at this time began to use quiescents (*matres lectiones*) to guide the reader; but they often put them wrong. The copyists, not perfectly understanding what they copied, and at the same time endeavouring not to write nonsense, committed faults innumerable. Thus the exegesis of Hebrew books becomes very deplorable, especially in their poetic parts. The messianic beliefs, which grew up in darkness, found plenty to feed upon. As these ideas increased, every passage that was not clear was supposed to refer to the Messiah. An elaboration of all human hopes, made up of a confused collection of scraps of passages and of phrases altered by copyists, became almost unintelligible.* When hope is desired, human nature can always find cause to hope for what it wishes; and what it wishes for seems always right.

The ancient historical records not included in the Torah were little read. The Books of Judges, Samuel, and Kings existed as we have them now, and fuller annals than we possess of the days of the kings of Judah and of Israel were not yet lost; accounts of the Prophets had also considerable material for their development. A levite (probably a singer †) in the Temple at Jerusalem undertook, towards the close of the Persian rule, to write a new sacred history by the help of historical records more

---

* Exegesis of the Gospels, and also in general of the early Christians.

† Kuenen, *Hist. critique*, i. 480.

compact than ours, which were still at his command. He filled up vacancies by legends about the Prophets,* and completed his work by documents in his possession concerning Zerubbabel, Ezra, and Nehemiah.† All that related to the ancient kingdom of Israel was now considered schismatic; so the historian confined himself to the religious history of Judah. Very little is said even of Elijah and Elisha. The author, who is especially interested in matters pertaining to public worship, insists that all the musical and liturgical services of the second Temple had come down from the times of David and of Solomon. As a general thing all that belonged to the second Temple he ascribes to the first. A number of the things he says are intended to form a foundation for the pretensions of the levites. He shows no political or military interest whatever. Israel by itself has never won a single victory; but Iahveh has sometimes slain thousands of its enemies.

The author of Chronicles is extremely narrow-minded; his intellectual perceptions are very poor. No writer is more reckless, more careless, in the use of his materials; none has sown more errors in the world than this obscure compiler. He does not seem to have been able to read correctly, and the manuscripts he had at hand were very defective. One

---

* Reuss, *Chron. eccl.*, p. 27 and *circa*, Kuenen, *op. cit.*, p. 467 and *circa*.

† The Books of Ezra and Nehemiah as we have them should be considered as completing the two books of Chronicles, very incorrectly called "Paralipomena."

can hardly imagine a poorer philologist, a poorer critic, or a man who knew less of paleography.* Sometimes his errors are voluntary; sometimes he makes changes of set purpose, to serve religious zeal and national pride. Some narratives are his own invention, and show the *fanaticus*, the inhabitant of the Temple. He is especially severe on those who interfere with the rights of the levites.† One man who has invaded levitical functions is struck at once with leprosy. The inauguration of the Temple is accompanied by a miracle, — the offerings are consumed by lightning. The site of the Temple has been pointed out by fire from heaven.

The credulity and exaggeration of this writer pass all bounds. The character of David is entirely transformed. He is no longer the wily chief, the bold condottiere, the skilful sovereign. He is a king who plans great constructions, and who is absorbed in the interests of priests, levites, and singers. The ecclesiastical colour given to the episode of Joash is due to the writer of the Chronicles. It is levites who restore the heir of David to his throne, and attest his legitimacy; the chant of the levites leads to victory.‡ Prophets can hardly be distinguished from the priests. The ancient historical writings of the Jews, as we have them retouched by later writers, are the work of the school of the Prophets. Chronicles is a

---

* See Kuenen, *op. cit.*, i. 457–495.
† Ibid., p. 488, &c.
‡ 2 Chronicles xx. 19, 21.

work wholly levitical; its one interest is worship; it is history written by a sacristan.

These products of Israelitish literature when on the wane, show complete literary exhaustion. Hebrew genius had uttered its last word when Greece was producing its masterpieces. Its style is gone. Aramean, flat and involved in its manner of expression, is superseding the national language. Only the literature of the Psalms now continues to be beautiful: the people have grown accustomed to their rhythm. Everywhere may still be heard the charming resonance of ancient parallelism; still the old *kinnor* (harp) gives forth its harmonious sounds. Nothing, indeed, was more easy than to compose a psalm at this period. The air was, as it were, full of sonorous rhythm; the poet had only to bring together at will the pretty couplets that were common property. This is why we find so many repetitions in the Book of Psalms, which are really reproductions of each other. They seem like portions of verse of the same lyric school, dissevered, then reunited.

Public worship became more and more solemn and pompous. To "praise the Lord" seemed man's first duty, the great end of his existence. A swarm of little songs of praise with music were brought forth daily. The words *hodou* and *hallelou Iah* were the basis of these levitical compositions, which did not cost their authors much pains. The Psalter came forth like a little Bible, — more beautiful, more touching, more harmonious than the Torah, or even than the writings of the Prophets. But in this collection, which has been like milk for babes to the Christian Church, there is complete lack of unity. These psalms were sung, they were not often written; they were seldom read, they were never recited. It is not Iahveh who speaks; it is the voice of man, who in these touching elegiac strains tells his sorrows, his hopes, his joys. In those days only what Iahveh himself was reported to have spoken was considered inspired. What we find most charming and most valuable in the Psalter seems to have made its completion a slow process, and to have retarded its admission into the canon of Scripture. The mighty voice of Iahveh, which is heard in the Prophets and the Torah, grew still more emphatic in the Psalms. Men listened in the days of which we speak for oracles and imperious commands from Heaven.

No doubt there had been collections of psalms made before this period; and assuredly the hundred and fifty which we have are not all the psalms that have been written. There must have been new hymns composed every day, — all psalms must have been long sung before they were reduced to writing. There were no doubt many collections of psalms. The basis of the five books of which our present Psalter is composed had no doubt been laid down before this period, though we cannot perceive the especial unity of character that belongs to each of these five divisions.

David was considered the great ideal choir-master

of the worship of Iahveh. The old leader of a band of brigands at Ziklag was now considered as a psalmist by profession; all the little poems which owed their origin to the piety of the levites were considered his work. Hymns, rites, and even the invention of musical instruments were attributed to him.* With the vague ideas which at that period prevailed as to the naming of books, the name of David must be put at the beginning of the Psalter, so that it came to be believed that the whole Psalter was his. Solomon was in like manner made the patron of all books of parable or wisdom. Then came the idea that Moses wrote the whole of the Pentateuch.† The separation of the Book of Joshua from the other five books made such an opinion seem possible. Improbability did not affect a world in which no notions of criticism had ever found a place. And, indeed, in this respect Greece herself was not very superior to Judea.

The true meaning of history was lost; no care was thenceforth taken to follow the line of events. Of these " the prophet-historians no longer presented a continuous succession." ‡ They changed their plan, and made history serve for edification or amusement.

---

* Ezra iii. 10; Nehemiah xii. 24, 36, 44, 45; 1 Chronicles xvi., xxiii–xxvi.; Ecclesiasticus xlvii. 9–12.

† The first text on this subject is Josephus: *Against Apion*, i. 8. Josephus, however, generally seems not to consider Moses an ἱστορικός but a νομοθέτης. *Antiquities*, iv. vii. 3. Cf. Ecclesiasticus xlv. 6; Deuteronomy xxxii., xxxiv.

‡ Josephus, *Against Apion*, i. 8.

Jewish romance, with its conventional literary machinery, its obligatory prayers and hymns, or the like, grew out of the new conditions of the Jewish world. The more or less authentic autobiographies of Nehemiah and Ezra are a species of romance after their kind; one part at least is fictitious. Zerubbabel had his story written in the same way.* Every personage destined to play whether a real or a supposed part in the narrative had been either cup-bearer, page, or body-guard in the court of an Achæmenid sovereign.† Beautiful prayers well composed, though a little declamatory, gave a pious tinge to the narratives. The author of Esther has deprived himself of these ejaculations and prayers, that he might not give a religious character to his story. The form of personal memoirs, even of personages who were not historical, came into vogue. Thus the primitive Book of Tobit took the form of a family history. The story of Tobit, if one only judged it by its manners, might belong to this period, but the text as we have it is more modern.‡ We can be certain at least that the book was not known earlier than the second century before the Christian era.

The *hagada* of the pages (guards) of Darius,§ which has been attached to the history of Zerubbabel, is

---

* 1 Esdras iii., iv; Josephus, *Antiquities*, xi. iii.

† See pp. 138, 139.

‡ *Orig. du Christ.*, vi. 554, &c.

§ 1 Esdras iii., iv. The original was certainly written in Hebrew.

certainly pleasing. Nothing can be better than the covert satire in the little picture of the king's concubine sitting beside him, taking his crown, putting it on her own head, and giving him a tap on the cheek, — all of which the king thinks charming.* The praise of wine and women is treated in the ancient manner, somewhat freely, and reminds us of Proverbs. The tone is easy, gay, and natural. It is the model of the *hagadas* we find in the Talmud and in the *Midrashim*, which modern parable-writers, especially the Germans,† have often imitated with skill. Glaring impossibilities, scarcely perceived by the writer; a genial *bonhommie*, which hardly cares even if you laugh at him; great *naïveté*, which scarcely under any disguise lets you understand that he hardly expects you to believe him, while he gives you to understand that older writings contain similar fables, — all this, steeped in the court atmosphere whether of a Persian king or of a caliph of Bagdad, in the reign of a foolish despot, who executes men without rhyme or reason, but allows any one to sing what they please to him, becomes a charming framework for fabulous histories by which Israel has justified the common saying that all literature runs at last into romance.

The Bible from about the year 400 B. C. has been made up of two parts, each closed at this period; nothing from that time has been added either to the

---

* 1 Esdras iv. 29, &c.
† Krummacher, for example.

Torah or the *Nebiim*. A further series, on the contrary, remained still open, — that of the *Ketoubim*, or Hagiography. This series contained Proverbs, Job, the Song of Solomon, Lamentations, and (if you will) the Psalms; and it subsequently received several important additions.

There was far more copying done at this period than formerly; and with copying came alteration. The writing was bad. The Aramean characters, which were much more cursive* than the Hebrew, were generally adopted. A number of letters got confounded with each other; the *d*'s and the *r*'s in particular showed no difference. The books of Ezra, Nehemiah, and the Psalms are full of errors, and only a careful paleographist can find a key to the enigmas they present in almost every line.

In copying, the writer also interpolated, — for copyists were not simply men who made copying their business, and mechanically reproduced their text. Thus a writer from whom we appear to have a psalm,† thought good to give us a conclusion to the Book of Job, by inserting the weak discourse of Elihu, ‡ — a discourse which concludes nothing. It repeats the same ideas till they are old and frayed. They become a poor rehash of former arguments turning in a narrow circle, like figures in a dream,

---

* See the Aramean papyri of the time of the Median kings. *Corpus inscr. Semit.*, 2d part, No. 144, &c.

† Psalm cvii.

‡ Possibly this belongs to the Greek period. רהטש = perhaps ῥάθυμος.

striking over and over again the same spot in the brain. Many books of the Bible have been disfigured thus.

As for places where glosses and various readings have found their way into the text, they are, we may say, innumerable. The variations are put generally at the bottom of a page, without anything to show to what passages they refer. Later copyists have transcribed them in a string one after the other, and have added them in a lump to the text. Thus it happens that in some psalms we find whole passages composed of variations in the readings of other psalms, as if they had gathered together all the glosses at the end of a page of the masoretic Bible, and had formed sense out of them at haphazard.* A psalm in this way may have become so unrecognisable that when the collection was made it may have been divided into two psalms; and the identity of the separated parts might never have been discovered but for the great modern advance in paleography.†

The predominance of Aramean as the language of the people early made it necessary to translate the Book of the Law into Aramean, when it was read in public. ‡ It seems that for a long time these translations were oral; the doctor of the Law improvised them as he pleased. Later, when the system

---

* See especially Psalm xl. 8; Psalm lxxiv. 9.
† See, for example, Psalms xiv. and liii.
‡ No conclusion is to be drawn from Nehemiah viii. 8.

of attending the synagogue became developed, the Chaldean Targums* were reduced to writing; the readings became regular. The Bible that the Jew knew by heart, and repeated to himself in solemn moments, was in Aramean.†

* An erroneous denomination, which came from Daniel ii. 4 misunderstood.
† Λαμμὰ σαβαχθανί.

CHAPTER XVI.

THE DEEP SLEEP OF ISRAEL.

FROM about the year 400 to the year 200 B. C. Israel seems to have been in a profound sleep; and it was not without some reason that in rabbinical chronologies these years are abridged to almost nothing, and the days of the Asmonean kings appear to follow close on the times of Nehemiah. Jerusalem as Nehemiah left it was a tomb. There the Torah ruled supreme; that is, in other words, life was in the grip of the most terrible instrument of torture that has ever been invented. The utopias (sometimes cruel) of ancient dreamers had been realised; theocratic authority had it now in its power to inflict death, confiscation, and exile. Emigration took place on a great scale.* The Jewish Torah only shows its merits when it has no secular arm to do its bidding. The Roman rule was beneficial, inasmuch as it deprived the priests of the right to inflict death. Abroad, the Jewish law worked better than in Jerusalem, for the cruel penalties it contained were there null and void.

* See p. 136. Could priestly authority at this period inflict death? Josephus (*Antiquities*, xi. viii. 7) seems to think it could. Ezra vii. 25, 26, seems to imply it also.

Everything was growing narrower, closer, smaller. In the latter years of Nehemiah we perceived a strong opposition to his reforms which had its centre in families of the house of Zadok, who were allied with Tobiah and Sanballat. But now there is absolute submission. The Torah has absorbed all intellectual power in Israel. The people cared to know nothing more; the Torah contained for them all science, all philosophy. The rest of the world was daily becoming enlightened more and more by the marvellous initiative of Greece. Judaism turned its back on this, and would only give to the study of profane truth (real truth) its few idle hours. That prodigious Psalm (cxix.) in which the author, in twenty-two sections of eight verses each (in all, one hundred and seventy-six verses), all devoted to praises of the Law, sets forth its excellences, is a complete compendium of the Jewish spirit at this period, — of its firm determination to see nothing beyond the Torah, to find in it all its hopes and all its consolations. The punctual observance of the Torah became a sort of amusement. From this time forward Judaism was acting out the Talmud. The Torah not only gave happiness, it gave pleasure; it was a game of patience for poor decrepit Israel.

The most dangerous moment for a nation is that in which it seems to have realised its own ideal; for then it begins to see the vanity of the end it has pursued: it finds that it has taken immense trouble to attain a poor result. When France had realised her revolutionary programme, she discovered the faults of the Revolution. The vices of an ideal plan do not manifest themselves till it is realised. The divers parts of the Torah which contained things to be desired in a utopia, when put into practice became chains too heavy to be borne. The Torah, when enforced by the governing power, was the tightest garment into which life was ever laced. Nothing could be produced under such conditions. Philosophy, poetry, science, — all were smothered. Even Greek genius, had it been so constrained, would have perished. Those who could not flee from Jerusalem were made brutish, deceitful, hypocritical, and wicked. A materialistic religion to which men mechanically conform, by obeying which a man becomes a saint before the eyes of all, is the worst of religions. What had become of the dreams of the great Prophets? They died in the moment of victory. It is not always best, even in worldly things, to succeed too perfectly.

The peace and prosperity which the Jews enjoyed during the reigns of the Persian kings were not troubled until about 355 B.C., under the reign of Artaxerxes III. (Ochus).* Then a horrible scandal took place in the Temple. The high-priest, Johanan or Jonathan, son of Joiada, killed his brother Joshua, who was endeavouring to supplant him in the favour of the Persian satrap Bagoses. Bagoses sought to avenge Joshua. He entered the Temple with an

* Josephus, *Antiquities*, xi. vii. 1.

armed force, which of itself was held a frightful profanation; he insisted that tribute must be paid out of the victims offered to Iahveh, — and for seven years the condition of the Jews was very evil.

Meantime Judea in the fourth century was little conscious of the revolutions taking place in the outer world. The Jews in general found the rule of the Achæmenidæ very mild. The profound peace in which they lived contributed greatly to the kind of hypnotic state into which an extraordinarily active people had fallen under the influence of the Torah. The Torah had indeed found the very soil it needed, — a State whose provinces engaged neither in wars nor politics. The reigns of Darius and Xerxes especially shone as a brilliant epoch in which the Jewish writers loved to place their national romances.* The Achæmenid monarchs had acknowledged that they owed their power to Iahveh. What more could be needed? Jerusalem might not grow rapidly, but the Jewish race spread like oil among all the little villages of Judah, Benjamin, and Dan, even into the country of the Philistines. Galilee was possibly already included. The relations of the Jews with the court at Susa seem to have been satisfactory. Judea suffered little from the faults that were mining the mighty empire. Despotism it did not find displeasing.† Was not Iahveh himself the mightiest

---

* Esther i. 1; 1 Esdras, iii. iv. The story of the pages (or guards) of Darius. Bel and the Dragon, its beginning.

† Cf. 1 Esdras iv. 3, &c.

of despots? The Jews in the far East seem to have found Persian despotism always in their favour. The story of Esther, if it has any foundation in fact, proves that under the blue sky of Persian rule there might be storms for the chosen people; but our belief is that this story is a pure *hagada*, and contains nothing of truth.*

The material condition of Jerusalem was mean and sordid; and that is why a city so full of interest for us was unknown to the Greeks at the time of their greatest wakening. The Torah permitted no free activity. There was no civil element in Jerusalem; nothing was to be seen there but priests and sacred ornaments.† The work going on at Jerusalem was done in secret; the best eyes in the world without could not have seen it. Herodotus and the logographers knew nothing of it.‡ The Persian *pekahs* in Jerusalem were prefects of the second or third class. The high-priests Eliashib, Joiada, Jonathan, and Jaddua § succeeded each other in complete obscurity, and their very names are not quite certainly known. Commerce and manufactures did not even exist. Life in the country round about Jerusalem was far preferable to life in the city. No man was rich except the priests, or those who had relations with the government. It is a great mistake to think that skill in the management of money, to which for the

---

* See p. 140.
† Josephus, *Antiquities*, xi. viii. 5.
‡ They also overlooked Rome completely.
§ Nehemiah xii. 10, 11, 22, 23.

last thousand years the Jews have been devoted, existed among them from the beginning of their history. The object of the Mosaic Law was to keep the people in a patriarchal state, to hinder the formation of large fortunes, and to arrest the development of commerce and industry, after the fashion of the Tyrians. The Jews never became rich till Christians forced them to be so by preventing their becoming landowners, and by entrusting them with monetary affairs which their own false ideas on the subject of usury rendered it improper for them to undertake themselves.

The intellectual condition of the inhabitants of Jerusalem was also on the decline. Nor was their moral condition any better. From this period all the faults with which Jews have been reproached began to show themselves. At once cringing and scornful, as regarded men in power, are the Jews of the Persian period. They are susceptible, easily wounded by ridicule, and cruel when they perceive themselves subjects of mockery.* Overweening in their self-complacency, they respond by hatred to a joke at their expense. Their ambition is of a low kind. They do not aspire to be satraps, but they wish to stand well in the satrap's sight. Nehemiah is proud of having been the king's cup-bearer; he thinks it has given him importance. The *anavim*, men of peace, servants of the Church, not born to

---

* Nehemiah iv. 1–5; vi. 14. Compare the fierce *massa* of Ezekiel against those who have made a mock of Israel.

be soldiers, are always craving official employments granted to them by a military power. They take strength where they find it. Ah, poor human nature!

Judea could not possibly be a military nation, and yet it was military power that she needed: without military strength no nation can exist. A soldier cannot be made by promises of a temporal reward; he needs immortality. If we cannot offer him paradise, there is glory, which is a kind of immortality. Napoleon's soldiers all knew that they would probably remain poor men; but each knew that that for which he laboured would be eternal, — that he would live in the glory of France. The Greek knew that his glory would be the thing that would last longest in the memory of men. The bravery of the Gauls arose from their admitting no difference between life and death. The Russian and the Turkish soldiers believe in a paradise that awaits them should they fall in battle. Men are ready to die on such conditions. The *mitnaddeb*, or volunteer, in ancient Israel, was a brave man after his fashion; he was no religious bargainer, doing well because Iahveh would give him his reward. Jewish pietism is too reflective; it might make martyrs, it could never make an army. The only races which have made great armies are those which believe in immortality. The Jew in the day of battle only thinks how he may escape.* He offers his purse to the soldier about to kill him; and

---

* אין משלחת במלחמה.

when he sees that this will not serve, he sees no sense in a game where a prudent man can make no use of all his means, and decides never again to expose himself in battle.*

One would suppose that a nation's destiny, shut up so strictly in very narrow ideas, would have found no outlet. The apparent end of Israel seemed to coincide with the moment of the greatest glory of Greece. Ezra and Nehemiah belonged to the age of Pericles; they were contemporary with Herodotus, Æschylus, Socrates, and Hippocrates. Whilst Israel was thankfully accepting the yoke of the Persian kings, and Iahveh was turning the heart of the great monarch in his people's favour; whilst a Jew was proud of being cup-bearer, spy, and menial to the King of Persia, — Greece was resisting Persia to the death, overcoming Darius, Xerxes, and Artaxerxes, and saving civilisation. The history of the people of Israel, had it been merely a continuation of Ezra and Nehemiah, would have been simply that of a rigorous sect of Mahometans, that of a powerful *Khouan*. But besides the Torah, they had the prophetical books. They read the Prophets almost as much as they did the Torah. They there learned what made them thirst for the future. Those dark prophecies of Isaiah, the second Isaiah, Zechariah, and Malachi, though often misinterpreted, stirred men's souls, and prevented them from falling into that sleep which is close upon the borders of death.

* Ecclesiastes viii. 8.

In religious history a text is valued, not by what an author meant to say, but by what the necessities of his time made him say. The religious history of mankind is made up of contradictions. Just now the Torah triumphs; but in history we must learn to wait. Four hundred years from this time, Christianity will again accept the teaching of the Anonymous Prophet of 536 B. C. Jesus will atone for Ezra, will rekindle the flame of prophecy in Israel, will enchant mankind by the prospect he will hold out to them of the kingdom of God, will lead captive Greece herself, and will procure for her a new life under a Christian form.

BOOK VIII.

THE JEWS UNDER GREEK DOMINION.

CHAPTER I.

ALEXANDER. — ALEXANDRIA.

WITH one of the most extraordinary sudden outbursts recorded in history, Greece (B. C. 333) went to war against the entire East, and in ten years had won a complete victory. The vast Achæmenian empire passed away like a dream. Greek armies had penetrated to Bactriana and to India. In Asia Minor, Syria, and Egypt were sown seeds of Hellenism which developed rapidly. The world changed its axis of rotation, as it had done two hundred years before by the victories of Cyrus. For once, the march of mind followed the march of arms. The rude Macedonians, who under the leadership of Alexander accomplished a campaign to be compared only to those of France under the Revolution and the Empire, were assuredly not men of letters nor great thinkers. But what matter? Ideas travel with men, often in a course just opposite to that in which it was meant to lead them.

A French army thrown into a foreign country to uphold an anti-French policy, takes with it the ideas of France. In past ages a Greek was everywhere a man of enlightenment, just as a Frenchman of our own day is everywhere a liberal.

Greece in two hundred years had founded a civilisation and developed an intellectual culture which greatly surpassed anything the world had seen up to that period. This culture was far from causing a decline of power in arms; for at the very moment when Greece was creating the framework of a civilisation that the whole world was subsequently to accept, she was victoriously resisting the whole strength of the Persian monarchy and inflicting on it defeat after defeat. Her political progress was immense. The citizen — the free man of a free city — made his appearance. At the same time morality established on reason, with no aid from the supernatural, proclaimed itself in all its dignity as a law revealed to every man. The truth as to the gods and as to Nature was almost discovered. Man, delivered from the foolish terrors of his childhood, was beginning calmly to contemplate his destiny. These were the days of Euhemerus, Epicurus, and Zeno. Science — in other words, true philosophy — was born. Some glimpses of the world had been caught; and although they had no result, the right foundation was laid. Copernicus, Galileo, and Newton did but complete the work, reduce it to order, and trace its consequences.

And as to art, O heavens! what new wonders now appeared! What a world of gods and goddesses, what a heavenly revelation! In this, more than in all else, Greece showed her power of creation. She invented beauty, as she had invented reason. The East made statues before Greece did, just as the East sooner than Greece contrived to rid itself of the continual intervention of gods. But Greece alone discovered the stability of Nature's laws; Greece alone found the secret of beauty, truth, order, and ideality. From that time forth man had only to go to her school: so it was with Rome; so it was with the Renaissance; and after every return of barbarism that is what every Renaissance will do to the end of time.

The period of which we treat was indeed a critical moment in the history of mankind. The foundation was already laid for science, philosophy, ethics, politics, the military art, medicine, and law. There was but one thing lacking to this admirable work, — one fatal leak, through which destruction was to make its way. Greece was weak as to her religion. She cherished all childish beliefs, even such as destroyed man's very manhood, and, like Italy after the Renaissance, she throve by the gainful falsehood. The Italy of the Renaissance saw religious imposture established, and she safeguarded the Pope, the chief of all impostures. Greece saw that the gods of the vulgar had no existence, but she employed her art in the service of a brilliant idolatry. Here Saint

Paul was right.* The sages of old saw the truth, but they confessed it not. They were too aristocratic, too artistic. Satisfied to see it themselves, they left the religion of the people in its degradation. They cared little, it may be, for questions affecting the well-being of the people, or for morality. They had not enough of what the prophets of Israel had in excess. They had no interest in common with the people. To the solicitudes of a Marcus Aurelius or a Saint Louis they were entire strangers.

As time went on, this rude religious condition became unbearable. It was the rift into which Israel forced its terrible wedge. And when the fulness of time was come, good and noble souls, disgusted by the farce of popular beliefs, went over to Christianity, — that is, to Judaism. But we are as yet far from that. In the second half of the fourth century before Christ, Greece was a beacon light of truth. Progress was all with her, and nations that did not look to her were those that had no future.

What especially characterised the Greek was his belief in glory, his confidence in posterity. The life of each individual is brief; but the memory of man is eternal, and in that memory he really lives. The important thing for a man is what will be said of him after he is dead; his present life is, as it were, subordinate to his life beyond the tomb. A man is wise who sacrifices himself to his reputa-

* Romans i. 18-32.

tion.* The Greek created an inestimable fund, of which he was the sole disposer. The strange thing is that this great paradox proved true. By inventing history † Greece invented the judgment of mankind, and in this judgment the verdict of Greece was without appeal. Any man in ancient times of whom Greece has failed to speak is doomed to oblivion, to annihilation. The man whom Greece remembered, to him belongs glory that is life. Kings bid high, in adulation and in good offices, to have a statue in Athens; and thus, in lack of immortality, which the gods reserve to themselves alone, there was something more than a transient lustre waiting him for whom everything is short-lived. A selection was made among the crowded ranks of mankind. Life had a motive; there was a reward in store for him whose aim had been the good and beautiful: he won the esteem of Greece!

A godlike youth, who seemed to the ancients an incarnation of Dionysus, and of whose heroic personality we moderns are reminded when we think of the triumphant return of General Bonaparte at the opening of the campaign in Italy, pushed his columns, light-bearing, through the dense darkness of barbarism. His personal character is not known to us from any reliable documents; ‡ but what of that? His deeds speak for him. Alexander's campaigns

* Dummodo absolvar cinis. (Phædr. iii. 9.)
† Herodotus, procem.
‡ The tradition of Bœotianism: *Bœotum in crasso*, &c. (Hor. *Ep.* ii. i. 244), comes from learned Greeks who were hostile to him. The same thing might have been said of Napoleon.

are an immense fact in the history of civilisation. The sphere of Greece was enormously enlarged; the East was penetrated to its very depths. Did Alexander encourage marriages between his Macedonians and Oriental women? We doubt it.* At all events, that was not the best way of regenerating the East; children born of marriages between Europeans and Asiatics are generally Asiatics themselves. Far more solid results were attained. Asia Minor, delivered from the Persian satraps, became an annex to Greece. It was the same with northern Syria; and though southern Syria kept longer its original character, it underwent the influence of a magnet outside of itself which disturbed all its movements. The valley of the Nile slept its unbroken sleep: it went on adorning its temples with bas reliefs, and sculpturing its rocks; but while it did so it was getting impregnated with Greek taste. The Delta, at all events, became one of the strongest positions occupied by Hellenism. If the basin of the Tigris and Euphrates was soon recovered by the Orient, we must remember that the Arsacidæ were always dominated by the ascendency of Greece. The title *philhellene*† was coveted by sovereigns in hither Asia. As far as central Asia and India may be seen undoubted proofs of the influence of Greek art and genius.‡

* It rests on very poor authority.
† Eckel, part i. vol. iii. pp. 330, 528, &c.
‡ Lassen, Wilson, Senart, Weber, Sylvain, Lévi. We must not, however, exaggerate the influence exercised by Greece over the art and literature of India.

The most surprising result of the Greek conquest is the depth of the traces it left behind. It was not an ephemeral march through foreign countries, as were too often the campaigns of Napoleon. Its consequences were lasting; they may be compared to those of Roman conquest. The divisions which followed the death of Alexander, unlike the majestic unity of the Roman Empire, hinder us from realising the changes that followed the Macedonian expedition. To this very day the Greek Church inherits this supremacy. It owes its title to the successes of Alexander, as the Latin Church owes hers to Roman conquerors.

If we may believe Josephus,* Alexander, after the siege of Gaza, visited Jerusalem, and paid especial honours to the high-priest, who showed him passages in the Book of Daniel which related to himself, and offered sacrifice in the Temple. This of course is mere romance, whether it be due or not to the invention of Josephus.† Alexander most probably did not turn aside from his course, and did not visit Jerusalem. Josephus also gives us to understand that there were many Jews in the army of Alexander, and that they took part in his expeditions, which led to their having in the new cities that he founded equal privileges with the Macedonians, and full liberty to practise their rites of worship, even those

---

* Josephus, *Antiquities*, xi. viii. 3–6. For Talmudic traditions (without value) see Derenbourg, *Palestine*, pp. 42–44.

† The mention of the Book of Daniel, at any rate, supposes the narrative to have a modern origin.

hardest to reconcile with the common law. This also seems improbable. The Jews who may have embraced camp life with its loose ways of living could not have been fair examples of the spirit of their people.* A man does not risk his life when he values it so highly. What Josephus says of Samaritan reinforcements seems more probable.† The Samaritans had military ways which the Jews had not.

However this may be, in 332 Greek domination in Jerusalem began. The first governor of Syria was Andromachus, who was killed by the Samaritans, we know not under what circumstances, and he was succeeded by Memnon.‡ Nothing, however, was changed in the internal life of the city. The high-priest Jaddua appears to have exercised in it almost absolute sway.

A new world needed new cities. As Alexander passed the spot where Antioch was subsequently built, it is said he had a vision of what a great centre of civilisation a city founded on so beautiful a site would become. Opposite to the Isle of Pharos he afterwards laid the foundation of that great city of all nations which was to bear his name in triumph to our day. Alexandria, which is still one of

---

* Ecclesiastes viii. 8.

† Josephus, *Antiquities*, xi. viii. 4, 6 The revolt of the Samaritans (Quintus Curtius, iv. 8; Eusebius, *Chron.* i. 11; Ol. cxii.) and what Josephus says is not very distinct. The Hecatæus of the Jews is spurious.

‡ Quintus Curtius, iv. 5, 8.

the world's great cities, was founded in 332, in the interval between the battles of Issus and Arbela, with a clear idea of what it was some day to become. The spot was fixed where East and West were to fertilise each other; one of the hot-beds of Christian growth was laid out in advance; and Greece herself in this distant colony was to develop a new and original side of her own genius.

The literary work of Greece was accomplished; her scientific work began. The old Greek republics had too little of the spirit that loves to work out conclusions, and were too dependent on public opinion, for facility of scientific research. These little democracies formed excellent centres for the creation of first thoughts,* in an age when every one philosophised, speculated, and generalised for himself with a child's fearlessness and serenity; but they were not fit to take up studies in common supported by the State. United efforts, organised bodies, were there impracticable. The monarchies that rose after the death of Alexander were much more favourable for patient scientific elaboration. Neither Athens nor any other Greek city had ever had an Institute or an Academy where learned men could have found books, or laboratories, or means of subsistence. The Museum at Alexandria offered them all this. Learned men thenceforward worked in continuity, worked

---

* We may say the same of the Italian republics of the Middle Ages, which brought to second birth all that Greek republics had brought forth originally.

to one end and under some control. Archimedes, Eratosthenes, Apollonius of Perga, Aristarchus of Samos, Hero of Alexandria, and Hipparchus were the Laplaces, the Berthollets, and the Gay-Lussacs of their day. Important progress was made in many ways. Unhappily, the fire kindled was a single flame; it lacked intensity. The Roman conquest gave little impulse to scientific curiosity. Learned bodies disappeared. A public which had an unconscious influence on learning ceased to exist. The great centre of light was extinguished by the gradual debasement of human intelligence which took place during the first centuries of our own era.

It was not on the lofty and cold heights of scientific truth that East and West were to embrace each other. They united in loving what was vague and conjectural. The mysticism which the East everywhere bears with it formed a far more favourable atmosphere for durable religious union. Neither the austere methods of scientific investigation nor the masterpieces of classic art could establish a common bond between such different races. Two genuine originals will not amalgamate. Things too perfect will not touch each other; or at least if they do, no spark comes from their contact which will set fire to the mass. The Hebrew genius of Isaiah's day and the Greek genius of the fifth century could never have penetrated each other. But Greece in its decay, and Hebraism, also in decay, could embrace; and we see in both the singular results of this interpenetration. The Jewish race having been transported in large numbers to Alexandria, showed there its best gifts. Alexandria was free from the limitations of Jerusalem. Something was to be born of the new union that would be not quite Christianity, but at least what we may term its preliminaries, its first attempt. Christianity itself in the second and third centuries of our era found in the land of Egypt a soil wonderfully prepared for its growth, which furnished it with some of its most important developments.

The city founded by Alexander had in this way a decisive effect on Judaism. There were, besides Jerusalem, two powerful magnetic attractions as it were, Alexandria and Antioch, which deeply influenced the Jewish mind. Hellenism and Hebraism stood face to face, and the battle was a sharp one. Alexander had not, like Cyrus, a second Isaiah to proclaim his coming. It is probable that if any one of Israel's seers of old had come to life during the siege of Tyre or that of Gaza, the words that would have fallen from his lips would have been words of deep dread and malediction. That Olympian Zeus, that god of the thunderbolt, borne everywhere by the new dynasty as the symbol of its power, proved a formidable rival to his fellow-divinity Iahveh.

CHAPTER II.

THE RULE OF THE PTOLEMIES.

THE twenty years of war which succeeded the death of Alexander (323) weighed heavily on Palestine as on the East. Laomedon, Ptolemy the son of Lagus, Antigonus, and Demetrius, one after the other seized it as their prey. The march of Ptolemy the son of Lagus through the land was terrible. In the year 319 this rude captain, already master of Egypt, captured Jerusalem by surprise, profiting by the scruples of the Jews which withheld them from defending themselves upon the Sabbath.* His object was to collect prisoners who should people Alexandria. He saw that the Jews were especially fitted for this kind of colonisation; and he especially valued their faithful observance of an oath. The Jews have always shown themselves most excellent in a new city. Old cities they do not like, for there they are sure to encounter national prejudices; while, on the contrary, they seem particularly fitted for carrying out the plans of a new nation in facing the unknown.

* Josephus, *Antiquities*, xii. i.

Ptolemy son of Lagus took with him a great crowd of captives from Jerusalem, the mountains of Judea, and Samaria. Some of them he placed in Greek settlements in Lower Egypt, but the larger number were confined to Alexandria. When they had sworn allegiance to the Lagidæ, Ptolemy granted them, it appears, a very favourable charter, which conferred on them the same rights in Alexandria as those of the Macedonians. However that may be, the Jewish captives found themselves well off in their new abode. They drew thither a large number of their countrymen by boasting to them of the advantages of the region and the liberality of Ptolemy. Some families of priests followed the current, although in this new state of things there was not much employment for them.* Distance from Palestine put no stop to the dissensions between the Jews and the Samaritans. Mount Zion and Mount Gerizim continued even beyond seas to be a fruitful source of hate and rivalry.†

The Jewish colony in Alexandria soon became very flourishing. The Jews showed their best qualities away from home, where they were not too much the masters. They were liked both for their modesty and their humility.‡ They made good traders and good domestics, were very industrious, with much liking for study. With their facility in acquiring

---

* Josephus, *Against Apion*, i. 7.
† Josephus, *Antiquities*, xii. i.; *Against Apion*, ii. 4.
‡ Μετριότης. Josephus, *Antiquities*, xii. ii. 2.

languages they soon learned Greek, and applied themselves to write it correctly. Their gentle demeanour made them popular among rich Greeks; those destined to follow the employments assigned to eunuchs wore the rosette in their ears in a manner that seemed to ask for pity.* The regularity of their lives and the strictness of their morals procured them situations as confidential servants in the inferior places to which alone they aspired. They made excellent clerks. A new city in which great activity reigned offered to these valuable qualities great opportunities for development. As they had no political objects of their own, the higher political classes established on the conquest found them priceless instruments in the work of administration and government.†

The battle of Ipsus (301) at length put an end to the anarchy that prevailed in Asia. The two great kingdoms of the Ptolemies and the Seleucidæ were consolidated. Palestine fell definitely to the share of Ptolemy the son of Lagus, and remained in his family about one hundred years. It was a prosperous time for Judaism, especially in Egypt. The dynasty of the Lagidæ was in general enlightened and liberal. The reign of Ptolemy Philadelphus especially (284–247) was long remembered, and romantic tales were associated with it. The status

---

* Collection Graf. (Catalogue, &c.: Vienna, 1889), Egyptian portraits, especially of Jews and Syrians.
† Josephus, *Antiquities*, xii. ii. 3.

of the captives brought by Ptolemy the son of Lagus seems to have been ill defined. Those of servile origin were numerous,* to whom Philadelphus gave their liberty. Throughout his reign he seems to have shown favour to the Jews. Ptolemy Euergetes was also held by them in kindly remembrance. It was asserted that on one of his grand expeditions he had even offered sacrifice in the Temple at Jerusalem.†

About the year 300 Antioch began to offer almost as many attractions as Alexandria. It has been asserted that Seleucus Nicator, grateful for the military services the Jews had rendered him, gave them in all the cities that he built equal privileges with the Greeks and Macedonians.‡ This may not be true; but it is certainly true that the Jews found in these new cities a fit field for their activity, and that they flocked thither in crowds. In Judea life was poor and hard; agriculture was wretchedly poor, and there was no commerce, while the tribute was very heavy. The emigrants had all the advantages of Judaism without its inconveniences. The Jewish colony at Antioch was never so famous as that at Alexandria; it was Christianity that raised Antioch, in the first century of our era, into a world-famous city of the first class.

The wars between Egypt and Syria had important

---

* Josephus, *Antiquities*, xii. ii. 1–3.
† Josephus, *Against Apion*, ii. 5.
‡ Josephus, *Antiquities*, xii. iv. 1.

consequences for the Jews. Palestine was perpetually trodden underfoot by the march of contending armies (264, and the years following). Greek monarchies, unlike the Roman conquest, could never insure peace to the inhabitants; and for that reason probably their subjects showed little zeal in defending them. On the other hand, the far East was waking up again. In 256 B. C. Persia broke off from the Hellenic world, and founded the dynasty of the Arsacidæ. Old Iran, however, was only half aroused. It was not till the time of the Sassanidæ [in the third Christian century] that it recovered its ancient national life. We are still four hundred years away from the peace that Rome gave to the world. Each year brought with it new terrors. The Samaritans, on their part, never ceased their enmity to Jerusalem. As soon as fortune smiled on them, they ravaged Jewish territory, made raids, and carried off captives.* Their military organisation gave them means of inflicting injury which the more pacific Judah never had; the Jews, however, retaliated by the most bitter abuse, — as Eastern Christians now are always complaining of the misdeeds of their enemies numerically feebler, and pouring upon them the fiercest invective.† Nevertheless, Judaism flourished in the main. The power of the high-priests was absolute throughout all classes of society.‡ The high-priests Onias I.,

---

* Ecclesiasticus i. 28.   † Ecclesiasticus l. 26.
‡ Philo, *Vita Mosis*, ii. 6.

Simeon I., Eleazar, Manasseh, and Onias II. presided over the nation with dignity.

In Jerusalem and its immediate environs Hellenic influence was weak, but it was very strong in neighbouring regions, especially beyond the Jordan. There, especially at Gerasa and at Pella, colonies of Macedonian* veterans had been planted, who liked to call places around them by the names they had known in their childhood, such as Pella and Dium.† The names of Mygdonia and Pieria owed their origin to similar transfers. The Orontes received the name of Axius, whence comes its present name (*el-Aasi*).‡

On the other hand many cities, to flatter royalty, changed their old names for those of their new conquerors: Alexandrias, Antiochs, Seleucias, Laodiceas, Ptolemaids, Philadelphias, and Phileterias sprang up in all directions.§ Greek mythology took the place of local mythology at Apollonia (Arzuf) and at Panium. The whole aspect of Eastern geography was changed. It is to be noted, however, that the old names were not lost. Acre, Hamath, Arzuf, Rabbath-Ammon, Gerasa, Edessa, are called at this day by their old Semitic names, and not by the

---

* Military colonies replaced the native population. Josephus, *Antiquities*, xii. iv. 1.

† Eusebius and St. Jerome. *Onom.*, at the name of Pella. Stephen of Byzantium on the word Γέρασα. Droysen, *Städtegrundungen Alexanders*, 1843, p. 17 (*Geschichte*, ii; *Anhang*, p. 601); Ritter, *Erdkunde*, xv. ii. p. 1025, &c., 1089, &c.

‡ For el-Aqsi, from the Syrian pronunciation of the *qoph*.

§ There were even several transitory Antigonias.

new titles given them whether by fashion, servility, or adulation.*

Galilee, which after the downfall of the kingdom of Israel seemed to all appearance lost to Judaism, returned about the epoch of Greek domination to the worship of Iahveh, and that not according to the Samaritan form, as might have been expected, but according to the worship of the Jews; so that Jerusalem became the religious capital of districts at some distance, and in order to go up to it on pilgrimage the Galilean Jews had to pass through the hostile country of the Samaritans.† Tyre and Damascus about the same time became filled with Jews, and almost rivalled Antioch and Alexandria in the importance of their " dispersion."

The Jews of the dispersion in the far East, who had never been willing to leave the banks of the Tigris and Euphrates, spread far into Media, into Osrhoene and Commagene. Jerusalem in these distant countries enjoyed an extraordinary prestige. The priestly families in those regions never severed their connection with the sacred city.‡ The godly sent presents thither; the chief revenues of the Temple were derived from this source. A large number of Eastern Iahvists established themselves in Jerusalem, and filled up the void left by the emigration to Antioch and Alexandria. Syriac was the

---

* *Mission de Phénicie*, p. 21, note 2; p. 790, note 4. It was the same with Herodian and Roman names; as Antipatris Ælia, &c.

† *Vie de Jésus*, p 242.

‡ Josephus, *Against Apion*, i. 7.

language spoken by these Eastern Jews; and this circumstance contributed not a little to make Aramean, which they called Chaldean,* the common language of the people.

* Philo, *Vita Mosis*, ii. 7. Cf. Josephus, *Antiquities*, xii. ii. 1.

CHAPTER III.

PROSEUCILÆ. — SYNAGOGUES.

THE Jews of Alexandria, no less ardent than Jews in other parts of the world, gave to their extraordinary inborn activity a different direction from that of the Jews in Judea. They concerned themselves little about the Temple at Jerusalem. Worship which could be followed out only in that one city was a secondary matter with them. A religion without ceremonial, temple, or priests had been an ideal of which the Prophets caught occasional glimpses. The worship established at Jerusalem was the great obstacle to the realising of these dreams. Jerusalem, a purely priestly city, was the place in all the world where such visions were least likely to be realised. But the prohibition against offering sacrifice elsewhere must yet bear its proper fruit. It was this prohibition, in fact, that led to a purer worship. If Jerusalem should be once suppressed, all ceremonial worship would become impracticable; Iahvism would turn to deism; the last trace of local worship would disappear.

All this came speedily to pass with the Jews of the dispersion, especially in Hellenic countries. Without giving up pilgrimages and dependence on Jerusalem,* the dispersed Jews, especially those of Egypt, gave up observance of the ritual. Their fundamental idea that Iahveh could only have one Temple was not to be taken by storm. They, however, made distinctions. They conceived the possibility of a Mosaic law without sacrifices. They came to think that a man could be a good Jew without having worshipped at Jerusalem.

What, then, should a pious Jew do in lack of the essential rites of worship prescribed by the Torah? Ablutions were still possible, and were not to be dispensed with. Men might pray with the heart, and give efficacy to their prayers by turning their faces towards Jerusalem. They might sing hymns of praise to the Divinity; and above all they might meditate on those portions of the Torah that bore on questions of philosophy and politics. A religious life shared in common has always been the imperative need of the Jewish people. In lack of temples they provided oratories, very like those founded about this time by the religious clubs and brotherhoods of the Greeks (ἔρανοι, θίασοι) and the Roman *collegia*.† These were enclosed spaces in the open air, orchards with tiers of seats as in a little theatre. They were not unlike the district chapels, or those of the lay brotherhoods, in old Italian towns. These

---

* Philo, *Fragm.*, Mangey, ii. 645, 646; Josephus, *Against Apion*, i. 7.

† See *Origines du Christianisme*, ii. 351, &c.

places of prayer were called in Greek *proseuchæ* (προσευχαί, προσευκτήρια).* They were generally situated on the bank of a watercourse or near the sea, for convenience of ablutions. They became very dear to pious Jews. There they met one another, there they talked of religion, or discussed the Law, and spoke of the happiness to be derived from its observance; and with this was presently joined a sort of catechetical instruction. These little oratories were the germ of the synagogue, and subsequently of the church. They were to have an immense development in the future.

The place of prayer, indeed, like the mediæval corporation chapels,† soon became little more than a gathering-place, or *synagogue*.‡ Now, the synagogue has been the most original and fruitful creation of the Jewish people. Religion comes to birth and development by human contact. The parish in our own day forms the special religious tie, almost the only tie, and the last that will be broken. The Jews in every little town, and in large cities the Jews in every quarter, had their place of meeting, often in the *proseucha*, but sometimes in a chamber fitted up for that purpose, like a hall of assembly, with

---

* Philo, *Vita Mosis*, iii. 27; *In Flacc.*, 6; *Leg. ad Caïum*, 20, 43; 3 Maccabees vii. 20; Josephus, *Antiquities*, xiv. x. 23; *Vita*, 54; Acts xvi. 13; Juvenal, iii. 296; Epiphanius, *Hær.*, lxxx. 1.

† For instance, the *Cambio* of Perugia.

‡ בית הכנסת, συναγωγή. The organisation of the synagogues and proseuchæ is clearly related only by Philo, the Books of the New Testament, and Josephus. But we perceive it in expressions in the *Pirke aboth*. Remember the expression הכנסת הגדולה.

benches, a seat of honour for the presiding officer, and a pulpit for the orator.

All this was remarkably developed in time.* In the third century before Christ, the life of the synagogue was just beginning.† Its institution was a consequence of the dispersion, and we have seen that during the first years of the Captivity in Babylon the house of Ezekiel was, properly speaking, a synagogue.‡ Men felt the need of seeing one another, of mourning together, and of discussing their common interests. Very quickly, indeed, the synagogue took on something of a worldly air. Here they received new-comers, made fresh acquaintances, or asked tidings of the absent. The power of association among Israelites, which is their strong point to this day, clung to this life of fellowship, full of common love and common hate, which, for the very reason that it had nothing to do with politics, had an intense influence on social life and on morality. The new-comer, who had once appeared in the synagogue, was known and helped. The synagogues corresponded with one another, and exchanged letters of recommendation.§ They formed a vast secret society, a sort of free-masonry, embracing all that portion of the world which lay round the eastern shores of the Mediterranean, which travellers, ‖ dis-

---

* See *Vie de Jésus*, p. 140, &c.

† Perhaps Psalm lxxiv. 8. ‡ See vol. iii. p. 316.

§ Ἐπιστολαὶ συστατικαί of Saint Paul and Saint James. See *Origines du Christianisme*, iii. 228, &c., 445.

‖ Yemen in our own day has something analogous. Jews can

seminators of religious ideas, found extremely useful. Synagogues played a great part in the foundation of Christianity. Even now in our own day they are the strength of Judaism,—a strength that others envy, the ground of many a jealous calumny, to which there is but one answer to be made: Go, and do thou likewise.

Saturday was naturally the day for meetings in the synagogue.* The day of rest was a day consecrated to the wants of the soul; and as it was agreed that the Torah embodied all wisdom, reading the Torah and meditation thereupon became a sort of weekly obligation.† Studied thus in common, the Law became a food of wondrous efficacy. Before long the Prophets were read as well as the Torah, and with them came interest and excitement greater still.‡ The Torah was not as yet divided into *parashas*, or sections, so arranged that it could be read through, either in three years or in one year.§ Just as in the Middle Ages Sundays were designated by the first words of the *introit* at the Mass, sabbaths were distinguished by the *parshioth* or *niftaroth*, which were read. The reading was done by members of the synagogue in turn,‖ for great was the

travel there only by going from synagogue to synagogue with letters of recommendation.

* Note σαββατεῖον. Josephus, *Antiquities*, **xvi.** vi. 2.

† Josephus, *Against Apion*, ii. 17.

‡ We have no proof of it before the time of Jesus.

§ Schürer, ii. 378, 379.

‖ Mishna, *Megilla*, ii. i. 4; iv. 1-6; Zunz, *Die Gottesdienstlichen Vorträge*, p. 3, &c.

dread of setting up in the synagogue official duties or a titled priesthood.

The reading of the Law was followed by a translation of it into the vulgar tongue, — Aramean or Greek, as the country might be.* Then a member of the congregation commented upon what had been read.† This was the origin of the homily and sermon. Jesus and the Christian religion proceeded from this custom.‡ Philo gives us masterpieces of this improvised exegesis, always arbitrary, always full of subtilty; but often also stamped with great love of man, and lofty moral feeling. The preacher, like the reader, had no official function; each man took up his task according to his knowledge or the inspiration of the moment.§ The meeting closed with a benediction pronounced by some member of the assembly, of priestly class if any should be present.‖ And all the people responded *Amen*. The Mass, as we see, already had a virtual existence.

The school was an outgrowth of these very exclusive religious institutions. From early childhood a boy was instructed in the Law under the severest discipline.¶ Parents were strictly charged with this duty, but it is probable that very early there were

---

* Mishna, *Megilla*, iv. 4, 6, 10; Zunz, p. 8; Schürer, ii. 380, 544.

† דרש or דרשה.

‡ *Vie de Jésus*, pp. 140–144.

§ Philo, *Quod omnis probus liber*, 12; *Fragments* (ed. Maugey), ii. 630.

‖ Berahoth, v. 4; *Megilla*, iv. 7, &c.

¶ Ecclesiasticus; Philo, *Legatio*, 16, 31; Josephus, *Antiquities*, iv. viii. 12; *Against Apion*, i. 12, ii. 25; *Vita*, 2; 2 Timothy iii. 15.

also schoolmasters to take the parents' place.* An ignorant person † was despised, and held incapable of being a pious Jew.‡ Religion therefore was, as it is in the Mussulman East of the present day, a complete civilisation, enfolding and imprisoning the entire person, body and soul, and restricting his education in the most absolute way.

How many great things have owed their being to these virtuous sectaries, of whom the world in their own day knew so very little, and yet who were busy in creating the future! The Sabbath, as a day of spiritual nourishment, no longer a day of mere bodily repose; the homily, or familiar preaching, the origin of a pastoral ministry; the church, that great school for things of the spirit, source of consolation, life, and guidance; the confessional school, with narrow culture no doubt, but strong, such as could be passed on to succeeding generations, — all owed their origin to the Jewish *diaspora*, when once dissevered from the absorbing worship of Jerusalem. Hellenic Jews gave to their place of meeting on the Sabbath the name of *synagogue*; the better word might have been the name afterwards adopted by Christians, *ecclesia*.§ Thus was the Church founded; or perhaps, we should

---

* There is however no trace of this before the Talmud.

† עַם הָאָרֶץ = ἰδιώτης.

‡ לֹא עַם הָאָרֶץ חָסִיד. *Aboth*, ii. 5.

§ The synagogue also was called ἐκκλησία. In Alexandrine translations the word קהל is more often rendered by ἐκκλησία than by συναγωγή. See the *Origines du Christianisme*, ii. 86, iv. 47, 48. A church in Arab lands in the East is still called a synagogue.

say, rather by founding the Church Judaism was preparing its own revolution. Antiquity had nothing analogous to the Church, except the *collegia*,* and the *collegia* never resulted in anything important. Religious fellowship, which has been the source of so much moral improvement and happiness, is the especial gift given by Judaism to the world.

To have true religious fellowship we must have a State which leaves to individuals the most complete liberty in everything but politics. The Roman Empire committed the fault of not being sufficiently liberal in that direction; hence came those terrible persecutions of the Christians, and the still more cruel persecutions carried on by Christianity when it had grown to be the official faith. The kingdom of the Ptolemies was a model in this particular.† Under the rule of the Greek Colony of Alexandria, as at the present day under the rule of the English at Calcutta, the most different religious bodies lived independent and happy. Old Egypt carried out its mystical religious beliefs, and no one interfered with its dreams. A kind of Christianity seemed near its birth. Gnosticism was making ready for its eccentric evolutions. At the Museum exact science enjoyed entire freedom. A State, both secular and neutral, played, in the midst of differences mutually hostile, the part of an inflexible impartiality.

* Mithraism alone, among the different forms of worship in these little chapels, seems to have met with some success.
† The narrative in 3 Maccabees is a fable written in imitation of Daniel. See below, p. 210.

CHAPTER IV.

THE GREEK TRANSLATION OF THE PENTATEUCH.

THE common use of the Hebrew language was very soon lost by the Jewish community in Alexandria. Reading the Law in Hebrew became difficult, and of no great service. Greek was the language spoken in the colony, and the Jews ardently studied it. It was inevitable that a Greek translation of the Law should be made, and it seems that this important task was executed in the second half of the third century before Christ. The Hebrew language was not then, as it became afterwards, an object of superstitious respect. The translators were hampered by no scruples; they were not conscious of being engaged in a rash work. The unity of style gives us the impression that the whole translation of the Pentateuch was made by a single writer, who adhered invariably to certain rules that he had marked out for himself. The language is the common dialect spread by the conquests of Alexander throughout the East; a number of little indications would have made us certain that it was written in Egypt, even if we did not know it independently.

As we have said,* the opinion that Moses was the author of the whole Torah had cut short the old book of the sacred history: the tadpole in its last transformation had lost its tail. Moses evidently could not have written the Book of Joshua; so the Torah ended after the portions that had been appended to the arrangement of Josiah. The translator gave special names to the five portions into which the Torah was divided, calling them Genesis, Exodus, Leviticus, Numbers, and Deuteronomy. The whole was called the Pentateuch (the five rolls).† These five little volumes from that time forth were what was chiefly read in the synagogues. Before long they were invested with respect almost equal to that bestowed on the original.

Philology and criticism were not a product of antiquity. A translation that should aim to render the true shades of an author's thought was unknown to that day. For this it would have been necessary thoroughly to understand the original; and such understanding was not then possible. The most learned *soferim* were, in presence of these ancient Hebrew writings, like the Parsee *mobeds* as they sat before their sacred books, when Anquetil saw them for the first time. A crowd of passages, especially in the poetic and prophetic books, were doubtful, or had been altered. The translators had not the great

---

* See p. 99.

† Τεῦχος [tool or weapon] was taken by the Alexandrian Jews as the equivalent of כנגלה. Mosaic of Hammam Lif (*Acad. des Inscr., contes rendus*, 1883, pp. 19, 20.

resources that modern science has since accumulated. They had no knowledge of the comparative method; they had no lexicons and no grammars.* They were satisfied to come pretty near the truth, and were guided by superficial analogies. All translations made in the Middle Ages or by Orientals are of this character; they thought their task accomplished when they had made a second text as obscure as the original; they matched words from their own language upon words of the language they were translating, concerning themselves very little as to the sense it made: it was the business of the reader to find the meaning for himself, if there were any. They fancied themselves very exact because they were perfectly literal. They never observed that since the genius of no two languages is quite the same, equivalent words set in the same order give a very different sense.† But in truth it would be unjust to require of these old interpreters to solve difficulties before which modern philology, with its highly developed instruments, is powerless. Literalness allowed them to leave in the dark what was dark before. Very often they seem to have thought that the obscurity of a passage came from some hidden mystery, which they were bound to protect, and so they contented themselves by giving the bald meaning of the Hebrew words.

* The Alexandrine translators, for example, had not the least notion of defective verbs.

† See some very judicious reflections of Sirach in Ecclesiasticus, prol.: οὐ γὰρ ἰσοδυναμεῖ . . .

The true translator ought always to have his mind free from preconceived ideas; but that was far from being the case with the author or authors of the Alexandrine Greek version. The spirit of their translation is Messianic in a milder way than that of the Chaldean paraphrase, but enough so to falsify, in a number of instances, a true view of the original. The Alexandrian translator is above all things an apologist; a champion of the work of Moses at any price. He is already impregnated with the spirit of the false Aristeas, Philo, and Josephus. He wanted to present the Law to the Greeks in a creditable shape; hence a whole crowd of petty modifications worked into his interpretation of the text, out of consideration for the delicate taste of the Greeks. Explanatory notes have been added, apparent obscurities have been softened, and the grand simplicity of the ancient authors is spoiled. The anthropomorphism of the text is carefully suppressed. God is not to be seen; all passages which speak of men having been permitted to see Iahveh are retouched with a timid hand.* "The angel of Iahveh" is substituted for "Iahveh" † in all cases in which the intervention of the Divinity might give a shock. Many improbabilities have been softened. Dates and numbers, almost always faulty, have been altered. It has been the object to ward off objections that might be raised by the Voltaires of

* Compare it with the Masoretic, יִרְאֶה
† History of Jacob.

the day. Certain precautions seem to have been taken against the quibbles that Orientals are so fond of, which might have given rise to ill-natured remarks among the wits of Alexandria.*

But in spite of all this the Alexandrine translation is one of the most important events in history. It was the Bible of infant Christianity; it was in one sense the Bible of mankind, for the Latin Bible proceeded from it, and Saint Jerome himself only in part supplied its place. Unquestionably the Latin Bible, with its rude Hebraisms, its sublime paradoxes, and its energetic vulgarisms, is superior to this Greek one of Alexandria, which never condescends to shades of meaning, in which lack of precision is a discord, which admits no poetic vagueness or mysticism. But although the Eastern Church has not done with its Septuagint all that our Church has done with its Vulgate; though the Latin Bible holds the first place for its incomparable beauty, — a robe of honour should be given to the Greek Bible, which almost everywhere prepared the way for the work of the disciples of Jesus. It is to the Western Bible what a church on Mount Athos is to a Gothic cathedral, what a Venetian mosaic is to the work of Giotto. The lovely eyes of the Virgins of the schools of Sienna and Umbria enchant us, but in the glass eyes of Byzantine mosaics a more remote antiquity

---

* Thus, it is believed that in the list of unclean beasts the word λαγώς, "hare," was altered to δασύπους, to avoid any puns on the family name of the dynasty, Λᾶγος, Λαγίδαι.

is gazing at us. The Alexandrian therefore who wrote Ἐν ἀρχῇ ἐποίησεν ὁ Θεὸς τὸν οὐρανὸν καὶ τὴν γῆν merits the highest praises of humanity. He divined the loftiest truth in history; namely, that Hebrew genius would conquer the whole earth through the Greek tongue, and in close alliance with Hellenism.

The translation of the Prophets soon followed that of the Torah. The practice of reading in the synagogues called for this addition, for very early it became the custom to read, at the close of the Sabbath assembly, a few pages from the Prophets. There was the wish, besides, to show the Greeks the wealth of literary treasures they possessed.* Other Hebrew books were one by one translated, and pious additions were sometimes made to them after the fashion of the time. The Book of Esther seeming to possess too little unction, prayers were added to remedy the defect. As soon as any important work appeared in Palestine, a translation of it into Greek was made at Alexandria, often after a very short interval;† and not unfrequently this Greek translation has been better preserved than the original. A knowledge of Hebrew became more and more rare at Alexandria, and towards 132 the son of Sirach found Hebrew culture in the Egyptian colony at a very low ebb.‡

The Greek Alexandrine version had an extraordinary success. From Egypt it spread into Syria, even

---

* Prologue of Ecclesiasticus (written about 120 B.C.).
† Ibid.   ‡ Ibid.

into Palestine; the Jews used it throughout the Grecian world.* It was the Bible of Philo and of Josephus, of Saint Paul and the early Christians, who made it the basis of their apologetic writings. Some of the Messianic arguments which converted the world came from blunders in the Alexandrine text, misread, misunderstood, and taken in connection with other blunders. The religious history of the world, as we have often said, is made up of repeated misconceptions.

Fable early fastened on the Greek version of the Pentateuch, and endeavoured to disseminate the idea that it was as good as the original.† The Jewish legends of those times all further the idea that the Jews wished to give themselves importance, and to show the Greeks that poor Israel, so humble as they saw it, once had relations with kings, nobles, and famous men of the Greek world. They therefore tried to make out that their Alexandrine translation had a share in the glory of the library at Alexandria, and in the literary tastes of Ptolemy Philadelphus. This prince they said was anxious to make his library complete. Demetrius Phalereus, his librarian, one day drew his attention to the Law of the Hebrews, and gave it the highest praise. This book was lacking in the collection of comparative

---

* Tertullian, *Apol.*, c. 18; Justin, *Apol.*, i. 31; *Dial.*, c. 71; *Novellæ*, 146; Talm. de Jer., *Sota*, fol. 21, c. 2 (Cæsarea).

† Philo, *Vita Mosis*, ii. 5, 6, 7; Josephus, *Antiquities*, prooem. 3, xii. 11; *Against Apion*, ii. 4; allusions in *Megillath Taanith*, fol. 50, c. 2; *Tract. Sopherim*, c. 1.

legislation. Philadelphus therefore sent to Jerusalem to ask the high-priest Eleazar to furnish him with the precious volume. The high-priest sent the scrolls, and with them seventy-two old men (six out of each tribe),* who were placed in a palace on the Isle of Pharos, each in a room apart from the rest; and in seventy-two days they produced each a version agreeing to the last syllable with that of the rest,† — an evident proof that the sacred book admitted but one way of being turned into Greek, and that inspiration had its share in the task. Those who did not go quite so far as this asserted that the version had been transmitted to the Council of the Jews at Jerusalem, who gave it their unreserved approval. At all events, the version was to be regarded as the perfect equivalent of the original.

The work being finished, Ptolemy gave superb presents to the translators, while to the Jews he accorded noble privileges. So everybody was well pleased.

These fables long passed from mouth to mouth, with various alternations of wonder and embellishment. An annual nautical celebration in the port of Alexandria, ending in a feast on the Isle of Pharos, was connected with the event.‡ We shall soon see how an apocryphal writing § composed in

---

* According to another version of the story, there were five old men for the five portions of the Pentateuch.

† Pseudo-Aristeas (ed. Schmidt, p. 306) tells the story a little differently.

‡ Philo, *Vita Mosis*, ii. 7. § See p. 221.

Egypt gave a pompous version of these fables. The Pharos became a sort of sacred spot; here Justin saw the ruins of the cells of the seventy-two translators.*

This foolish story had prodigious vogue among the Christians of the second century, who appealed to the Alexandrine version in their controversies, and enthusiastically accepted a tale which gave it all the authority of an inspired work.† From that time forth they felt authorised to reason from the Alexandrine version, as if it were the Hebrew. Now, the proofs of the Messianic office of Jesus were much stronger in the Greek version than in the Hebrew; many of the passages cited most triumphantly were only due to false renderings in the Greek. The miracle of the Septuagint took its place side by side with those of the Old and New Testaments as an integral part of sacred history.

Having thus become the basis of Christian Apology, the Alexandrine version, from the second century down, excited the keen animosity of the Jews. What they had one and all admired, they now declared to be a perversion of their scripture.‡ A fast, it is said, was established on the 8th day of the

---

* Pseudo-Justin, *Cohort. ad Græcos*, § 13.

† Justin, Clement of Alexandria, Irenæus, Tertullian, Origen, and the author of the *Cohortatio ad Græcos* attributed to Justin. Οὐ δὴ ξένον ἐπιπνοίᾳ Θεοῦ τοῦ τὴν προφητείαν δεδωκότος καὶ τὴν ἑρμηνείαν οἰονεὶ ἑλληνικὴν ἐνεργεῖσθαι (Clem. Alex. Strom. i. 22). Cf. Talm. of Jer., *Megilla*, fol. 62, c. 4; Talm. of Bab., *Megilla*, fol. 9; Tract. *Sopherim*, c. 1.

‡ Justin, *Dial.*, c. 68, 71.

month Tebeth, "because on that day the Law was written in Greek, in the days of Ptolemy; darkness at that time covered the heavens for three days."* Elsewhere the day when the five old men wrote the Law in Greek for Ptolemy is represented to be equally disastrous to Israel as the day when Aaron made the golden calf.† After the Talmudic period, the Jews gave up the use of Greek, and the Alexandrine version went quite out of their remembrance.

* *Megillath Taanith*, fol. 50, c. 2.
† *Tract. Sopherim*, c. 1.

CHAPTER V.

LITERATURE OF THE ALEXANDRINE JEWS.

During those years of peace in Alexandria the development went on with entire freedom. Intercourse among the various races was close, and fertile in results. The Hellenists, who were the dominant class, showed great toleration for the turn of mind natural to Orientals, which had much looser fibre than their own. The Jews by their humility and their supple temper pleased their proud but kindly masters.* The Jews made good clerks, good stewards, good under-managers. During the reign of Ptolemy Philometor, especially, the Jewish colony in Egypt was in constant favour. Of course we have to allow much for exaggeration and the desire to give themselves importance, in what Jewish historians tell us on this subject.† Vanity and a sense of inferiority made the Jews extremely sensible to small favours from a sovereign, and led them to attach to these an exaggerated importance. Like all little people honoured by the favours of the

* See the story of Joseph and Hyrcanus, p. 248 et seq.
† Josephus, *Antiquities*, xiii. iii. 4; *Against Apion*, ii. 5.

great, they wish to lose none of the credit of these advantages, and eagerly lay stress on all that seems likely to enhance them.* We have already pointed out their tendency to swell the list of foreigners of distinction who visited their Temple.† A provincial is ambitious of relations with as many men of note as possible, and treasures among his life's most precious possessions the memory of the honours he has received from them; when he returns from Paris, he likes to have it thought that he has met many people of consequence, and has been on intimate terms with them. Thus Josephus is proud that his countrymen in Alexandria "lived on terms of familiarity with kings;" he gives us to understand that in the reigns of Philometor and Cleopatra Jews were masters at court; and that, to use his own expression, "those two sovereigns confided their kingdom to Jews." According to him, two Jews, Onias and Dositheus (Johanan), were at one time generals-in-chief of the Egyptian forces. It was Onias who, after the death of Philometor, secured the throne for Cleopatra and her children in opposition to Physcon.‡ All this is doubtful; but what is certainly true is that during the period of the

* Observe how eager are Jewish newspapers in our own day to make great mention of any Jews who have been decorated, have had interviews with sovereigns, or have acquired any other distinction.

† Euergetes is said to have sacrificed at Jerusalem after a victory. This fact is told us twenty times.

‡ Josephus, *Against Apion*, ii. 5. Josephus mixed up with his story a miracle very like that on which the narrative in 3 Maccabees is founded. A feast is also established in honour of this miracle.

struggle between the Seleucidæ and the Lagidæ the Jews throughout the East took the side of the latter, and regarded the defeats of the northern kingdom as victories in the cause of order and legitimacy.*

Jewish vanity has covered these early traditions of Judaic Hellenism with such a tissue of imposture that it is very difficult in this obscure story to discern what is true from what is apocryphal. What seems certain is that during the reign of Ptolemy Philometor (170–150 B. C.) the Jews of Alexandria made a close compact with Hellenism, were seized with a spirit of emulation, and began to write in Greek in imitation of the Greeks. Their first attempts in this line were not very happy. Up to this time Jews had had no notions of literary criticism. The false reasonings which they heard on Homer and the old Greek writers disturbed their biblical exegesis, which was defective enough already. A superficial acquaintance with the origin of Greek mythology and history, as it was taught at Alexandria, threw them into a senseless syncretism. The mania for speculating about Orpheus and Trismegistus led the Jews to imagine endless fables about Abraham. They had long ceased to understand the true spirit of their ancient Scriptures. The most superficial likeness was sufficient to make them identify stories in the Bible with features in the Greek mythology, or with ill-understood data of ancient

* Daniel xi., xii.

erudition.* Wretched historical compositions, sometimes wholly fraudulent, but yet accepted with all confidence by Jewish Christian apologists, were the result of this fever brought upon Israel by a too rapid inoculation of Hellenism. Demetrius,† Aristeas,‡ Cleodemus or Malchus,§ seem to have been really in earnest in their pretended historical lucubrations. Eupolemus ‖ and Artapanus (or at least the Jew who concealed his identity under this absurd name) put no bounds to their charlatan fancies. Artapanus¶ tells us that the Egyptians received from the Jews all their knowledge and all their institutions. Abraham taught astrology to King Pharethothes; Joseph rendered numberless like services. The most celebrated temples in Egypt were built by the sons of Jacob. All the Egyptian worship was due to Moses: he was the Musæus of the Greeks, the master of Orpheus; he invented navigation, architecture, the military art, philosophy; he divided Egypt into thirty-six administrative districts ($\nu o\mu o\iota$); he taught the Egyptians to honour

---

* I have treated this subject in my monograph on Sanconiatho, *Mém. de l'Académie des Inscriptions*, xxiii. 2d part, p. 241, &c.

† Clement of Alexandria, *Strom.* l. xxi.; Eusebius, *Præp. ev.*, ix., xxi., and xxix.

‡ Eusebius, *Præp. ev.* ix., xxv.

§ Josephus, *Antiquities*, i. xv. Some of the above-mentioned compositions may be of Samaritan origin.

‖ Josephus knew him (*Against Apion*, i. 23), but mistook him for a pagan.

¶ Josephus appears to have used his work without naming him (Freudenthal, *Alex. Polyh.*, 169-171).

God, and instructed the priests in hieroglyphics; he was the same as Hermes, — and so on.

These childish fables were sometimes told in verse. Histories of Jerusalem and Shechem * were related in bad hexameters, and a certain Ezekiel made a miserable tragedy out of the exodus from Egypt.†

Criticism was so little known in antiquity, even among the Greeks, that these puerile compositions were taken seriously by some of the Egyptians. It was impossible that a public so curious as that of Alexandria should not have felt interested in the past history of the Jewish people, and should not have made its studies upon the Jews (Περὶ Ἰουδαίων), when it had its treatises on the pettiest populations.‡ The celebrated Manetho most certainly wrote about the Jews, and the passage which Josephus § quotes from him may very probably have been really his, though it may also have been interpolated into the copy of Manetho's text, which Josephus was making use of. The same thing may be said of Lysimachus,|| of Cheremon,¶ of Hecatæus,** and perhaps of Hermippus.†† Many exaggerated praises of the Jews which Josephus borrows from these writers really

* Eusebius, *Præp. ev.* ix., xx., xxii., xxiv., xxxvii.
† Ibid., ix., xxviii., xxix.
‡ See Ch. Müller, *Fragm. hist. græc.*, iv. idex.
§ *Against Apion*, i. 26, 27.
|| Josephus, *Against Apion*, 34, 35.
¶ Ibid., 32, 33.
** Ch. Müller, *Fragm. hist. græc.*, ii. 391, 392, 393.
†† See later, p. 216.

proceed from them; but they themselves had borrowed them from Jewish fabulists.

One circumstance, besides, made the circulation of these falsehoods particularly easy. The great compiler, Alexander Polyhistor, writing towards the year 75 B. C. upon all sorts of subjects, did not omit the Jews, and composed a Περὶ Ἰουδαίων.* This Περὶ Ἰουδαίων was a mere uncritical collection of extracts.† Alexander had not a fortunate hand; he stumbled on the weak literature we have just described. Almost all the apocryphal stories told about the Jews were borrowed from Polyhistor; it is through him, or, if you prefer, through Clement of Alexandria and Eusebius, who borrowed from his compilation, that they were saved from the oblivion they well deserved.

A certain apologetic motive generally mingles in the composition of these works. The Israelites, standing face to face with a public either hostile or ignorant of their past, were naturally inclined to boastfulness. They were sophisticated, too, by fre-

* He speaks of the Jews also in other places.

† A strong argument against the authenticity of the Περὶ Ἰουδαίων is that Josephus did not know of its existence. The quotation in *Antiquities*, i. xv., is not taken from it. We therefore ask ourselves whether it may not have had its origin, like the Exegesis of Aristobulus, among the crowd of apologists in the second century of our era, not far from the middle of which lived Saint Justin. According to this hypothesis, all the authors quoted in the Περὶ Ἰουδαίων must have been manufactured by the author of the apocryphal compilation. This it is hard to admit, because of the agreement of these authors with Josephus (*Against Apion*, i. 23); φαληρεύς may be a marginal addition, which has been included in the text.

quenting the Greek schools. Proud as they were of their national literature, and now made familiar with the course of ancient Greek literature, so well known to the grammarians of Alexandria (those were the days of Aristarchus and Crates of Mallos), the Jews could not fail to make comparisons; and naturally they gave the preference to the writings of their fathers. They maintained that the Hebrew Scriptures were the more ancient, which was true; but they supported this assertion with much bad reasoning. The great objection made by the Hellenists was the little space held by the Hebrews in the classical writers of Greece, who alone deserved confidence.* To make up for this silence (which is surprising to us also), they invented wholesale a series of citations favourable to Israel. They insisted that the ancient Greeks had known and esteemed the Jews; that they spoke of them as a noble people; that they related things about them infinitely to their honour. Wherever patriotism is intense, it makes these encroachments upon truth. They quoted especially Theophilus, Theodotus, Mnaseas, Aristophanes, Hermogenes, Euhemerus, Conon, Zopyrion, and Demetrius Phalereus.† They confessed, indeed, that these mentions of Israel in Greek antiquity were not so numerous as they should have been. This was the outcome of a sort of fear, of a respectful timidity, such as one feels in approaching

---

* Josephus, *Against Apion*, i. 22.
† Josephus, *Against Apion*, i. 23.

sacred things;* oftenest, however, a base envy is the real source. Many classic authors (it was said) had known the Jews, but had abstained from mentioning them from a feeling of jealousy.† Oh, how perverse of them! To repair as far as possible the consequences of this conspiracy of silence, Jewish writers set to work to manufacture texts of eminent authors, that they might buttress a history which in the past stood solitary as a wall. Pagans would have only Greek authorities,‡ and Jews provided them. As they refused to recognize the truth in Hebrew, they were furnished with witnesses in Greek which they could not reject.

In the time of Alexander and of the first Ptolemy lived a man of high esteem for learning, Hecatæus of Abdera, whose writings, on Egypt especially, were of great authority. In his works he spoke of the Jews with great justice and impartiality. This led the Jewish forgers to foist their falsities on him. They attributed to this man of learning in a preceding century a Περὶ Ἰουδαίων or Περὶ Ἀβράμου, which was naturally *ad majorem gloriam Judæorum*.§ It is generally believed that the forger did little more than embroider upon authentic passages of Hecatæus a whole series of his own inventions. His principal

---

* Pseudo-Aristeas, ed. Schmidt, p. 259. Cf. Eusebius, *Præp. evang.*, viii. iii. 3; Josephus, *Antiquities*, xii. ii. 3.

† Josephus, *Against Apion*, i. 22, 23.

‡ Josephus, *Against Apion*, i. 22.

§ Quotations in the Pseudo-Aristeas, Josephus, Clement of Alexandria, and Origen. See Ch. Müller, *Fragm. hist. græc.*, ii. 391-393.

object is to prove that the nobles of the Greeks had been in full sympathy with the Jews, and had admired the purity of Israelitish worship.

The East as well as Greece was called upon to bear witness to the antiquity and veracity of the books of Israel. Egyptian, Chaldean, and Phœnician writers, — why might they not serve as well as Greeks? Now, such testimonies abound.* Already, perhaps, the Jews were busying themselves with Berosus, Manetho, and the arguments that might be drawn from the *Chaldaïca* or the *Ægyptiaca* in defence of Moses. In general, the entire apologetic of Josephus goes back to the Jewish school in Alexandria in the second century B. C., as the attacks of Apion (in the first half of the first century after Christ) were a mere repetition of things said in Alexandria ever since the time of Philometor.

Pythagoras stood so high in the opinion of philosophers at that period that it was a great object to prove that he had known the Jews, and had imitated them. It was asserted that the essential elements of his noble doctrine were derived from the Jews. The historian Hermippus, author of a life of Pythagoras written about 225 B. C., had already (it was said) indicated something of the kind.† But that is very doubtful, though the uncritical spirit of the

---

* Josephus, *Against Apion*, i. 23.

† Josephus, *Against Apion*, i. 22; Origen, *Against Celsus*, i. 15. Possibly the words Ἰουδαίων καὶ are an addition made by some Jew. Josephus in all probability used volumes that had been read and annotated by Jews before his day.

time allows us to think that even pagan writers availed themselves, in such matters, of very superficial resemblances.

If we may believe the Christian Apologists, there lived in the days of Philometor a learned Jew attached to the peripatetic school, named Aristobulus, who addressed to the king an exposition of the writings of Moses. The pretensions of the Jews were then carried to their height.* The peripatetic philosophy was entirely derived from Moses. Long before Alexander, even before the days of the Persian kings, there had been translations of the Scriptures; Pythagoras, Socrates, and Plato were acquainted with them, and had borrowed from them. Plato especially in his Republic had imitated Moses. Homer and Hesiod also owed him much. Aristobulus had employed the usual exegesis of the Hellenistic Jews, which consisted in forestalling by allegorical explanations any objections that might be drawn from the anthropomorphisms in the Bible. Where it is written "God spake and it was done," he explains that the divine force was exerted, as Greek philosophers had taught, and Orpheus and Aratus. The six days of Creation, and the day of rest for the Almighty that followed them, are also symbols. These assertions are not incompatible with the exegesis and criticism of the Alexandrine Jews in the days of Philometor; but the authenticity of the

---

* Clement of Alexandria, *Strom.*, i. xv. xxii.; v. xiv.; vi. iii.; Eusebius, *Præp. ev.*, viii. ix. x.; xiii. xii.; *Hist. eccl.*, vii. xxxii. 17, 18.

Book of Aristobulus suffers from other great difficulties.* We consider it to have been an apocryphal work, composed in the second century of the Christian era, about the time of Saint Justin and Tatian. The assertions of the author are not made in simple good faith; they are those of a charlatan, and as foolish as those of Artapanus. He knew very well that Plato, Homer, and Hesiod never copied from the Hebrew Bible; but he wrote what he did for ignorant men, hoping to throw dust in their eyes.†

The allegorical exegesis of which the Jews of Alexandria made so strange abuse was, in their way of employing it, a downright monstrous falsehood. To forestall the contempt with which Hellenic rationalists might have treated certain traits told with a grand simplicity in the ancient Hebrew scriptures, they made haste to say, "Oh, no! that

---

* Aristobulus quotes the Σοφία Σαλ. (Cf. Delaunay, *Philo*, p. 45, note 1.) Now, the Σοφία was written at the close of the second century B. C.

† Clement of Alexandria was the first to quote the work of Aristobulus. It is a very surprising circumstance that Josephus and Saint Justin had neither of them known of such a book. The fables of the Pseudo-Aristeas, particularly the part which Demetrius Phalereus must have taken from the Greek translation of the Bible, are mentioned by the author. All his quotations are found elsewhere in the writings of the Apologists, and in a better condition. (See especially Schürer, ii. p. 814.) The dedication to Ptolemy Philometor is especially improbable; the falseness of the statements and the quotations is too easy to verify. Such works could only have been produced in a literary circle of a very low type, where an extraordinary lack of skill was permitted to have its way. The forger, in choosing his author's fictitious name, may have had in view Aristobulus, "the preceptor of Ptolemy," who figures in 2 Maccabees i. 10. Cf. Eusebius, *Præp. ev.*, vii. ix.

never happened. Those things are types and metaphors." The innumerable passages in which Iahveh acts in an anthropomorphic manner were explained and twisted; they were said to be symbolic, or examples of the old figurative style. All apologists are alike. Is it not by means of childish allegories that apologists in our own day endeavour to escape from the pressure of common-sense, or rather from the fetters of a theological past? These proud churches once burnt thinkers who tried by such poor makeshifts to ward off the impossibilities of the current exegesis; but now, at bay, they betake themselves to the same expedients to which they once were merciless. Thus the world moves on; but through all the absurdities that perish, poor reason, which never allows anything to be quite lost, still pursues her way.

CHAPTER VI.

COMMENCEMENT OF PROSELYTISM. — PIOUS FRAUDS.

ALL this seems puerile; but it is really grand, full of promise for the future, and touches us with a certain pathos. The end, as is often the case, was worth far more than the means employed to attain it. Israel was attaining to an idea which had indeed been that of its ancient prophets, but which seemed to have become strange to it since the return from the Captivity, — the idea of propagandism, of making proselytes. A true feeling of charity appeared with the desire to do good, and the effort to better the condition of their neighbours, to bring them into the same state with themselves, in which they felt so happy. Judaism was so excellent! It was the true religion; why should it not be the religion of all? Judaism is only the worship of one God, and the practice of morality. Every good man ought to become a Jew; true religion has only two enemies, — polytheism and a corrupt life.

To become a Jew, — one must understand what that meant. Some, indeed, considered all the good men upon earth as sons of the God of Israel. Others went further still. All the names given to God are synonyms; a good pagan monotheist might remain a pagan, provided he observed the natural law, of which the Jewish Law is the most perfect expression. To preach to the heathen became from that time forth one of the fixed ideas of the Jews in Alexandria. Literary fiction was almost always the form adopted in the writings of this propaganda, the writer's object being to make pompous praises of the Law proceed out of the mouths of unbelievers. Ptolemy Philadelphus was considered in those days the model of a well-educated and intelligent king. What an advantage for the truth, could it be proved that Ptolemy Philadelphus had an especial esteem for Judaism and for its Law!

Accordingly, this was what a pious Jew of Alexandria undertook to do; and he took for the framework of his fiction the origin of the Greek version of the Bible, and the fables that had grown up around it.* A certain Aristeas — a high officer in the court of Ptolemy Philadelphus, and a pagan in belief — writes to his brother Philocrates, also a pagan, but a man of fine intelligence, impartial, and anxious to know everything worth knowing in his day, and tells him his impressions of the excellence of the Law of

---

* The latest edition is that of M. Maurice Schmidt in Merx's *Archiv*, i. 241-312. See also Lumbroso, *Atti dell' Acad. di Torino*, 1868-1869; and *Recherches sur l'écon. polit. de l'Égypte sous les Lagides* (Turin, 1870), p. 351, &c.; and Papageorgios, *Ueber den Aristeasbrief*, Munich, 1880. The document exhibits some very remarkable Egyptian peculiarities.

the Jews. These men were enlightened pagans, and consequently deists. There is but one God, under various names. "They worship God the Creator, who watches over everything. Him all men adore; we, in particular, calling him Zen or Zeus."* Aristeas, by reason of his duties at court, has been directly concerned in the completion of the work of the Seventy. He has seen the great consideration with which the seventy-two learned Jews have been treated, the splendid presents that the king, by advice of Demetrius Phalereus, has given them, and the superb palace built for them at Pharos, that they might not be disturbed by the noises of the city. Jerusalem, the writer thinks, belongs to the King of Egypt. The Jews live there fully independent, in the comfort and prosperity due to their own virtues; for when one is as good as they, he must be happy. Never was any nation so prosperous; their land is fertile, their seaports excellent, their government perfect, as it must be with a people by God rewarded here below. Aristeas has seen this with his own eyes, having been one of the embassy sent for the seventy-two learned Jews, and to carry presents to the high-priest. The Jewish Law is a law that conforms to Nature; its deep meaning is the very reality of things.† It throws light unlimited on all sorts of subjects. Philadelphus on eight consecutive days invited the learned Jews to his table. He put to

---

* Schmidt, pp. 255, 256.
† Τὴν σεμνότητα καὶ φυσικὴν διάνοιαν προῆγμαι. Schmidt, p. 283.

them all manner of questions in politics, ethics, and practical wisdom. They answered in a way that filled the king with admiration. Thus the most enlightened of sovereigns and the wisest of his counsellors esteemed the Law, and praised it highly. What a recommendation was this for Hellenist deists, convinced of the folly of idolatry, whom the author supposes to be numerous around him!

It is not doubtful, indeed, that there must have been many such Greeks in Alexandria; cultivated men, whom philosophy had led to a sort of deism analogous to the eclecticism of Cicero a hundred years later. Theophrastus, in his "Treatise on Piety," had proclaimed the precepts of the purest religion. The Stoics in many points were like enlightened Jews.* Agreement, therefore, between Judaism and Greek deistic sects had apparently become possible; but the time was not yet ripe. Men of learning disliked Judaism; the middle classes, worthy people but without culture, amongst whom Christianity found the soil for its growth, were too few. The world was still too aristocratic. To promote so useful an evolution, so far from the domain of reason, there needed the wide top-dressing of democracy, with which the Roman Empire fertilised the world.

On the part of Israel, the concessions were very great. The needs of the propaganda brought about a certain shock of reaction, which showed itself so

* *Orig. du Christ.*, v. 305, 306.

strikingly in the early days of Christianity. It was felt that to win souls Judaism must be simplified; that its complicated religious observances could not suit everybody; that the law destined for Gentiles must be reduced to what were beginning to be called the precepts of Noah, — that is, to the precepts of natural morality, and the addition of a few points which the Jews considered as nearly of the same rank, — rules concerning marriage, abstinence from unclean meats, above all, from blood. These made the conditions of Christian fellowship in what is called the First Council at Jerusalem.* Nothing was said of circumcision, or of observance of the Sabbath, — such essential parts of Judaism for the Jews.†

Alexandria had the glory of inaugurating this movement, whence came the Sibylline Books, Essenism, and Christianity.‡ Alexandria thus took up a position the very opposite to Jerusalem. The idea of winning over an unbeliever to the Jewish faith by facilitating his admission and mitigating for his sake the rigours of the Law, would have seemed monstrous in Judea. In Egypt it made headway in all directions. The Jew was content at first to proclaim the excellence of his Law; as yet there were no conversions. The proselyte would soon

---

* *Saint Paul*, p. 79, &c. [Acts xv.]

† Sibylline Books. Pseudo-Phocylides.

‡ Christianity abolished not only circumcision, but also the Sabbath. Sunday is not the Sabbath. *Saint Paul*, p. 263; *The Gospels*, p. 376; Marcus Aurelius, pp. 509, 523.

come, and bring into the new religion he embraced his good faith, his tenderness of heart, and his piety as a new disciple. This simplified Judaism, purely deistic and ethical, was naturally friendly to Greece, and aimed to be on good terms with her. The Jew in Palestine knew nothing about Greece, or else despised her. The Egyptian Jew knew her and admired her. Indeed, what did Moses teach? He told of a God who rewards good and punishes evil. And what morality did he teach? That eternal morality which the sages of Greece taught likewise. It only needed, therefore, that Jew and Greek should understand each other. This school of Hellenising Jews, so puerile in argument, so irritating to us by its historic falsehoods, thus proved itself great, fruitful, providential. It was essentially the offspring of the Second Isaiah, and it prepared the way for Christianity. A monotheistic and moral propaganda was gradually organised. To save it men recoiled before no violence. Theirs was the cause of truth and right. This may excuse in them a few pious frauds, a few fabricated verses.

Since pagan Hellenists, they thought, would only accept the authority of their own writers, it occurred to them, as we have said, to get together a collection of classic passages favourable to the life and Scripture of the Jews. They chose the most highly honoured names out of ancient Greek literature to give the holy doctrine a favourable hearing with the pagan masses. Sometimes they took single verses out of ancient texts, or fragments which seemed to serve the cause; sometimes they altered passages; sometimes they made up statements out of the whole cloth. This propaganda, masking in pagan guise, was doubtless held to be a deed of piety and merit.

Like all great literary centres, Alexandria established two grades (so to speak) in the public of letters, — masters or professors, living apart and holding their learned discussions among themselves, under the rules of criticism of the day; and a sort of cultivated inferior class, which knew things only by halves, like our own newspaper public, open to any sort of credulity. In such an atmosphere literary frauds had the finest of chances to see the light. The Alexandrian who had heard of Orpheus was dizzy with delight when verses of Orpheus himself were quoted to him, shaped to the very ideas of his own age. He had no thought of verifying them. The official teacher probably never heard of these frauds; at any rate, he did as we all do when we hear of some low-down imposture, — he made no protest.

The poem of Aratus, which was nearly a hundred years old, had an immense success. They made much especially of the first line in it, —

Ἐκ Διὸς ἀρχώμεσθα,*

and that other hemistich, —

τοῦ γὰρ καὶ γένος ἐσμέν,†

---

* Eusebius, *Præp. ev.*, xiii. xii. 10, &c.
† Acts xvii. 28.

both of which express an elevated thought. More or less fabricated are the lines attributed to Æschylus, Sophocles, Euripides, Philemon, Menander, Diphilus, Orpheus, Hesiod, Homer, and Linus.* It is supposed, and not without probability, that most of these mystifications proceeded from the Pseudo-Hecatæus.† The poem attributed to Orpheus is not without a certain beauty. Orpheus, having reached the end of his career, makes a kind of confession to his son Musæus. He retracts all his previous poems consecrated to polytheism, and proclaims the one true God. Linus also, in a piece attributed to him, expresses some very fine sentiments.‡

The ancient gnomic poet, Phocylides of Miletus, enjoyed a great reputation in respect to his moral precepts. A sage of Alexandria, a brother in spirit of Jesus son of Sirach, chose the form of Phocylides to make a collection of maxims of natural morality, in which the part played by Judaism is very weak, and the precepts of Noah are reduced to precepts on health and cleanliness.§ The Sabbath itself is

---

* These verses may be found in the *Cohortatio ad Græcos*, and in the *De Monarchia*, falsely attributed to Saint Jerome, in the *Stromata* of Clement of Alexandria, and the *Præparatio evangelica* of Eusebius.

† Schürer, *Gesch. des Jüd. Volkes*, ii. 810, 811. Many of the fabricated verses imply a very advanced theory of the end of the world. *De Monarchia*, 3 (Pseudo-Sophocles).

‡ Quoted by Aristobulus.

§ See *Saint Paul*, p. 80, &c.; J. Bernays, *Gesamm. Abhandl.*, i. 192–261; Schürer, ii. 824–827. This document has never been quoted either by Jewish or Christian apologists; but its affinity with the Sibylline poems is striking (*Carm. sibyll.*, ii. 56–148), and it seems much more Jewish than Christian.

omitted in this little code, whose object was less to convert the reader to Judaism than to make him a good man, a believer in God and in future retribution. The name of the celebrated philosopher Heraclitus * was used in the same way. Forged letters were a favourite method of proceeding. These books were much read. The apocryphal correspondence of Diogenes † was also interpolated by some Jew, desirous of inculcating his own principles of natural morality, touched with a mitigated Mosaic tinge. Later, the names of Hermes, Æsculapius, and Hystaspes were thus misused. There is nothing to prove to us that in ancient times these mythical names sheltered any writings of a monotheistic tendency.

* Bernays, *Gesamm. Abhandl.*, i. 70, &c.; *Die Heracl. Briefe*, Berlin, 1869; Schürer, pp. 827, 828.

† Bernays, *Lucian u. die Cyniker*, Berlin, 1879, pp. 96-98; Schürer, p. 828.

CHAPTER VII.

THE RULE OF THE SELEUCIDÆ IN PALESTINE. — FIRST APPEARANCE OF ROME IN THE EAST.

ABOUT the year 220 B. C. the kingdom of the Seleucidæ at Antioch gained a decided superiority over the Ptolemaic kingdom at Alexandria. This revolution was the result of the accession of a very remarkable sovereign, Antiochus III., rightly surnamed "the Great," who seemed to revive in some measure the genius of Alexander. What the kingdom of Antioch needed was possession of Cœlesyria, Phœnicia, and Palestine. The brilliant campaign of 218 put all these countries into the hands of Antiochus. But his success was only ephemeral. The following year the battle of Raphia restored Palestine to Egypt for fifteen years. In 202 Antiochus reconquered it more effectually; the battle of Paneas (198) may be taken approximately as the date when Jewish countries, or those under Jewish influence during the tolerant dominion of the Ptolemies, passed under the rule of the Seleucidæ, which was far more stringent. There were, indeed, several later changes of fortune. In 193 B. C. Palestine again fell under the dominion of Egypt, as the marriage portion of the daughter of Antiochus;* but the die was cast. Jerusalem for fifty years was to receive from the shores of the Orontes electric shocks which would rouse her from her torpor into ten times her former energy.

During this period, when the country seemed rent in pieces, the condition of the populations of Palestine — overrun as it was by armies, by turns defeated or victorious — was something dreadful.† A chief object of the war was to make slaves, who brought a good price in markets along the Mediterranean. Demoralisation was extreme; good faith was almost lost. Military tacticians were for a space masters of the world, as in the fourteenth and fifteenth centuries in Italy. There was no petty chief, if he thought himself a man of some ability and had a few mercenaries at his command, who might not hope to carve out for himself a kingdom peopled by wretches on whom he could lay burdens. In short, the condition of things was much like that in the fifth century, when barbarous tribes divided western Europe, without heed to the wishes of the native population. The campaign of 202 was especially disastrous for the inhabitants of Cœlesyria and Judea. The Egyptian general Scopas had placed a strong garrison in Jerusalem, where the Syrians besieged it. The struggle was terrible. The con-

---

* This is found in Daniel xi. 17.
† Josephus, *Antiquities*, xii. iii. 3, 4.

servative and orthodox party seems to have remained faithful to the Lagidæ;* but the Hierosolymites among the common people † soon went over to the party of Antiochus,‡ and helped him to get rid of Scopas.

It was said that Antiochus, in return for these services, loaded the Jews with favours; that he embellished their Temple and enlarged its porches, and granted the priests what they desired above all things, — official sanction for the requirements of their law. The city had been almost deserted. Antiochus repeopled it, and set his prisoners free.§

If we may believe certain very suspicious documents cited by Josephus,‖ the confidence of Antiochus the Great in the loyalty of the Jews went further still. Being doubtful as to the attachment of the people of Lydia and Phrygia, he is said to have given orders to transport from Mesopotamia and Babylon to these countries two thousand Jewish families with all belonging to them,¶ to form the nucleus of an industrious and loyal population. This is extremely

---

* This we infer from Daniel xi. and xii.

† פָּרִיצֵי עַמְּךָ, Daniel xi. 14.

‡ Josephus is eager to prove that the Jews have always been entirely faithful to their masters, even when vanquished; yet he is every time forced to admit that they have made singular haste to pass over to the winning party.

§ Josephus, as above. The letter of Antiochus is probably spurious, but the situation it describes is real.

‖ Josephus, *Antiquities*, xii. iii. 4.

¶ It has been supposed that this was the origin of the manufacture of carpets (*Ushak*). But no; according to Josephus these Jews were all agriculturists.

doubtful; what is certain is that the Jews retained a very kindly remembrance of Antiochus the Great. He took his place later as one of the princes who had conferred privileges upon them, and certified to their fidelity.

If the work of Antiochus the Great had proved permanent, — if he had established in Syria an empire as firm as the Ottoman empire in after years, with Antioch for its capital, — the religious destiny of mankind might have been greatly changed; but a very important event was looming in the distance. During the last years of Antiochus the Great, every magnetic needle in the East seemed disturbed. A new power was entering on the world's stage. Rome, proud of having humbled Carthage, was resolved that nothing without her permission should thenceforth take place in countries bordering on the Mediterranean. All Greek kingdoms and confederations became virtually subject to her; ancient democracy, daughter of Hellenism, was struck dead.* The political work of Alexander was destroyed. Greek liberalism, ruined by its own faults, was to be stranded for two thousand years.

Greece first taught the world liberty and the dignity of man; but in everything she created, discipline was wanting. Her ancient republics never found the way of escape from incurable anarchy. Boastfulness, sheer folly, and the rash adventures of superficial politicians, have in such communities too great

---

* Daniel xi. 18. An allusion to the battle of Magnesia.

advantage over serious purpose, good sense, and moral scruple. And the Greek, always a man of high breeding in his own country, appeared before the world in the character of a Macedonian warrior, often cruel, — as it was in the French Revolution, which began with the widest sympathy for foreigners, and ended by irritating its warmest friends by its display in arms and its vainglorious soldiery.

Up to this time nothing had ever hinted the immense strength Rome was now exhibiting to the astonished world. Her military display was not extraordinarily great; but terrible was the resolution, the obstinacy, the energy, which were felt to lie behind those legions, — those ambassadors, that represented her invincible strength. The Senate seemed a deity, far off and hidden from sight, whose decrees were carried out with the inflexibility of fate. The cool determination of her aristocracy and the self-sacrifice displayed among her people were alike admirable. Never was there seen less of philosophy, more of public spirit, — in other words, more resignation to inequality. Never once did the heroes of these legions ask why they were being taken to the ends of the world. "They toil, they suffer, — from want of food, from want of fire," says a Jewish writer.* Doubtless they did so, but this is the virtue that history rewards. The patrician who commands these legions may be the least lovable of men, a bitter tory, a bad man, stiff, awkward, and hard-hearted, ready

* See vol. iii. pp. 401-404.

to become a robber when he can; but what of that? He does the work of God. If there had still been prophets in the dark days, those who had called Nebuchadnezzar the servant of Iahveh would have given the same name to the eagles which flashed to right or left like the thunderbolt, fulfilling their appointed tasks.

In many ways the legions, though they knew it not, carried progress with them,—which is, indeed, the true will of Iahveh. Almost everywhere throughout the East the native populations were weary of these Macedonian dynasties. The vast coalition, Antiochus at its head, had at bottom nothing national. The Greeks and the Syrians had never coalesced into one nation, like the Gauls and Franks under the kings of France. The energetic resistance Scipio met with was from the troops rather than from the people. In general, these last profited from the preponderance of Roman rule. Petty monarchies, like that which was soon to arise in Judea, could not have existed if the rule of Antioch had still been held in respect. The same is true of the numberless free cities of Syria, whose independence began about 125 B. C.,— that is, at the time of the great decline of the Seleucidæ. Besides, the political weakening of Hellenism did not lessen its influence as a factor in civilisation. The diffusion of Greek manners, customs, and speech did not slacken during the second century before Christ. About the year 100 the Phœnician language almost disappears; Greek wholly supplants it in inscriptions.* The powerful protectorate that Rome held over the countries of the East did not extend to intellectual, moral, or religious matters. In these, Rome was always neutral. She created one great thing, — the secular State, indifferent to all besides material order. In those ancient days, at least, she was a thousand leagues from any idea of religious persecution. The family *sacra* and respect for local gods never entailed such grave consequences as did the assumed revelation of an absolute God, for whom one takes up arms against all the world.

Antiochus was not always so wise. These Semitic gods were rich, and they avenged themselves on those who laid hands upon their riches. Antiochus, to replenish his empty treasury, conceived the unfortunate idea of pillaging a Temple of Baal in Elymais, and the people of that country murdered him (187).† His son and successor, Seleucus IV. (Philopator), was accused of having meditated the commission of a similar outrage in the Temple at Jerusalem, by means of his minister Heliodorus.‡ To all appearance, this story is destitute of truth. Religious liberty was not as yet openly violated. All else the Jews suffered patiently, repairing with their

---

* A bilingual inscription in the Piræus, *Revue archéol.*, January, 1888, pp. 5–7.

† Strabo, xvi. i. 18. There is another version in Aurelius Victor.

‡ 2 Maccabees iii. 7, &c. (Compare 4 Macc. iv., and Daniel xi. 20.) All that concerns the splendid gifts made by Seleucus IV. to the Temple at Jerusalem (2 Maccabees iii. 3) has no foundation.

national love of order the injustice of which they were victims, and making the best of the public affronts they might receive. The point of honour was nothing to them. Anything could be borne provided prayer was free, and incense each day might ascend before Iahveh.

CHAPTER VIII.

MIDDLE CLASS. — SACERDOTAL NOBILITY.

In fact, during the first part of the time when the Seleucidæ held sway in Jerusalem, men of piety had little to complain of. Greek fashions were making progress; but the old school, the grave "noble fathers" of the ancient sort, continued to flourish. The high-priest played the part of a real king, set public works on foot, fortified the city, and prepared it to resist a siege.* Nobody dreamed, however, that such a city had any military value. The Greeks looked on Jerusalem merely as a Temple, and in keeping with the etymology of that period wrote its old name of *Jebus* as if its first syllable were *Hiero* (*holy*).†

The Jew was above all things a pious man, but he was also a man who loved order; a man of action, acquitting himself well in all affairs intrusted to him; ‡ excellent for every kind of subordinate work, on the one condition that he was suffered to observe

---

* Ecclesiasticus i. 1-5.

† Τὸ ἱερὸν προσαγορευόμενον Ἱεροσόλυμα. Polybius quoted by Josephus, *Antiquities*, xii. iii. 3.

‡ Josephus, *Antiquities*, xii. xii. 4; προθυμίαν εἰς ἃ παρακαλοῦνται.

his Law in peace. What the Torah formed with wonderful success was a well-regulated *bourgeoisie*, a middle class, pious and reasonable, — like the Protestant Puritans in England and America, vehement defenders of the Sabbath, and excellent bankers. The idea of rising to the highest rank and taking a place among their Greek conquerors was beyond the reach of such a man. In his resigned humility he was satisfied to enjoy the good things that God accorded him in return for his faithful observance of the Law. The Jew never dreams of worldly honours, until money has come to be the one thing in the world, and a substitute for the great prizes that in old times were only gained in war.

It was not that there were not Epicurean Jews, voluptuous, ambitious, almost void of religious feeling. The simplicity of Jewish ideas has always tended to the two extremes. An atheist in Israel touches elbows with the fanatic. It is in the families of the high-priests that we most find these scandals. The money that passed through the hands of pious sacrificers made them rich, almost the only rich men of the nation. The opinion of the Jews about nobility — that the only nobility was that of the priesthood * — gave them great facilities for rich marriages. Sometimes there mingled in all this a sordid avarice, which was downright robbery of the poor. The farming of taxes, that perpetual running sore of the East, gave rise to crying abuses.

---

* Josephus, *Against Apion*, i. 7.

The leading men in each province contracted under bonds for the tribute due to the king of Egypt or Syria, made slack payment, and left their provinces exposed to outrage, while they themselves made scandalous fortunes.

The high-priest Onias (second or third of that name) kept for himself the tribute collected for the overlord, and thereby came near bringing down upon Jerusalem the greatest suffering.* His nephew Joseph, son of Tobias, a man skilful in intrigue, profiting by his father's faults, insinuated himself into the good graces of Ptolemy by baseness and buffoonery, such as have succeeded with khedives in all ages. He acquired immense riches, and had a son named Hyrcanus,† who far outdid his father in rascality and sycophancy. After a life full of adventure, part of which was passed in battles with the Nabathean Arabs, Hyrcanus built in the rock near Heshbon a fortified place of safety, which to this day is the wonder of travellers.‡ He called it *Souri*, or "my rock," § which in itself was impious, because a true Jew would have given the name *Souri* to God alone. He had not time to finish this luxurious den of robbers. We can see

---

* Josephus, *Antiquities*, xii. iv. This episode is a singular one in the last days of the rule of the Ptolemies, and is in strange contrast with other documents of that period which have no historical value. Josephus probably found it in some family records.

† A nickname (one given to a dog) taken from the district Hyrcania (Mazenderan or Taberistan), near the Caspian. See Pape.

‡ Now *Aaraq el-Emir*. See Vogüé, *Temple de Jerusalem*, pp. 37–42.

§ A trace of this name is preserved in "Wadi-el-Syr."

how even there fear and dread pursued him. There are covered passages and holes for hiding scooped out in the rock, so that he might be safe from the most cunning treachery. Hyrcanus had made his fortune by Egyptian favour; but seeing that the Seleucidæ were getting firmly established, and that their rule was becoming assured, he dreaded lest he should be given up to the vengeance of the Arabs, and killed himself about the year 175.

For a Jew to commit suicide was a great sign of the times. In the view of ancient Iahvism it was both a crime and an absurdity. Hyrcanus son of Joseph was no doubt one of those Jews who had imbibed Greek ideas with Greek manners. Never had suicides been so numerous as now. Political opinion was merciless, and its sentence was generally anticipated.* Hyrcanus is the Jew materialist, whose life is summed up in "vanity of vanities." His unfinished palace in the desert is like a page of Job, — a lamentation over life; a reproach to God, who, careful only of his solitary grandeur, has made human destiny so mean, so absurd, so miserable.

May not Ecclesiastes have been written at this time? It is certain that Aaraq el-Emir is the very spot wherein the Koheleth shows all its truth, all its value. Hyrcanus must have been a man especially fitted to comprehend the state of mind of a disillusioned Solomon. But let us wait. Fanaticism has not yet set on fire the Jewish blood.

---

* As in the case of Hannibal, Mithridates, &c.

During the two centuries which yet separate us from Jesus, religious indifference will play a large part in Israel; not until the first century of our era will the lukewarm be cast out. Agrippas and Hanans will then have no place in Jewish life. Between the Christian and the zealot no space will be left for the moderate man.

We need not be surprised that even amid such pious surroundings great abuses flourished without provoking much reaction in the higher ranks of the priesthood. Very religious times and very religious countries are apt to suffer great scandals among their clergy, without being greatly shocked by them. The clergy are much more lax in pious countries than in a public of unbelievers. The Middle Age saw enormities of simony, indulgences, masses for the dead, and was not induced to revolt against the Church as by law established. That Temple where everything was for sale, its vile pontiffs (*cohanim*) lovers of pleasure, atheists, and materialists, who preyed upon the piety of the faithful, cheated God, and took for themselves all the clear profit of the sacrifices, had not as yet provoked any strong remonstrances. The people believed God considered himself honoured by the homage of such rascals, and money was brought them without the slightest misgiving. A pious man is apt, unintentionally, to attribute strange tastes to the Divinity; one might suppose, to see how piety sometimes reasons, that nonsense is a kind of sacrifice made to God of what he values most, — an act of homage, which sets at naught all exercise of private judgment.

There were, besides, among the higher priests some very respectable men, and that sufficed to maintain the honour of the priesthood. The old men, the Council of the Seventy (Sanhedrim), governed. It is about this time that Jewish tradition places the Great Synagogue, a somewhat mythical institution,* around which grouped themselves, as round a primitive church, memories of an orthodox transmission of the Torah. *Asou seïag lattora*, " make a hedge about the Law," build up around it walls of defence, was in brief the religious teaching of that period.† All private speculation was forbidden; no revival of the prophetic spirit was foretold by any sign.

The high-priest, Simon the Just, is considered to have been the last member of the Great Synagogue.‡ He left behind him a memory of high honour.§ He is almost the last Biblical figure seen against the dark background of sacerdotalism, before the days of the great debasement of Judaism under the Asmoneans and the Herods.‖ To him the Temple owed many

---

* See Derenbourg, p. 29, &c., resuming and correcting Herzfeld.

† *Pirké aboth*, chap. i.   ‡ *Pirké aboth*, chap. i.

§ The date of Simon the Just has been made uncertain only by the blunder of Josephus (*Ant.* xii. ii. 4), who made a mistake of a century. Simon the Just lived about 190. The pompous eulogy made of him by Jesus, son of Sirach, was undoubtedly written by a contemporary. See *Breviarium Philonis* under Antiochus the Great; Derenbourg, p. 46, &c., resuming Herzfeld.

‖ Ecclesiasticus l. Compare Derenbourg, p. 47, &c.

embellishments, and the city also many public works, especially such as concerned its water supply.* He was in fact a religious politician, if it be true that his words were, "The world rests upon three things, — the Torah, worship, and good works." † The accounts we have of him are that he was a man of gentle piety, opposed to the exaggerations of mysticism.‡ The majesty with which he exercised his functions in religious worship was long remembered. The son of Sirach gives us the most perfect picture we possess of the Hierosolymite worship of those times : § —

> How was he honoured in the midst of the people
>   In his coming out of the sanctuary!
> He was as the morning star coming out of a cloud,
>   And as the moon at the full!
> As the sun shining upon the Temple of the Most High,
>   And as the rainbow giving light in the bright clouds;
> As the flower of roses in the spring of the year,
>   As lilies by the rivers of water,
> And as the branches of the frankincense-tree
>   In the time of summer;
> As fire, and incense in the censer,
>   And as a vessel of beaten gold set with precious stones;
> As a fair olive-tree budding with fruit,
>   And as a cypress-tree which groweth up to the clouds, —
> Was he when he put on the robe of honour,
>   And was clothed with the perfection of glory.

---

* Ecclesiasticus, l. 3, 4. Χαλκός is certainly an error. It should be Λάκκος.

† *Pirké aboth*, chap. i. 2.

‡ See the pretty story of *Nedarim and Nazir* (Derenbourg), pp. 51, 52.

§ Ecclesiasticus l. 5, &c.

When he went up to the holy altar *
    He made the garment of holiness honourable;
When he took the portions from the priest's hands
    He himself stood by the hearth of the altar,
Compassed with his brethren round about †
    As a young cedar in Libanus; ‡
And as palm-trees compassed they him round about.
    So were all the sons of Aaron in their glory,
Holding the oblations of the Lord in their hands
    Before all the congregation of Israel.
And, finishing the service of the altar
    That he might adorn the offering of the Most High, the Almighty,
He stretched out his hand to the cup,
    And poured out of the blood of the grape.
He poured out at the foot of the altar a sweet-smelling savour
    Unto the most high King of all.
Then shouted the sons of Aaron,
    And sounded the silver trumpets,
And made a great noise to be heard
    For a remembrance before the Most High.
Then all the people together hasted
    And fell down to the earth upon their faces,
To worship their Lord God Almighty,
    Imploring the Most High.
The singers also sang praises with their voices;
    With a great variety of sounds was made great melody;
And the people besought the Lord, the Most High,
    By prayer before him that is merciful,
Till the solemnity of the Lord was ended,
    And they had finished his service.
Then he went down, and lifted up his hands
    Over the whole congregation of the children of Israel,

---

* He is certainly speaking of the Great Day of Atonement. See Derenbourg, p. 49, note.

† The levites were often called אחים. Psalm cxxxiii. and the Book of Kings.

‡ Read κέδρων. See Fritzsche, *Handbuch*, p. 299.

To give the blessing of the Lord with his lips,
And to glorify and rejoice in his name.
And they bowed themselves down to worship a second time,
That they might receive a blessing from the Most High.*

The little Mishna treatise *Pirké aboth* begins a list of doctors of the Law in Palestine with the name of Simon the Just; its list, however, belongs for the most part to the days of the Asmoneans.† Each doctor has appended to his name a sentence with which it is supposed he was familiar. Trivialities are mixed up with elevated sentiments. There are echoes of the Sermon on the Mount among them. Antigonus of Soco, who seems to have lived about the time of Antiochus the Great, was most assuredly a man of wondrous wisdom, if he really said: "Be not like slaves who serve their master in hope of receiving a reward: but be like those slaves who serve their master without looking for a recompense, and the dew of Heaven will rest upon you." ‡

---

* From the authorized English version, which is almost identical with M. Renan's French translation. — TR.

† There are other similar lists. See Mishna, *Pea*, ii. 6. See Derenbourg, p. 33, note.

‡ *Pirké aboth*, chap. 1.

CHAPTER IX.

JESUS, SON OF SIRACH.

THE clearest Israelitish voice that has reached our ears from that period is that of a Hierosolymite named Jesus, son of Sirach,* who about the year 180 B. C.† wrote a book of Wisdom, in imitation of the ancient books believed to be by Solomon. With allowance made for a few blemishes, this book does honour to the age and to the race from which it sprang. It is a code of maxims for an honest man of the middle classes, taking in a high degree a practical view of life, and not in the least misled by supernatural fancies. Wisdom consists in fearing God and in keeping his commandments. He who does not believe in God is a fool; for God's justice may be seen daily in striking instances, —

---

* The Hebrew text is lost. The Greek version made by the author's grandson about the year 130 B.C. is very poor. The same version, to which glosses have been added, is given us in the Latin Vulgate. The Syriac version, a translation from the Hebrew, is in many places better than either the Greek or the Latin. See Grieger in the *Zeitschrift der D. M. G.* 1858, p. 536, &c.

† Shown in the Prologue of the Greek translator. Euergetes ["benefactor"] is here Physcon.

things that leave no room to doubt, if we give heed to them.

Of this we could wish the author to bring forward proofs, to summon his witnesses; but this, unfortunately, he has not done. He insists that lack of wisdom is always punished; that God is good to men of virtue, and severe only with the evil.* But he gives us no proof that it is so. The punishment of the wicked is that they sometimes fall into misfortune. But what becomes of the righteous? The son of Sirach thinks he has observed that riches ill-gained never profit the gainer. But he also owns that sometimes the wicked man succeeds; for he implores the good man not to be envious of his deceptive prosperity.† The author, being himself keenly alive to the value of public opinion, represents to the wicked that one of their punishments will be the shame that they will feel when all their misdeeds are laid open and their hidden vices are revealed in the synagogue, or, if you like it better, before the eyes of men.‡ That seems but a small thing. In truth, the theory of rewards and punishments, as presented by the son of Sirach, has made no advance since the earliest days when Israel began to think for itself.

* Chapters xvi. xxiii. &c. The Greek text having many omissions and transpositions, what we quote will have its figures taken from the Latin, except where we say otherwise. [The figures do not always correspond with those in the English version. — TR.]
† Chap. ix. 16. Cf. Psalm lxxiii.
‡ Chap. i. 27.

Ideas, especially those concerning Sheol, have not been altered.* "The fire and the worm," which the author has borrowed from the Second Isaiah,† are still only figures of speech.‡ For one moment a gleam of hope seems to penetrate the nether regions. Wisdom speaks of going down to illuminate the dead who are in the other world still hoping in the Lord.§

But, alas! this passage was not written by the son of Sirach; it is an interpolation after the great crisis in the days of the Maccabees, which soon changed all the ideas of Israel concerning the final destiny of man and immortality.

Never was there a smaller dose of religion administered than is done by this pious layman, two centuries before the time of Jesus. "Ecclesiastes" itself is not more free from spiritual ideas. Sacrifices and pious observances are with him of little value; it is an honest life which is everything.‖ Priests must be paid very scrupulously,¶ but outside of the Temple priests have no religious precedence. Sacred history may be filled with marvels, but the author seems to think that in his day the fountain of prophecy and miracle is dried up.

---

* Chap. xli. 4 (Latin 7, wanting in the Syriac).

† Chap. vii. 19. Compare Isaiah lxvi. 21. See vol. iii. p. 194.

‡ Compare Mark ix. 13, &c.

§ Chap. xxiv. 45. *Penetrabo omnes inferiores partes terræ et inspiciam omnes dormientes et illuminabo omnes sperantes in Domino.* This is wanting both in the Greek and Syriac. It is possibly Christian.

‖ Chap. xxxiv. 21, &c. xxxv. Compare vii. 11.

¶ Chap. vii. 33–35.

Science and philosophy, so brilliantly cultivated by the Greeks, are unknown to Jesus, the son of Sirach. The science of the Hebrew *sofer*, who was versed only in his old Scriptures,* seemed enough to him. The earth and the heavens have been marvellously made,† but the son of Sirach stops there; his superficial admiration does not induce him to examine into them. His ideas on physics have made no progress since the days of Job. Curiosity on such subjects he deems useless and dangerous.‡ Medicine alone among the sciences may be good, but prayer is better.§ All that takes place in the universe is the direct work of God, whose object in all things is to do good to the good, and evil to the wicked.‖ All things considered, the lot of man is sad. The philosophy of life professed by the son of Sirach does not greatly differ from that of Ecclesiastes. All is vain, fragile, hollow, and must pass away, except God.¶

Prosperity and adversity, life and death,**
Poverty and riches, come from the Lord.

The gift of God remaineth with the godly,
And his favour bringeth prosperity forever.

There is that waxeth rich by his wariness and pinching,
And this is the portion of his reward when he saith,

* Chap. xxxix. 1, &c.
† Chap. xlii. 15, &c.; xliii.
‡ Chap. iii. 22-26.
§ Chap. xxviii. 1-15, — a shade of irony.
‖ Chap. xxiii.; xxxix., end.
¶ Chap. xl.; xli. 1-4.
** Chap. xl. 14, &c.

"I have found rest, and now will eat
Continually of my goods that I have acquired."

And yet he knoweth not what time shall come upon him,
And that he must leave those things to others, and die.

Be steadfast therefore in thy covenant, and be conversant therein,
And wax old in thy work.

Marvel not at the success of sinners,
But trust in the Lord, and abide in thy labour.

For it is an easy thing in the sight of the Lord
On the sudden to make a poor man rich.

The blessing of the Lord is in the reward of the godly,
And suddenly he maketh his blessing to flourish.

Say not, What profit is there in my service?
And what good things shall I have hereafter?

Again say not, I have enough, and possess many things,
And what evil can come to me hereafter?

In the day of prosperity there is a forgetfulness of affliction;
And in the day of affliction there is no more remembrance of prosperity.

For it is an easy thing for the Lord
In the day of death to reward a man according to his ways.

The affliction of an hour maketh a man forget pleasure,
And in his end his deeds shall be discovered.

Judge none blessed before death;
For a man shall be known in his children.

This is still the same repeated balancing of contradictions that we find in the Book of Job. It contains something, however, that we do not find in Job, — namely, that an hour of suffering or enjoyment at the time of death may counterpoise the entire life, and set right the balance of divine justice. This is admirable. But before long this compensating hour between the life of trial and death will prove inadmissible. The martyr puts to shame the old Hebraic theory. Who could say that the Jewish hero, who endured the most cruel death rather than prove faithless to the Law, had his recompense in this world? The hour of reparation must necessarily be put beyond the grave. And from that moment the gulf was crossed. The dogma of rewards and punishments in a life to come, which the old sages would never accept at any cost, made its victorious entry into the mind of Israel.

The triumph of Jesus, the son of Sirach, is in his code of maxims for the middle classes. His is wisdom after the pattern of Franklin; and that is the way this book, a commonplace one in itself, has been twenty times more powerful in the world than books that are greatly its superior. Very severe home discipline braces family life, — as in Rome, or in Sparta. The author is austere in the extreme; not only does he insist on strict monogamy, though the Torah allows a man several wives: any frailty on man's part he finds worthy of condemnation.* The family is founded on honour for the father;† filial piety will insure long life; an ungrateful son is a monster. The mother is also to be honoured, or rather to be treated with consideration: her position in the family is a subordinate

---

* Chap. xli. 27. † Chap. iii.

one.* Daughters are to be strictly guarded.† In general, the son of Sirach puts little confidence in the virtue of women. He neither loves them nor esteems them.‡ While admitting exceptions, he finds them, in general, unbearable, quarrelsome, greedy; they are scolds and scandal-mongers. They need to be scrupulously watched. The very best of them should be kept under lock and key.§ All the troubles of men come to them through women; and the son of Sirach draws the conclusion from the first chapters of Genesis that through woman death entered into the world.‖

The part played by the father in family life is thus made a melancholy one, full of dangers, full of cares.¶ At home he must always be grave. He must never show his daughter a smiling face;** and he must never caress his children, play with them, or laugh with them.†† A child must be, from the very first, curbed by violence ‡‡ and daily subjected to blows. Children's natural gaiety and all their little tricks are evil. They must be humbled, and kept down sternly by the rod.§§

Separation between men and women in such a

---

* Μητρὸς ὠδῖνας μὴ ἐπιλάθῃ (vii. 27); Greek: Forget not the sorrows [birthpangs] of thy mother.

† Chap. vii. 26, &c.; xxvi. 13; xlii. 9–11.

‡ Chap. vii. 26–28; xxiv. xxv. xxvi.; xxxvi. 23, &c.; xlii.

§ Chap. xlii. 6, 7. ‖ Chap. xxv. 33.

¶ *Est tibi filia*, &c. (vii. 24, 25).

** Chap. vii. 26. †† Chap. xxx. 9, 10.

‡‡ Κάμψον ἐκ νεότητος τὸν τράχηλον αὐτῶν (chap. vii. 23).

§§ Chap. xxii. 6; xxiii. 2; xxx. 1; xlii. 5.

home life was necessarily complete. The ideal of the son of Sirach is realised at this day in any rigorous Mussulman village. The man of wisdom, as the son of Sirach paints him, is a Mussulman with his grave carriage,* careful above all to preserve his respectability, clean in his person, sensitive as to his reputation, visiting none but people as punctilious as himself, paying great attention to his guests, a man of moderate opinions, of minute ideas, if I may so express myself.† He is a faithful friend.‡ His deportment is modest; what he hates most are the flippant manners of men of the world, their talkativeness, and their proud bearing. He shuns the company of men of fashion and of rich men with a supercilious air.§ To offer resistance to men in power is as useless as trying to stem a current; ‖ a wise man keeps out of their way: he does not care for offices, he lives by his labour, happy in being neither poor nor rich, and equally removed from avarice and prodigality. Like the Ecclesiast, he does not object to giving himself occasionally a good time, knowing that in Sheol there will be no pleasure.¶ But all excess is hateful to him: wine is an excellent thing, if drunk with moderation; but it is perhaps the saddest cause of troubles and of follies.**

* Chap. xxxii.
† Chap. ix. 22 (Greek); xii.; xxi. 23, &c.
‡ Chap. vi.   § Chap. xiii.
‖ Chap. iv. 26.   ¶ Chap. xiv. 16, 17.   Read τρυφήν.
** Chap. xxxi. 22, &c.

This *bourgeois* aristocrat does not like to look upon the poor, but he considers it one of the fundamental principles of religion to be benevolent to them. To give alms is a duty.* But, as things are, the division of classes seems to him to result in a struggle to the death between them.† The ills of humanity are mitigated by the good works of the godly man, who is assiduous in visiting the sick, helpful to the weak, kind to his servants, and ready to forgive injuries. ‡ This, it may be seen, is almost the entire moral teaching of the Gospels, needing only the strong upward flight that Jesus gave it. The proper virtue of humility is already indicated. The quiet, sober, well-behaved man, who governs his tongue, who never swears,§ who never speaks a coarse or vulgar word, who gives up to his adversary rather than quarrel with him,‖ shall be master of the world. This is the religion of the respectable, the well-to-do, the man of right balance. The ungodly man is a worldling and a free liver; he talks loud, his laugh is uproarious. The godly man is humble, poor, wise, and industrious; his ways are diametrically opposed to the vanity of the worldling. He loves agriculture ¶ and useful labour. Avarice is an absurdity,** and great riches are little profit in the end.†† To praise a man for his wealth, his handsome

---

* Chap. iv. vii. Ἐλεημοσύνη in the sense of alms, vii. 10.
† Chap. xiii. 22, &c.   ‡ Chap. xxviii. xxix.; xxxi. 31–33.
§ Chap. xxiii. 7–14.   ‖ Chap. viii.
¶ Chap. vii. 16.   ** Chap. x. 30.
†† Chap. xiv.

person, or his clothes is mere frivolity. A poor man who has learning and good behaviour is indeed a pearl among men.* We may easily observe in all this an analogy to the ideas of the Jansenist *bourgeoisie* in France in the seventeenth and eighteenth centuries.

Of course, the son of Sirach has never a doubt as to the lawfulness of slavery. In all that concerns the manner of treating the slave he is sometimes very indulgent,† sometimes very harsh,‡ and even more cruel than the author of Proverbs.§

> Fodder, a wand, and burdens are for the ass;
> And bread, correction, and work are for a servant.
>
> If thou set thy servant to labour, thou shalt find rest;
> But if thou let him go idle, he shall seek liberty.
>
> A yoke and a collar do bow the neck;
> So are tortures and torments for an evil servant.
>
> Send him to labour that he be not idle,
> For idleness teacheth much evil.
>
> Set him to work, as is fit for him;
> If he be not obedient, put on more heavy fetters.
>
> But be not excessive towards any,
> And without discretion do nothing. ‖

Although the synagogue is not directly mentioned by the son of Sirach as a separate building,¶ the

---

* Chap. x. 29, 30; xi. 1, &c.   † Chap. vii. 22, &c.
‡ Chap. xxxiii. 25, &c. (Greek, xxx.) xlii. 6, 7.
§ Proverbs xxix. 19.
‖ The three following verses apply in case a man has only one slave (see the Syriac), in which case he becomes a sort of brother. The Greek text is doubtful.
¶ Passages like xxiii. 34, xxxviii. 37, show the transition (see the Greek, ed. Fritzsche).

ideas and customs that belonged to it already exist. Reprimands, false reports, and gossip flourish, as they will in every community,* — I was about to say, as they do in every convent. At any rate, the state of religion described by the son of Sirach comes nearer to pure religion than anything before his day. There is no sacrifice, no augur. He puts no faith in dreams. His worship is that of an enlightened man, who places justice and honesty above everything.† With his looks always cheerful,‡ his accounts always balanced,§ such a Jew will effect a peaceful conquest of the world. He may, indeed, but only for form's sake, recall the grand hopes held out by the Prophets, or pray for the realization of the promises made to Israel, or speak of a day when the Gentiles shall recognize Adonai as their God.‖ His admiration for the great men of Jewish story ¶ is wholly retrospective. The son of Sirach is a man well satisfied. Like the author of the *Koheleth,* he is a modern Jew, useful to the society in which he lives, getting his living out of his surroundings, resigned to the vanity of all things, and not unwilling to enjoy the passing hour, because he knows nothing of the infinite in which it is engulfed. Of such men is not born the kingdom of God. The son of Sirach is the forerun-

---

* Chap. xix. 13; xx. 1, &c.
† Read attentively chapters xxxiv. xxxv. (xxxi.-xxxii.).
‡ Chap. xxx., 2d part.
§ Chap. xlii., init. Comp. chap. xxix.
‖ Chap. xxxvi., the whole.
¶ Chap. xliv. 1.

ner of a Mendelssohn, virtuous and modest; or of a Rothschild of an older day, growing great by good order and honesty, shaming those who live riotously, and who aim to dazzle the world. Say not that in all this there is no heroism, and that out of such a life will never come an enthusiast or a martyr. In the heart of a Jew are many little leaves folded down closely one over the other. The son of Sirach wrote ten or fifteen years only before the time of the Maccabees, two hundred years only before the birth of Jesus.

The "Wisdom" of Jesus, the son of Sirach, had great success in Jerusalem, and its text was long preserved.* About the year 130 B. C. the grandson of the author, having been carried into Egypt, was a witness of the great movement which had turned all the Hebrew books into Greek; and, to complete the series, he translated his grandfather's work. But it is evident that his own knowledge of Hebrew was small, and his Greek translation swarms with errors.†
Another Greek text, enriched by glosses, has come down to us through the Latin Vulgate. The Syriac version, which was also made from the Hebrew, gives us in very many instances the original far better than the Greek.‡

---

* Saint Jerome, *Præf. in libros Salomonis*, leaves room for doubt.

† For example, in xxiv. 25 he has confounded אור and אך; and xxv. 14 ראש has been misunderstood.

‡ Observe especially the mention of Job (xxxviii. 1; Cf. Ecclesiasticus xlix. 11). The text of the son of Sirach must surely have been וגם וכד את איב כן הסיערה. It is well known that the Hebrew text

The Talmud quotes many sentences from a certain Ben-Sira,* several of which correspond with those of Jesus, the son of Sirach. But very soon apocrypha took its share in the work, and there were in Hebrew collections of gnomic maxims that have nothing in common with the collection which the Church piously read for centuries under the name of "Ecclesiasticus." The work of the son of Sirach had an immense popularity in the Church, being of the earth, earthy. It was also the manual of Christian instruction, and the practical guide of an honest, commonplace Christian. The number of whippings to be laid to its account must be incalculable. Wisdom, as they called it, was a real torturer of children.

offers à propos to זם, a singularity indicated by a qeri. The author had preserved this anomaly in his text. His grandson has added the ם to א׳ב, and then of a נ undecided (not final) he has made a ב; בהסיערח א׳בם, τῶν ἐχθρῶν ἐν ὄμβρῳ. The Syriac and the Arab translator who followed him have preserved the true text. See the book of Job xxix.

* מירא is perhaps the true form ; compare Ἀκελδαμάχ (Acts i. 19).

CHAPTER X.

THE STRUGGLE FOR HELLENISM IN PALESTINE. — ANTIOCHUS EPIPHANES.

ABOUT 175 B. C. the victory of Hellenism on all the eastern shores of the Mediterranean was complete. The Jews in Palestine alone resisted it with obstinacy. Yet even there the passion for Greek fashions was deep-rooted; all the more lively and frivolous elements of Jewish society, the young and the intelligent, turned towards the sun which was to enlighten the world. But the old party, who exclusively admired the Torah and was hostile to Greek rationalism, was more stiff than ever. We shall see that pious party triumph, and make the Jewish people unique in history. Egypt, Phœnicia, Syria, Asia Minor, Italy, and even Carthage, Armenia, and Assyria, in a great degree, became Hellenized. Palestine alone opposed a resolute NO to this seduction. It continued to speak in a Semitic idiom, and to think Semitic thoughts. It had very little to do with Greek science. It knew nothing of the literature that was received with rapture by all the enlightened among mankind, nothing of that supreme law of reason and beauty which was now established in the world.

Greek life consisted of several essential parts, — a sort of exterior discipline, requiring public establishments; and at certain hours an activity in common, to be engaged in by all its young men, a theatre for public life and literary culture, baths, a gymnasium, and open porches for bodily exercise. The first consideration with a Greek was due care of his own person. To be sure, cleanliness and hygiene play a large part in the life of every Oriental who respects himself (be he a Jew of the old school, or a Mussulman); but the Greek training required much more. Wrestling and prescribed gymnastic exercise are repugnant to Orientals. The nudity compelled by the Greek palæstra was shocking to them. They considered it as leading on to vices of which Greece,* unhappily, was far too careless. In the gymnasium, circumcision was often a butt for ridicule.† The emulation entailed by these games seemed to zealous Israelites a pernicious thing, — so much sheer loss to a true sense of their own national glory.‡

Accordingly the city of Jerusalem was divided into two parties. One half, madly eager to imitate Greek customs, neglected nothing that would assimilate its deportment, its dress, and its language to

---

* 2 Maccabees iv. 12.
† *Saint Paul*, 66, &c.; Marcus Aurelius, 556.
‡ 2 Maccabees iv. 15.

those of Greece. To this party of Græcomaniacs were opposed men of piety, men of narrow ideas, those called *hasidim*, hostile to Greek civilization even in what was excellent, who wrote only in Hebrew or Aramean, and on the lines of their ancient literature. This gulf between these parties led to another, deeper still. The majority of the Jewish community were fervent Jews; but there were lukewarm ones among them, many who were barely Jews, who hated the strict way of life enjoined by the Torah. This irreligious group was a ready mark for a propaganda coming from without, especially when the drift of the day was all in the same direction. The *hasidim*, on their part, formed a coterie, a "synagogue," entirely apart.*

The Torah, carried out as civil law by Jewish state authority, must have been intolerable, and very naturally. It was a code drawn up by utopian theorists for an ideal society, not a system of common law, formulated, but open to reform. One sees how it worked under the Asmoneans when the power of the nation was really in the hands of the Jews. At the period that we have reached, this was not quite the case, but very nearly so. The Persian and Greek governors cared very little about the local affairs of the communities they ruled over, and so they ended in being petty tyrannical States. Things went on very much as they do in the Ottoman empire in non-Mussulman communities, where each individual

* 1 Maccabees ii. 42 (edit. Fritzsche).

is under the absolute power of his own clergy. A pious Jew was therefore subject to the Torah, admirable for its social aspirations, but one of the worst codes to live by that were ever seen. This created some very difficult situations. It is not surprising that Greek law, which like Roman law was purely rationalistic, should offer an open door of escape from these impracticabilities.

Neither the Lagidæ, who never practised for Hellenism the method of compulsion, nor Antiochus the Great and his successor, who were tolerant, made any attempt to interfere in this burning family quarrel, or to exercise an influence on behalf of either party. It was otherwise when the throne of Syria came to be occupied by Antiochus Epiphanes,* a man of restless temper, of no firm purpose, liberal at times, but always violent, who marred even a good cause by his intemperance and want of judgment. The Jews, possibly prejudiced, found his countenance haughty, his air fierce, his heart so hard that nothing which usually softens men — neither women nor religion — could bend him. They said he was moulded of nothing but pride and fraud.† His lack of dignity, and his deeds like those of a debauched scapegrace, would have been of no great consequence to the world if he had not imperilled his authority by enterprises that never came to anything, in which the most melancholy mischances

---

* Polybius, xxvi. 10.
† Daniel viii. 23, &c.; xi. 21, &c., 37.

awaited him. He loved Greece, and he looked upon himself as the representative of the Greek spirit in the Orient. The god who was the object of his predilection, and whose worship he considered it his duty to promote, was that majestic deity, the Olympian Zeus,* who is better served by calm reason than by rash acts of violence. He had no conception whatever of the character of the country he reigned over, — a country of deep-seated political and religious diversities, where no centralisation could be effected unless the local worship should be publicly respected, being as it was the equivalent of what were elsewhere patriotism or a citizen's attachment to his city. He committed the very gravest fault a sovereign can commit, which is to interfere with the religion of his subjects. He was very intelligent and generous, and his tastes were all for greatness.† He made Antioch a brilliant centre, though not to be compared with Alexandria in science and serious literature. He was in some sort the second founder of that city, which up to his time had not greatly developed.‡ Thanks to him, Antioch took her place among the most splendid cities of the world. She became one of the brightest spots whence flowed rays of Hellenism. The temptation was strong to make this lofty civilisation of reason prevail over countries which till then had known only an inferior culture,

---

* The *Olympicon* of Athens was his. Polybius xxvii. 10.
† Diodorus Siculus, xxix. 32; xxxi. 16; Livy, xli. 20.
‡ See Ottfried Müller, *De Antiq. Antioch.*, pp. 34, 35, 53–65.

and over religions that almost all seemed to have some flaw of superstition or fanaticism. It is probable that if Antiochus the Great had not united Palestine to the empire of the Seleucidæ, the enterprise of Epiphanes, aiming only to Hellenise northern Syria, would have succeeded. But Judaism presented an invincible opposition. In attacking it, Epiphanes struck against a rock. He did not indeed content himself with curbing the excesses of fanaticism, with guaranteeing liberty of dissent, or with making all forms of worship subservient to one civil law. He vainly sought to suppress Judaism, and force the Jews to acts they held to be idolatrous.*
He has been compared to Joseph II. of Austria, but the comparison is not exact; for Joseph II. only upheld the rights of the secular State in opposition to the encroachments of the theocracy. Epiphanes was a true persecutor, and as his character lacked balance, resistance impelled him to madness and folly. His contemporaries, punning on his royal name, called him Epimanes. It seemed, indeed, as if at times he had fits of well-defined insanity.

His is the first persecution which befel the theocracy that had proceeded from the teachings of the Jewish prophets. Antiochus acted on the same principle as the Roman emperors, some of the best of them; but he was less excusable, because Juda-

---

* *Rex Antiochus demere superstitionem et mores Græcorum dare adnisus, quominus tæterrimam gentem in melius mutaret, Parthorum bello prohibitus est.* — Tacitus, *Hist.* v. 8.

ism was confined to one small country, while Christianity was a widespread evil menacing the empire itself. The incessant fire of complaint and recrimination between Church and State has never ceased up to our own day. There is indeed a difference between a form of society claiming to be founded on a divine revelation, and that broad human society which acknowledges only the bonds of law and reason. Marcus Aurelius, who was a very different man from Antiochus Epiphanes, was, like him, the persecutor of a theocracy. The excuse for these great men is that a theocracy, where it has the upper hand, persecutes its adversaries even more cruelly than they have persecuted it. Antiochus, before coming to the throne, had passed his youth as a hostage at Rome. Possibly he may have acquired in his intimate intercourse with great Roman families a positive tone in his ideas, a contempt for all religions except national superstitions, which in after years was to make the Roman Empire the worst enemy of theocracies throughout the world.

CHAPTER XI.

THE PERSECUTION OF ANTIOCHUS. — THE ABOMINATION OF DESOLATION.

ANTIOCHUS, from his accession (175 B. C.), showed his dislike of the Jews, at least for those of strict piety, the *hasidim*. All employments were given to Jewish liberals, several of whom, to court the favour of the king, renounced their religion, and did homage to Zeus Olympius. Such apostasies were numerous.[*] The renegade became the recipient of all kinds of favours; places and lucrative employments were reserved for him.[†] Circumcision alone remained, a painful reminder of his old estate, exposing him to disagreeable remarks in public places. He endeavoured to remedy it by a painful operation described by Celsus;[‡] after which he assumed a supercilious air, appeared everywhere in Greek costume, endeavoured to be in all things the model of an accomplished Greek, despising Mosaic customs and his old-fashioned co-religionists.

---

[*] 1 Maccabees i. 11.
[†] Daniel xi. 30-39; 1 Maccabees ii. 18; cf. *Les Apôtres*, p. 330.
[‡] 1 Maccabees i. 11-15.

One may conceive the horror and the grief felt by a faithful Hierosolymite when he beheld such a being, who was often tricked out with official titles and handsomely rewarded for his apostasy. Day after day the epidemic of Hellenism was making havoc; the fashions of Antioch spread as by enchantment; in Jerusalem a majority was won over to the new ideas.* The accession of Antiochus, whose opinions probably were well known beforehand, gave to the Greek party irresistible strength. The head of the party in opposition was Onias III., who was then high-priest. He was a firm and pious man, who under Seleucus Philopator had vigorously defended the treasures of the Temple; † his son Joshua (or Jesus), who according to the custom of the Hellenists had changed his name to Jason, was at the head of the Greek party. The effort of that party was to deprive Onias of his office, and put Jason in his place. Jason made the king enormous promises of money. He also engaged to do all in his power to Hellenise Jerusalem; especially he promised to build a gymnasium, and a young men's club-house. The inhabitants of Jerusalem were to be registered as Antiochians, and considered citizens of Antioch. Antiochus accepted these proposals. Onias was deposed, and Jason was made high-priest.‡ The Hellenising process was pushed to its limits. The gymnasium was built; young men rushed to it in

---

* 1 Maccabees i. 11–15.   † 2 Maccabees iii. 1, &c.; iv. 1, &c.
‡ 2 Maccabees iv. 7–10. Josephus is in error.

crowds; even priests left their service at the altar for training in the *palæstra*. It was a fever of innovation and transformation; every man was anxious to conceal the fact of his circumcision, and to give himself the air of a Greek. Never had the fate of Israel been in more peril than at this evil epoch (about 172 B. C.). A little more, and the Hebrew Bible would have been lost, and the Jewish religion blotted out forever.

No scruples arrested the career of Jason. In the year when the festival of Melkarth took place at Tyre (the feast was held every fifth year), he sent a rich gift to the idol to show his breadth of mind and generosity. Those who carried his gift were more timid than their high-priest; they paid over the money, but they did it in such a way as to insure its not being directly employed in the Tyrian worship.

Jason was only three years in power. A certain Onias, who preferred to call himself Menelaus,* and who is sometimes said to have been Jason's brother,† supplanted him in 171 by promising still larger gifts of money to Antiochus. To pay this virtual tribute he laid hands on the treasures of the Temple, and committed all manner of crimes.‡ Old Onias had retired to Daphne near Antioch; he was an honest

---

* Possibly the mode of writing had something to do with this. According to the Hebrew alphabet at that day, the name חניא would be very like מנלא.

† Josephus, *Antiquities*, xii. v. 1; cf. xv. iii. 1.

‡ 2 Maccabees iv. 27-50.

man, who did not hesitate to speak his mind. Menelaus had him assassinated. Thus perished the last high-priest of the house of Zadok. Since the return from the Captivity at Babylon not a single high-priest had been taken from outside the race of Saraiah.

Jason, though deposed, continued his intrigues. There seemed to be a positive rivalry between the two wretches, to see which could do most harm to his country. It is very hard to follow the thread of their proceedings. But it is certain that in 170 Antiochus on his return from one of his expeditions into Egypt passed through Jerusalem, where he shed torrents of blood; and, prompted in his misdeeds by the odious Menelaus, he pillaged the Temple, and carried off the most precious things in it to Antioch.*

The situation was horrible: all moral feeling seemed destroyed; God seemed verily to have turned away his face from his people. And there was worse to come. In 168 Antiochus made a fresh expedition into Egypt, whence he was soon turned back, being baffled by the circle of Popilius Lænas.† He returned northward in a rage, and all his fury fell on Jerusalem.‡ Possibly the relations of the conservative

---

* 1 Maccabees i. 20-24; ii. 9; 2 Maccabees v. 1-21; Josephus, *Antiquities*, xii. v. 3; *Against Apion*, ii. 7.

† When Antiochus was at Alexandria, he was met by deputies of the Roman Senate, who demanded that he should make peace and withdraw from Egypt; and as he eluded the demand with evasive answers, Popilius haughtily drew a circle round him in the sand, ordering him to give an answer to the Senate before he stirred beyond that line. Antiochus was paralysed, and obeyed. — TR.

‡ Daniel xi. 30, 31.

Jews with the Romans, already apparent, were the secret cause of this sudden change of policy, which at the first glance seems inexplicable. He now aimed at the total extinction of Judaism. His plan of execution was clear and thorough; it was to drive out the old population, and to replace it either by a purely Greek colony, or by new-made Hellenists.* Nothing was more common at that day than such a substitution. Almost all the Macedonian cities in Syria owed their origin to a *veteres migrati coloni* more or less brutal. We shall soon see the Jews practising the same method † when they become the stronger party. Antiochus charged one of his fiscal agents, named Apollonius, to see that his plans were carried out. Many Jews quitted Jerusalem; many who remained were put to death, their wives and children being sold as slaves. The rest apostatised. Pagans were brought in to fill the void left by the expulsion or extermination of the Jewish population. There were several months — nay, several years — when Jerusalem did not reckon one true Jew as its inhabitant. It seemed as if Adonai had been false to his promises; every prophecy had come to nothing.

The Syrians apparently put no great confidence in the new colony with which they had peopled Jerusalem; for they caused the walls of the city to be

---

* 1 Maccabees 1, 29–40; 2 Maccabees v. 23–26; Josephus, *Antiquities*, xii. v. 4. Compare Daniel vii. 25; viii. 11, &c.; ix. 27; xi. 31, &c.; xii. 11.
† At Jaffa and Gezer.

broken down, considering Jerusalem a permanent support to the cause of Judaism, and they commanded a citadel to be constructed on the hill opposite Mount Zion.* They called it "Akra," and it was to serve as a place of retreat for the Hellenic population and the renegades in case of danger.† This precaution was not useless. In the long struggle which followed, Akra always remained in the hands of the Syrians. It was not conquered by the Jews till twenty-six years later, in 141 B.C.‡

Jewish worship ceased. The daily sacrifice, or *tamid*, was at an end. The Temple itself was fitted up so as to suit the new occasions. The patron divinity of the Syrian propaganda, the Olympian Zeus (Jupiter), was substituted for Iahveh. The

---

* The mount on which is Nebi Daoud, the pretended Zion of traditional topographers.

† 1 Maccabees i. 31, 33-36; Josephus, *Antiquities*, xii., v. 4. Passages like 2 Maccabees iv. 12, 27, are anticipations of the event.

‡ The position of Akra is a matter of controversy. One meets with sheer impossibilities if one would place this large castle near the Temple or on the Mount of Ophel. "Akra" is a word synonymous with "acropolis." To make of it a lower town is equally inadmissible. The strong position of the hill west of Jerusalem suits exactly. It is true that Akra in Maccabees is identified with "the city of David," or Zion (1 Maccabees i. 33; ii. 31; vii. 32; xiv. 36); but it is quite likely that the error by which Zion was transferred from the eastern to the western hill, an error fully adopted by Josephus, may have been already adopted in the time of the Maccabees (see above). It is true that the first Book of the Maccabees (iv. 37-60; v. 54; vi. 48-62; vii. 33) identifies Zion with the hill on which the Temple was built. Perhaps the identity of the City of David with Zion was not always kept up. See especially 1 Maccabees vii. 32, 33, where the City of David and Zion are clearly not the same; and, above all, 1 Maccabees xiii. 52: τὸ ὄρος τοῦ ἱεροῦ τὸ παρὰ τὴν ἄκραν.

ornaments of the interior of the Temple had been pillaged two years before; the altar of incense, the candlestick with seven branches, the table of the shew-bread, had been carried away. We do not know what alterations the pagans made in the Holy of Holies; the doors were shut. According to Greek custom, the great altar before the Temple was the most important thing. Here something of the gravest import took place. A statue of Olympian Zeus was placed on a pedestal immediately behind the altar,* so that it was to him the sacrifices were offered. This statue was an unspeakable horror to the Jews. They long remembered the date at which it was erected, the 15th day of the month Kislev, in the year 145 of the Seleucidæ,— consequently in December of the year 168 B. C. They designated it with a profusion of the coarsest epithets; they called it משמם שקוץ, "filth of devastation," which the Greeks translated into βδέλυγμα τῆς ἐρημώσεως, "the abomination of desolation," according to the Latin.†‎ Evil was now at its height. Iahveh was dethroned by his Greek rival, who on the very threshold of his Temple was receiving in his stead the smoke of sacrifices. Never before had there been witnessed such an abomination. Nebuchadnezzar had destroyed

---

* See p. 319, below.

† Daniel ix. 27; xi. 31; xii. 11 (cf. viii. 13); 1 Maccabees i. 54, 59; 2 Maccabees vi. 2; cf. Matthew xxiv. 15. In Daniel, ix. 27, read כְּנַף שִׁקּוּץ מְשֹׁמֵם. The Masoretic copyists have ill divided the word, and have added the first מ of משמם to שקוץ, which has led them to put כנף in the constructive case.

the sanctuary, but now a strange god has installed himself in the very abode of Iahveh, takes his place, usurps his honours. Oh, horrible! most horrible!

Similar altars to Olympian Zeus were raised in all Jewish cities in the neighbourhood of Jerusalem.* Iahveh was pursued even into his sanctuary at Gerizim. There the name "Zeus Xenios" prevailed. The Samaritan population probably offered less resistance than the Jews. We do not hear at this date of any Samaritan martyrs.†

While Greek worship was thus established throughout Judea, Jewish worship was sternly prohibited. Circumcision, the observance of the Sabbath, and other Jewish injunctions were forbidden under pain of death. The government watchfulness in these matters was most severe. War was declared against the book that was the prime cause of these evils; all copies of the Torah that could be found were destroyed. Inspectors once a month passed through the country to seize scrolls of the Law, and to see if any new case of circumcision had taken place. At the Bacchanalia all persons were obliged to take part in the festival, crowned with ivy.‡ The law forbidding the use of pork gave rise to many annoyances. The courts of the Temple became the scene of heathen orgies; pagans came there with their

---

* See 1 Maccabees i. 46, 49, 50, 57, 58; ii. 15, 23.

† The passage in 1 Maccabees iii. 16 might lead us even to suppose that the Samaritans made common cause with the Syrians against the Jews.

‡ 2 Maccabees vi. 2–7.

concubines, and gave themselves up to debauchery. Horrible things, no doubt exaggerated, were told. Two mothers were brought before the judges charged with having circumcised their children. They were hung up by the breasts, and then flung from the city wall. Some people who had taken refuge in a cave, there to keep the Sabbath, allowed themselves to be suffocated by smoke rather than defend themselves.* Many legends of martyrs now arose. Old Eleazar, who refused to avail himself of a small deception to save his life;† the mother who witnessed the execution of her seven sons,‡ encouraging them to the last, — are the first of those stories which were to make the victory of Christianity.§ The Acts of the Martyrs, like all other branches of Christian literature, have their root in Israel.

The terrible shock that such a tragic state of things must have produced in the national conscience of unhappy Israel would surely find expression in earnest prayers and elegiac poems. The form in which prayer and elegy expressed themselves in Israel was the psalm. There were doubtless compositions of that kind in those days, some of which were probably written down.‖ But are there any

---

* 2 Maccabees vi. 4-11; Daniel xi. 33, 34, 35.

† 2 Maccabees vi. 18, &c.

‡ 2 Maccabees vii. 1, &c. Compare what is called the Fourth Book of the Maccabees, and the *Origines du Christianisme*, v. 303, &c. On the Jewish texts see Zunz, *Die gottesdienstlichen Vorträge der Juden*, p. 124.

§ The improbabilities are the same, — Antiochus presiding over the executions, &c.

‖ Traces may be found in 1 Maccabees i. 25, &c., 38, &c., 51, &c.

such in our collection of Psalms? This is one of the points on which it is hard to pronounce an opinion. The soul of Israel had not changed, but it had changed its language; and we think that any poems composed in the days of Antiochus would not be hard to distinguish from the more ancient classics.*

* Psalms xliv., lxxiv., lxxix., lxxxiii., seem especially suitable to these days; but after all there is nothing to prevent their being regarded as more ancient. The *anavim* had often found themselves in similar situations. These psalms are in most beautiful classic language, in the purest style, though often, as in Psalm lxxiv. especially, full of difficulties caused by errors of copyists. Now, the language in the days of the Maccabees had become very corrupt, and the poetic spirit seemed lost; the style was flat and prolix, after the Aramean fashion, offering no difficulties except where the writer is pleased to involve the expression of his thoughts. We can judge of it by the Book of Daniel, and by original fragments in the first Book of Maccabees, and by canticles which it was the fashion of the day to introduce everywhere, whose tone is very feeble. Notice also the insipid prayer in Daniel ix. 4, &c., and compare with the canticles in chap. iii. If the times of the Maccabees had produced any psalms, they would have formed a group easily recognisable in one of the five books which form our present collection; or rather they would form a collection by themselves, and would not have been attributed to David. Could the "Psalms of Solomon," somewhat later than the days of the Maccabees, have ever been confounded with the Psalter of David? Everything leads us to the belief that the canonical collection of the Psalms was finished, and even translated into Greek, at the date of the Maccabees (Ecclesiasticus, prologue, and xlvii. 6, &c.). There were some other books added afterwards to the canon (Daniel, Ecclesiastes, and Lamentations), but the ancient Biblical volume was closed forever; no one dared add to its pages. The style of the Greek translation of the Psalms is uniform; it is the work of one writer. The Maccabean Psalms, if we had any, would conflict with the others in their Greek as well as Hebrew. Let us add that the Psalm that seems most Maccabean (lxxiv.) is quoted in the First Book of Maccabees as an old prophetic text. Compare the allusion to Psalm xcii. 8, in 1 Maccabees ix. 23. Let us add further that the "Psalms of Solomon" speak of the Canonical Psalter as closed, and attribute the whole of it to David.

The age was not literary; the language spoken was flat and debased. The greatest change that was taking place was in the line of religious sentiments and opinions. Israel was dragging her old anchors. Old positions were no longer tenable. The kind of shut-in horizon that Israel had had before her eyes till then must widen at all cost. Israel had been fashioned hitherto by dreams of the infinite, while bounded by a narrow wall. The wall was about to fall. Israel was about to teach the world that immortality till now unknown, — which, indeed, it has never professed as dogma to this day.

CHAPTER XII.

THE EVIDENT NECESSITY OF REWARDS IN A FUTURE LIFE.

THE idea that virtue must meet with its reward is the most logical of all ideas in the human breast. That virtue is in fact rewarded would be a very bold assertion, to which the Israelite was brought by his unshaken confidence in divine justice. God desires what is right, and he commands it; consequently he rewards it. He is all-powerful. If he should abandon those who do his will, he would be illogical, a deceiver and the author of injustice.

But when does this reward of the just and this punishment of the wicked take place? That question would have seemed absurd to an old son of Shem. He knew of no other life for man but this. He rejected all forms in which other nations pictured to themselves a life beyond the grave, as mere chimeras. He was led to this conclusion by a certain good sense, and by the high idea he had of the divine majesty. God only is eternal; man lives but a few years at most; an immortal man would be a god, a rival of God himself, an impossibility. Man can only prolong a little his ephemeral existence through his children, or if he has no children, by a monument (*Shem*, "name"), which will retain his memory in his tribe.

This assertion that virtue is rewarded here below is at once encountered by unanswerable objections. The assertion is not true. In fact, in whatever age of the world, and in whatever society we place ourselves, compensatory justice is constantly violated. More versed in social science than the ancients, we can go further, and assert that it is not possible it should be otherwise. Injustice is to be found in Nature itself. Let us suppose society as perfect, and the art of medicine as advanced, as we will, — there will always be accidents, which justice cannot control. A man dies in the devoted attempt to save another; no one can argue that absolute justice in this present world has been displayed in the fate of that man. Old Israel tried all sorts of sophisms to get out of this difficulty. Very ancient times took refuge in collective justice: sons are punished for the crimes of their fathers; a community is punished for the misdeeds of some of its members. But such justice is so defective that the most orthodox Israelites gave it up at last. Job declares that the violent man, whose children are little esteemed, is not really punished, because he knows nothing of it in Sheol: he ought himself to have beheld his own disgrace. Ezekiel completely gives up this collective theory, and declares that every man is punished or rewarded for his own actions and those alone. In those days men had to take refuge in very weak explanations.

Sometimes the facts were denied. A psalmist tells us that throughout a long life he has never seen the son of a righteous man begging bread.* Or, again, they made distinctions. It is true, said men of wisdom, the good man is often poor; but better is it to be happy with little than to share in the prosperity of the wicked. Such prosperity so quickly passes away! Sometimes they fall back on the mysteries of men's consciences, or sins committed in ignorance. God is a judge so strict as to find iniquity in the man who seems the most virtuous. Then there was the theory of a brief probation: God is sometimes pleased to put his servants to the proof; but in the end he compensates the evil that he has done them. All possible cases were imagined. Job, the perfectly just man, is overwhelmed by terrible misfortunes, but God restores to him two-fold all his lost prosperity: instead of three thousand camels he has six thousand; instead of seven sons he has fourteen.† He dies at the age of a hundred and twenty, full of years and honours. Tobit's misfortune is still less merited, for it comes upon him when he is engaged in a work of charity. But he has no reason to complain: he is cured; he sees his son well married; he experiences the highest possible joy, for he witnesses the ruin of

---

* Psalm xxxvii. 25.

† Here Renan improves astonishingly upon his model: Job's "seven sons and three daughters" still remain to him, the report of their death having (apparently) been premature. — TR.

Nineveh, the enemy of his race; and he dies at a good old age. Judith, after her heroic act, is rewarded by the prosperity of her people, and by the honours they bestow on her. She too lives to be a hundred and twenty.

The vicissitudes of the history of Israel were explained in the same way. Terrible calamities, without doubt, fell upon the nation for its sins. These were a father's chastisements, smiting because he loves. The future has in store for Israel, as for Job, infinite compensations. The world, which now belongs to the violent, shall be his some day; the people who have despised him shall kiss his feet.

Reasoning of this feeble kind calmed through centuries, for better or worse, the restless conscience of Israel. Content was easy and cheap when the honour of Iahveh was in question. But in reality the conflict of soul was terrible. The history is a ten-centuries' effort to arrive at the idea of ulterior compensations. The prophet, representative of Iahveh, perpetually wrestles with his God, who draws him on by promises that he does not keep. The pious Israelite continually reproaches God for breaking his word, and for having no favour but for his enemies. What can be more scandalous, if Israel be really the people of God, than to find it everywhere downtrodden by the heathen? All the power of Iahveh was employed to turn the caprice of pagan despots to the benefit of the Jews, and to procure for pious Israelites comfortable posts with the conquerors of the world. It seems as if this were small game for the Almighty. The poor son of Sirach is at his wits' end. A good man dies who has always been unfortunate. He can only give wretched replies to this. "Does one know what has passed in his last moments? One hour of happiness blots out years of suffering; the evil that has gone by is a dream, is no more." All this is but poor comfort. But times were calm; men were then rich and tranquil. The wealthy Jew takes his wealth as recompense enough: he easily consents to lay no claim on God for paradise. A rich man feels no need of another world. Judaism, indeed, planted in the midst of the sad, sad life of antiquity, gave its followers so much happiness that they passed lightly over many an obscurity.

But things changed on the day when the persecution of Antiochus began. On that day the Jews saw apostates rewarded, and the faithful who would not forsake the Law expire in the most cruel torments. It was too much. The explanations that had hitherto seemed only a little lame became entirely inefficient. They went on repeating by rote that all this was happening to them because of the people's sins.* But this was blank evasion. Do what they might, how could they persuade themselves that those just men had in this present life received their reward? Between their torture and their death, where was there a chink in which to place their paradise? The son of Sirach himself would have found it hard to slip

---

* 2 Maccabees vii. 18, 32, 33, 38; Daniel, ix. 4, &c.

in his quarter of an hour's compensation. No, no! it is impossible. The martyr has not his reward in this life. He is rewarded, — that is certain; and therefore his reward must be in another life, in another world. There is another life, another world,* where the kingdom of God will be realised. Of that world the holy men now oppressed will be kings. Martyrs who have aided to found that kingdom shall rise again! The wicked, no doubt, will also rise again; but it will be to be cast into the Valley of Gehenna, "where the worm dieth not and the fire is not quenched." † There were two opinions, however, about this last; some maintained that the wicked would not rise again, that their punishment would be extinction.‡

It was by this heroic assurance that Israel came conqueror out of a difficulty whence there was no other issue. Never was a dogma formulated in a more unanswerable manner. Belief in the resurrection proceeded so logically from the development of Jewish ideas that it is needless to examine whether it had any foreign origin. Persia believed in the resurrection before the Jews did; § and we must confess that the Book of Daniel, in which it appeared for the first time as a Jewish doctrine, is full

* העולם הבא.

† See vol. iii. p. 421; Ecclesiasticus vii. 18, 19.

‡ 2 Maccabees vii. 14. *In resurrectione justorum.* See *Orig. du Christ.*, v. 276, and i. 280.

§ J. Darmesteter, *Ormazd et Ahriman*, p. 306; cf. Theopompus, ap. Diog. Laerti, proœm. 8.

of traces of Persian influence. But men do not borrow what they need for their salvation. The martyr was the creator of a belief in another life. The Seer of Patmos never dreams of his reign of a thousand years but for the martyrs; Daniel feels the need of a resurrection only for the martyrs. The date of this belief among the Jews is therefore fixed. Jesus, the son of Sirach, who wrote but a few years before the crisis invited by Antiochus, had no idea of it.* But the author of Daniel, who wrote during the time of anguish, has said, —

ורבים מישני אדמת-עפר יקיצו אלה לחיי עולם
ואלה לחרפות לדראון עולם

"*Many of those who sleep in the dust of the earth shall awake, some to everlasting life, and some for shame and everlasting contempt.*" †

This at least is clear. Israel has reached the last outcome of its centuries-old struggle, — the KINGDOM OF GOD, a synonym of the future life, and the RESURRECTION. Having no idea of a soul surviving separated from its body, Israel could reach the dogma of another life only by supposing man to return to life complete, body and soul. The souls of the just ‡ require the bodies of the just. The unity of man was thus better respected than it has been often

---

* It is needless to add that there is no trace of the doctrine before this. The testimony of Job rests on an alteration of the text.

† Daniel xii. 2.

‡ 2 Maccabees vii. 9, 11, 14, 23, 29, 36; xii. 43, &c.; xiv. 46. *Song of the Three Children*, Dan. iii. 86. πνεύματα καὶ ψυχαὶ δικαίων. (Cf. Matthew xxvii. 52.) This song was, in my opinion, part of the original Book of Daniel.

since, in many so-called spiritualistic schools. But where do these souls go to enjoy their reward? Into a metaphysical paradise, which monotony and weariness would render almost as unbearable as hell itself? No, they remain alive to reign with the saints, to share in that triumph of righteousness which they have brought to pass, to make part of the everlasting kingdom in the bosom of a regenerated humanity.

This is the idea which has converted the world. Belief in a future life was founded by the nation which of all others had the least belief in the immortality of the individual, and which held out longest against luring men to morality by forged tickets of admission to a life which has no reality.*

We must not regard the advent of these ideas as the proclamation of a dogma made on infallible authority. For a long time yet, or rather, we might say, always, Israelites will remain faithful to the old school, or will consider belief in immortality as a pious notion, which men may either accept or reject. The Sadducees in this respect held to the old tradition. Israel could continue its wondrous work of making perfectly good men without any reference to immortality. There would always be Jews who would think themselves rewarded by wealth, ease, and the pleasures of this life; but logic required to be satisfied. It was not possible that the nation which has shown more disinterested action than any

---

* The same may be said of monogamy, which Judaism so largely contributed to found; and yet Israel has never suppressed polygamy.

other, and done most to spread through all the world the thought of immortality, should remain ignorant of what we consider one of our life's first principles. Riches and length of days, which seemed a sufficient reward to the second Isaiah,* seen in that light must seem something childish.

For let us not deceive ourselves: man is governed by nothing but by his conception of the future. Any nation which *en masse* gives up all faith in what lies beyond the grave will become utterly degraded. An individual may do great things and yet not believe in immortality; but those around him must believe in it, for him and for themselves. In the movement of an army there is personal courage, and there is also the common impulse. Faith in glory and all our pursuings of the ideal are but another form of faith in immortality; they make people do a thousand things, the cost of which will never be repaid them until after death; every noble life is built, in great part, on foundations laid in the life beyond. Now, faith in glory is marred by the short-sighted views of history apt to prevail among us at the present day. Few people act with an eye to eternity. I own I have grave doubts as to an individual immortality; and yet I almost constantly act as if I held in view things beyond my life. I like to think that my work shall live after me; it seems to me that I shall live more then than now. But these feelings are becoming rare. One wants to

* Vol. iii. p. 428.

enjoy one's glory. In his lifetime he tastes it only in the blade; after death, he will not gather it in the sheaf.

I have tried to explain in my book on the "Origins of Christianity"* how the Jewish belief in the resurrection and the Platonic dogma of the immortality of the soul were combined in the second and third centuries after Christ, in a way that left many discrepancies. In reality, in the belief of a Christian, and of one who is called a spiritualist, the Platonic dogma is most prominent; the resurrection of the body is rather an embarrassment, — something postponed, like an idle decoration, till the end of his appointed time. I have tried to show, on several occasions,† how if our ideas *à priori* about justice have any value, Jewish ideas of the resurrection are more likely to be true than Platonic ideas, which are founded on an error, — the assumed separability of body and soul. This is no place to insist upon that point. The Jewish conception has at least its philosophic side: it supposes that man of himself is not immortal; that immortality, if he is to enjoy it, comes not from his own nature, which is essentially mortal, but solely from the grace of God, whose glory it is to be just.‡ It is a miracle which God

---

* *Origines du Christ.*, ii. 97, 98; vii. 505, 506.

† *Vie de Jésus; Dialogues philosophiques; Examen de conscience philosophique.*

‡ Christian theologians have also maintained that immortality is not essential to the nature of man, but is the gift of God by an especial act of grace.

owes it to himself to perform, despite the maxim that "All which begins must end." If the universe, which in millions of centuries will have come to its maturity, should undertake by an act of will to do justice in some such way to the innumerable human creatures who will then have lived, we may imagine the living again of individuals; and, as the sleep of a million centuries is no longer than an hour's sleep, that would seem as if it happened at the very hour of death, — "in a moment, in the twinkling of an eye."

But these dreams are carrying us too far. Let us come back to our heroic Israelites, who submitted to extreme tyranny for a Law whose entire recompense is summed up in a good old age. We shall never know all that sprang to life during those days when Antiochus Epiphanes rehearsed the part of Nero, and by persecuting religion gave it strength and put his seal upon it. All birth is effected in a crisis; that which was latent and potential comes forth only by pressure of the wedge of necessity. The Jewish faith, resting on the immoral doctrine that a man on whom misfortune falls is guilty, is obliged to recede, to speak the word which for centuries it so obstinately refused to utter, — עולם חי, "life eternal." Faith in the Messiah, in the Apocalypse, hitherto retarded in its growth, will henceforward march on with giant strides. It is Christianity, indeed, whose foundation has now been laid. The two leading ideas of Jesus — the kingdom of God and resurrection from the dead — are completely formulated. The martyr-spirit is created. The mother and her seven sons will be known throughout the world, and will be considered exactly like Christian martyrs. The "abomination of desolation" has roused the nation's anger to its height. All honour to enthusiasm! All honour to the martyrs! It is they who free humanity from all her difficulties, who speak boldly when she cannot free herself from doubt, who teach the true meaning of life, — the pursuit of abstract ends, and the true argument for immortality.

CHAPTER XIII.

THE NATIONAL UPRISING.

Such changes are not the work of a day. Many sincere Jews under these dreadful circumstances continued to believe that every one in this life is rewarded for his good actions. To fight for his life, for his home, for his Law, and to obtain glory and eternal remembrance,* seemed motives sufficient to these men. "The righteous shall be in everlasting remembrance": what can be more grand? The nobility of man is that he can be rewarded with words, — his inconsistency is his glory. A doctrine according to which man would naturally do anything mean to avoid death as the worst of evils, and so save the greatest good, — namely, life, — led him instead to heroism and martyrdom. We have seen legions of martyrs accept death for a Law which the plainest facts seemed to convict of falsehood; now we shall see legions of heroes rise, form themselves into armies, hope against hope, and fight with as much

---

* 1 Maccabees ii. 51; iii. 20, 21. In general, the first Book of the Maccabees holds to the old Jewish point of view on Messianism, or the resurrection. Read especially the few words spoken by Judas Maccabeus at the moment of his death.

fanaticism as if they had the Christian's paradise or the houries of Mahomet in plain sight.

The levitical families were, as we have seen, the hearthstone of Jewish fanaticism; without them it is likely that Judaism and the old Hebrew scriptures might have disappeared under the rigours commanded by the Syrians. Among them there were little groups of *hasidim*, or pious men, living together in their poverty, proud of their exact observance of the Law, contemptuous of the rich, the worldly, and those who aped the manners of the Greeks. The greater part of these families quitted Jerusalem when the persecution began, and went to dwell in the towns and villages of Judea. A certain Mattathiah, a priest of the family of Joiarib,* left Jerusalem thus with his five sons, and settled at Modin,† a village near Lydda, at the foot of a mountain.‡ He had also, it would seem, brothers who accompanied him.§ They were all men of energy, whose sedentary life at Jerusalem had not stifled their bodily activity, or even their military spirit. Poverty had here exercised its great privilege of keeping up their moral

---

* It was a mistake to call this family by the name of its most illustrious member (Maccabees). The books of the Maccabees do not contain the word *Asmonean*, which appears in Josephus, in the Mishna, and in the Targums. Josephus considers 'Ασαμωναῖος (השמני‎ה or שמני‎ or אשכני‎) as the great-grandfather of Mattathiah.

† Now *El-Medieh*, or *Harbet el-Medieh*, as M. Victor Guérin found it.

‡ We are not to conclude from 1 Maccabees ii. 70; xiii. 25, that Mattathiah had landed property at Modin. These are mere anticipatory revisions.

§ 1 Maccabees ii. 17, 20.

and physical vigour. While rich men were seduced by alien manners and modes of worship, the poor saved the soul of Israel, and openly proclaimed a principle yet unknown among the Jews, — "We must die for the Law." It was perfectly logical. Was not the old Torah in its living portions a code of the rights of the poor, a guarantee that those rights should be perpetually revived?

One day Mattathiah witnessed a dreadful spectacle. An apostate Israelite came forward to offer sacrifice on the pagan altar which the king's friends had set up. An officer of Antiochus stood at the side of the altar. Mattathiah was seized with terrible wrath. He sprang upon the Israelite, killed him, killed likewise the royal officer, and overthrew the altar. Old examples in sacred history* seemed to authorize this fashion of proceeding, which so boldly placed the interests of religion above all law.

After this deed Mattathiah had only to take to flight. He persuaded all who had zeal for the Law at heart to follow him; his sons, vigorous and high-tempered, formed a firm body-guard. All took refuge in the wild mountains of Judea, formerly the scene of David's adventurous life, and soon to be witness of the preaching of John the Baptist. They took with them their wives, their children, and their flocks and herds; the caves in that region offered them an asylum, and at least they were safe from the odious authority of the Syrians.

* Numbers xxv.

Many other Jews had taken the same resolve, and soon the wilderness of Judea was almost peopled with *hasidim*.* The Syrians attacked them, and were greatly favoured by the ill-advised scruple, which forbade the Jews to defend themselves on the Sabbath-day. Mattathiah, it appears, was dissatisfied with this extreme scrupulosity, and made it a rule that fighting for the Law was not to violate the Sabbath. The fanaticism of these refugees was frightful; what they sought was to kill, not the Syrians, but the renegade Jews. Mattathiah went throughout all Judea, overthrowing altars, slaughtering apostates, and circumcising by force children whose parents had not dared to fulfil the rite. The greater part of those who had shown a yielding temper fled from these madmen, and sought refuge with the Syrians in Akra. Others, through hypocrisy or hesitation, received the insurgents favourably, and when they thought they were the stronger took their part.†

Old Mattathiah, feeling his end draw near (167 B. C.), appointed (it is said) his son Simon, surnamed *Thassi*, to take the lead in counsel, and his son Judas to be military chief. The family remained closely united at a time when fratricidal disputes were the scourge of reigning families. John surnamed *Gaddis*, Eleazar surnamed *Avaran*, and Jona-

---

* 1 Maccabees ii. 42. 'Ασιδαίων is the true reading.

† This is the sense of ונלון עליהם רבים בחלקלקות, Daniel xi. 34. "Many shall cleave to them with flatteries."

than surnamed *Happous*, figured in due season beside their brothers, and helped them in their work; and there was never among them the smallest sign of rivalry.

Much the most celebrated man of the family was Judas, known by the name of *Muqqabaï* (Maccabeus) the meaning of which is probably the "Hammer of God."* He was a genuine man of war, with courage at once daring and cool, devoted to his cause like a fanatic, and apparently void of all personal ambition. We are so little fond of fanatics that such a character rarely enlists our sympathies. On the other hand, great deeds in history absolutely without self-interest are so very rare that it would impoverish our human Pantheon to exclude such men. Judas Maccabeus took no part in politics; he left that share of the work to his brother Simon. He was content to conquer and to die. All honour to Judas! He was a saint. He had all the qualities and all the faults of greatness founded upon faith. Such greatness surpasses in devotion anything attainable by mere reason. But, then, we think of stains that we cannot pardon, — the contempt of others' liberty even in the act of defending liberty itself. Most assuredly, the officers of Antiochus were wholly wrong in forcing these poor Jews to offer sacrifice to their Jupiter. It was Mattathiah's perfect right, it was

---

* The final αιος seems to suppose a final ' —, like יעבר for עבריח, טובי for טוביח. It is a very common practice in the Books of Chronicles. If the surname of Judas had been simply מקבה, the Greek transcription would have been Μακκάβας.

even his duty, to refuse this for himself. But he had no right to kill one who was less of a hero than himself. Every one is judge of his own conscience; he may not impose its dictates upon others.

We hasten to say, however, that under these conditions there would be no religious heroes. Godfrey of Bouillon, Simon de Montfort, or Charles of Anjou required to believe that their enemies were doomed to hell. We are too liberal, too well brought up, to express ourselves with the same conviction. I think that M. de Mun* is at least five-sixths in the wrong. But my philosophy also teaches me that he must be one-sixth right; and if I had one of his partisans before me, my good breeding would oblige me to seek out this sixth, in which I might fully agree with him. It was well that Judas Maccabeus was not so well-bred. He was surely a pillar in the world's history; he saved Judaism, he saved the Bible, which would both have been lost but for him. Even if mankind shall hereafter completely reject faith in Judaism and Christianity as an error, he will not merely be one of those great reactionaries who were purely and simply deceived, — he will have been one of the world's necessary heroes; he will have saved one of the disciplines which have best served the education of mankind.

Desperate men who are ready to sacrifice their lives, resolved to take no account of the laws of possibility, — who look on death, nay, even on de-

---

* The Legitimist leader in France. — Tr.

feat, as an advantage, — are generally scourges to the nations whose cause they defend; but sometimes they are in the right. Judas Maccabeus had no regular force to oppose to the well-disciplined Syrian legions; but yet he dared to measure himself against them.* In a first battle, probably fought near Jerusalem, Apollonius was killed; Judas took his sword, which served him ever after in all his battles. The *hasidim* had scarcely any arms; but the spoils of the vanquished supplied them. Seron, general-in-chief of the Syrians, put a second army in the field: Judas cut it to pieces in the defiles of Beth-horon. His activity never slackened. He went from village to village, gathering up all who had not apostatized. Throwing himself suddenly by night upon the disloyal villages, he would set them on fire, supply himself with provisions, and massacre the apostates. Throughout the land nothing was talked of but his exploits; to some he was an object of terror, to others of joy and hope.†

This lasted about two years. During this time Judas and his companions were becoming trained soldiers. The Syrians had never really struck root in the country. The Temple had fallen into great dilapidation.‡ The renegades founded nothing. The difficulties of the lavish and short-sighted administration of Antiochus became more and more serious.

---

* 1 Maccabees iii. 10–12.
† 2 Maccabees viii. 1, &c.
‡ 1 Maccabees iv. 37, &c.

The revolt in Judea was a fact of public consequence. It was necessary to suppress it.* But the treasury was empty. The taxes in the eastern provinces of the empire — Babylonia, Elymais, and Media — were in arrears, probably because the Parthians had seized these provinces. One piece of bad news succeeded another from the East.† Antiochus resolved upon a great expedition in that quarter. At his departure (166 B. C.) he conferred a sort of vice-royalty for his provinces west of the Euphrates on a certain Lysias, who appears to have been nearly connected with the royal family of Syria.

* 1 Maccabees iii. 27, &c. Tacitus, *Hist.* v. 8.
† Daniel xi. 41.

CHAPTER XIV.

THE BOOK OF DANIEL.

Those who neither took sword in hand for the salvation of Israel, nor took up the life of brigands, endeavoured by preaching and writing to animate the zeal of their co-religionists and to keep up their hopes. One book of this time was of especially important consequence, and won from the first its place in the sacred canon, which might have been thought to be definitively closed.

Among the mythic names of ancient sages who had kept unimpaired their Israelite superiority while passing their lives among the heathen, shone in the first rank the name of Daniel.* No other man had entered so deeply into the purposes of God.† It was this seer, faithful to the Law and pre-eminent for wisdom, that some pious writer now resuscitated to console his afflicted people, — to show them the end they were approaching, and to make the splendours of the future gleam before their eyes.‡

---

* See vol. iii. p. 112.

† *Daniel* = " God's judge," —*judex Dei, qui habet judicia Dei.*

‡ There is no doubt as to the modern authorship of this book. Sirach does not speak of Daniel, in a place in which he would certainly

It was imagined that having been brought when a child out of Judea, in the captivity of Jehoiachin, Daniel was brought up together with three companions in the service of Nebuchadnezzar's court. The four young lads in this realm of iniquity show surprising skill in never violating the Law, in never eating forbidden meats, and never taking part in heathen sacrifices. The Law is a marvellous thing, even if we only consider its rules of health. The little Jews, notwithstanding their abstinence, are found fairer and fatter than the children educated with them. Thrown into a furnace because they would not join in an act of idolatry, the fire does not harm them; they walk in the midst of the flames, and in this situation compose prayers and hymns.* The wisdom of young Daniel is prodigious. He alone can interpret the strange dream of Nebuchadnezzar; and he is placed at the head of the diviners of Babylon. Again, under Darius the Mede, who is one day taken by the fancy to compel the religious unity of his empire (the same thing that was attempted by Antiochus), Daniel is flung into a den of lions, where no harm happens to him; and Darius makes an edict that in all his

---

have spoken of him had he known (Ecclesiasticus xlix.). Persian and Greek words in the book are numerous,—כשדי ("Chaldean"), taken in the sense of "magician," &c.

* The prayer of Azarias has only come down to us in Greek, but it did exist in the Hebrew from which it has been taken. Notice the evident rent in the narrative: chap. iii., verses 24, 25, allude to verses 22-26 in the Greek. Concerning the "Song of the Three Holy Children," cf. p. 283, note ‡.

dominions men should "tremble and fear before the God of Daniel."

For those who are not familiar with historical criticism the author of the Book of Daniel presents an inexplicable psychological phenomenon. His ignorance of the history of the later centuries seems inconceivable, if we do not realise how completely the Jews were wanting in annals for these four hundred years. People seem to fancy that all centuries have possessed historical handbooks and dictionaries, and they do not understand the guess-work of a writer who is speaking of the past, when he has nothing of the kind to assist him. As for Nebuchadnezzar, the author of "Daniel" is supported by ancient Hebrew documents; but he has no idea whatever concerning the end of the Assyrian empire, or of the Persian epoch. And, in truth, he does not care; he only wants pretexts for allusions. Chronology is as unimportant to him as it is to a preacher who tells little stories to brighten up his catechising, and to edify his hearers. After Nebuchadnezzar comes a certain Belshazzar, a personage purely fictitious, who takes a fancy to give a feast, using the sacred vessels from the Temple at Jerusalem (this also is one of the misdeeds of Antiochus). Mysterious Chaldean words appear written on the wall;[*] and in fact that very night he is slain, and Darius the Mede,[†] the son of Xerxes, (!) takes his place.

---

[*] מנה תקל ופרסין. These are the words seen on the balances. See Clermont-Ganneau. *Rec. d'Archéol. orientale*, t. i. pp. 139, 159.

[†] It is really Darius son of Hystaspes, whom the author considers

The successor of Darius is said to be Cyrus the Persian. The author knows only four kings of Persia,* — Cyrus, Darius son of Hystaspes, Xerxes, and Darius Codomanus. He really knows in detail only the history of the fifty years before he wrote, after the death of Antiochus the Great; † all the rest is but the fancy of a Jewish *hagada* pushed to an extreme, with no regard to probability or even possibility. Nebuchadnezzar, because of his pride, is changed into a beast for seven years; then, having given glory to God, he regains his reason and his dominions, which during these seven years have patiently awaited his recovery! The intellectual culture of those to whom such a book was addressed must have been wretched.

Strange as it may seem, this author was the historian who was the master of Bossuet, and Bossuet was once our master in history. Adopted by Bossuet into his "Histoire Universelle," the philosophy of history in the book of Daniel has come down to our own day, at least in France, as the basis of the philosophy of history officially taught. This surely is an excess of university classicism. In one very real sense, however, the Book of Daniel was the first attempt at a philosophy of history. The idea of a plan in history demands, as we think, many explanations. It is nevertheless true. For the will of

---

the founder of the Medo-Persian empire. The Greeks also called the wars of Darius *Median wars* (Cf. 2 Stephanus, *Thesaurus:* Μηδικός). [Darius is called "Son of Ahasuerus" (Xerxes), chap. ix. 1.]

* Chap. vii. 6; xi. 2. † Chap. xi. xii.

God and "the decree of the Watchers"* we substitute the universal force, the hidden source of life and progress, that is at the bottom of all evolution. As Bossuet says truly: "All is surprising if we look only at the special causes; yet all goes on according to a regular plan." †

History therefore is a process which we must explain as a living whole. The half-crazy Jew who has told us his dreams on this matter was far inferior to the Greeks in the quality and culture of his mind; but religious emotion suggests to him what the Greeks almost never had,‡ — namely, a fellow-feeling for humanity. To him the development of humanity is a drama conducted by the Eternal to a certain end. The final goal of humanity is what he sees; and in this he probably sees the truth.

The historic theory of Daniel starts from the dream of Nebuchadnezzar. The king has dreamed of a colossal statue, whose head was of gold, the arms and breast of silver, the belly and the thighs of brass, the legs of iron, the feet part iron and part clay. A stone thrown by no man's hand strikes it, and it is crushed. The stone that has struck the image becomes a mountain, which fills the whole earth. The four metals are four empires, — the Assyrian, the Medo-Persian, the empire of Alexander, and the empire of the Seleucidæ as it was under

---

* Daniel iv. 17.
† Bossuet, *Discours sur l'Histoire universelle*. iii. 8.
‡ Except Polybius, the contemporary of our Jew.

Antiochus.* The stone, the supernatural instrument to destroy the empire of Antiochus, is the little Jewish revolt which is destined to change the face of the world. There will no longer be an empire great like those four; for the kingdom of the Jews shall be everlasting, and shall never be replaced by any other.

A succession of visions † makes the author's idea clearer still. The four empires of the dream are here represented, first, as four beasts, who come forth out of the sea, — a lion, with wings like an eagle; a bear; a panther; and a terrible beast having teeth of iron and ten horns,‡ in the midst of which rises a little horn, which speaks blasphemy (Antiochus), tries to change religion, makes war on the saints, and has the advantage until the solemn moment comes when the empire shall be given to them. This mighty act of Providence is making ready. The thrones are prepared; an old man (the Ancient of Days) takes his seat thereon amid floods of light; myriads upon myriads surround him; the judgment is set, and the books are opened. The beast with ten horns is killed; his carcass is cast

---

* The calculation is sometimes made differently, — the Assyrian, Median, Persian, and Greek empires. But he who sees the visions does not distinguish between that of the Medes and that of the Persians (observe viii. 20). He distinguishes, however, between the empire of Alexander and that of the Seleucidæ, though the latter proceeded from Alexander. (xi. 2, &c.)

† Chap. vii., &c.

‡ In the symbolism of Apocalyptic writings, when a horned head signifies an empire, each horn denotes a sovereign.

into the fire. Then appears in heaven a supernatural being like unto a SON OF MAN,* — that is to say, like a man; he is brought before the old man. To him is given an everlasting kingdom, to be shared by all those who serve him; his kingdom is a kingdom without change, a kingdom that shall never pass away; his reign shall endure for ages upon ages.

When will that great day of divine judgment come? On this point the author is designedly enigmatical. His numerical combination, however, appears to signify three years and a half,† a time not long to wait for. Yet a little patience, and the everlasting kingdom will be established.

This empire, not represented like the others under the form of a beast, but by the most noble of forms, that of man, is the Jewish empire, the empire of the saints. It may also, if you like, be called the kingdom of the Messiah, the everlasting representative of the triumph of the Jews. The expression "Son of Man" was soon misunderstood, and became a synonym of the Messiah; so that, it is said, "Son of Man" became the especial title by which Jesus called himself.‡ Paradoxes and equivocal phrases are generally the steps that lead to dogma. To the author of the Book of Daniel, who has only a vague

---

* In the language of that time, especially in Aramean tongues, בן־אדם ("son of man") means simply "a man."

† Chap. vii. Compare Revelation xi. 2; xii. 14; xiii. 5; where the same formula is interpreted as forty-two months.

‡ See the *Vie de Jésus*, pp. 131, &c., 284, &c.

idea of the Messiah, the "Son of Man" represents only the divine kingdom which will be established in Jerusalem when the followers of Judas Maccabeus shall have destroyed the kingdom of the Seleucidæ. Then will the last great kingdom be established, and there will justice reign.

In another vision* a ram represents the Persian empire. A he-goat comes out of the West, without touching the earth; he kills the ram, and tramples on him. The he-goat is Alexander, whose empire is divided into four kingdoms. From one of these four kingdoms proceeds a sovereign mad with pride, who desires to make war on God, overthrows his sanctuary, massacres his saints, and suspends the daily sacrifice. How long will this horrible time last, — this reign of the abomination of desolation?† The duration of the scandal is fixed at two thousand three hundred evenings and mornings (the *tamid* was celebrated evening and morning), which makes one thousand one hundred and fifty days, a result (according to the approximative arithmetic used by the author) about the same with the previous three and a half years. To about the same time amounts a calculation by a week of years, where‡ the interval between the close of the high-priesthood (the death of Onias),§ the cessation of the *tamid*, the installation of the idol (the abomination of desolation), and the end of these

---

* Chap. viii.
† See above p. 272.
‡ Chap. ix.
§ Daniel ix. 26. Instead of אֵין לוֹ, read אֵיב בך.

abominations is reckoned at half a week of years, — that is to say, three years and a half, the "week" being seven years.

The last vision * is very strange. It is history told in dark words of the East, from the close of the Persian empire to the time of writing. All that concerns Antiochus Epiphanes † is told at length. This sovereign is spoken of as the worst of men, — ignoble, perfidious, unmoved by any feeling but that of pride, faithless even to the gods of his fathers, for whom he wishes to substitute, out of flattery to the Romans, a strange god, the Capitoline Jupiter.‡ The Jewish fanatic exults over his defeats, and the insults put upon him by the Romans.§ The monster is destroyed. Bad news reaches him from all sides. He sets out furiously. He goes to meet his end. No one will help him.‖

All at once, in fact, the horizon of the scene contracts. The author passes from things that have happened to conjectures as to things that are to come : —

And in that time shall Michael ¶ stand up, the great Prince [archangel] which standeth for the children of thy people ; and there shall be a time of trouble, such as never was since there was a nation ; and at that time thy people

---

* Chaps. x. xi. xii.

† From xi. 21.

‡ Dan. xi. 38, 39, — a very obscure passage.

§ xi. 20.

‖ Chap. xi. 14 and 45. At times it would seem as if the author knew of the death of Antiochus in the East.

¶ The great revealer is here supposed to speak.

shall be delivered, every one that shall be found written in the book.* And many of them that sleep in the dust of the earth shall awake, some to everlasting life, and some to shame and everlasting contempt. And they that be wise shall shine as the brightness of the firmament; and they that turn many to righteousness, as the stars for ever and ever.

But thou, O Daniel, hide the words, and seal the book even unto the time of the end. Many shall run to and fro, [read?]† and knowledge shall be increased.

In a last epilogue,‡ the time of the accomplishment of the prophecy is again fixed, — first, at three years and a half; secondly, at one thousand two hundred and ninety days, which is about the same thing.

Such is this extraordinary book, — a strange mixture of the sublime and the commonplace, the outcome of intellectual abasement and of the most profound moral movement that the world has ever seen. It puts those rhetoricians who at a glance set a well-written phrase above an ill-written one, completely at fault.

The Book of Daniel is the best example we have of the alternation there is in the history of man between intellect and morality. Compared with Isaiah, the Book of Daniel shows complete literary falling off. Its language is detestable, — flat, prolix, incorrect, and sometimes untranslatable; and yet Jewish thought has made in these few ill-written pages mar-

---

* Cf. Isaiah iv. 3, — all those whom God has predestined not to be killed.

† *Beaucoup le liront et l'intelligence s'augmentera* (in the French).

‡ Chap. xii. 5-13.

vellous progress: it has passed beyond its first stage, which is simply monotheistic, to its Messianic stage, in which it has charmed all mankind by the offer of infinite hope. All things are born out of corruption. The decay of one thing is the beginning of another. The literary weakness of a work is no reason why it may not have a foremost part to play in the history of mankind. The Christian Scriptures, so very poor in the eyes of those who take for their highest type of excellence the writers of some great literary period, are profound and touching when one looks on them as writings for the people.

Ezekiel and Zechariah had already substituted for the old prophetic visions, so clear and in a certain sense so classical, a style of vision far more complex. Since the Captivity no prophet had spoken his prophecies in the open air. Reading is not the same thing as hearing. In reading we put up with enigmas that need reflection, with elaborated riddles, in which ideas are forced together without any thought of coherence. In Daniel this fault is carried to an extreme: a horn speaks, and has eyes. There is nothing artistic in the composition of these puzzles, which serve to express the writer's thought. There is everywhere incongruity, the very opposite of the Greek laws of harmony. That sense of the divinity revealed in the human form set forth in Greek sculpture is completely wanting. The fanatical author of these visions has but one thing in view, — to stamp his thought in by rude force; to make a powerful impression on his reader. In this he has succeeded; and no doubt he was a witness of the extraordinary impression produced by his work.

Its success was immediate* and immense. The taste of the time in Grecian countries — in Egypt, for example — and in Eastern lands was for sibylline enigmas on the political events of the day. They fancied these petty riddles; it was a recreation to make out their meaning. Oracles delivered in that manner had great publicity. They circulated promptly; they were even bought and sold.† The strong sectarian temper among the Jews made it easy to circulate these occult writings, which passed clandestinely from hand to hand.

In this way the Book of Daniel spread everywhere. Aramean and Greek translations put it at once within reach of every reader.‡ All those whose views and opinions tended towards Messianic belief made it their constant reading. The orthodox synagogue itself received it among the sacred writings,

* The Book of Daniel was soon quoted: Baruch i. 15-18; *Carm. sibyll.*, iii. 396-400; 1 Maccabees ii. 59, 60; Josephus, *Antiquities*, x. x. xi.; xi. viii. 5.

† Alexander, *Orac. Sibyll.*, ii. 314-323, 562-567.

‡ In its present state the book is a mixture of Hebrew and Chaldean. This has no critical importance; it only arises from an accident coeval with its origin. Some copyist, fancying that Aramean was the language of the old Chaldeans, thought proper (in v. 4 of chap. ii.) to give the discourse of the Chaldeans as he supposed in their original language, which he copied from the Aramean Targum. ארמית was no doubt not in the original text; it is a marginal note, or else a head-line. Then the copyist went on copying from the Targum, and did not return to Hebrew till chap. viii. See p. 2, second note, the same thing in the Book of Ezra.

without, however, including it in the volume of the Prophets. Jesus must have been well-read in this as well as in the Book of Enoch; from these he took his leading ideas and forms of speech, especially the phrase "Son of Man." The early Christians fed upon it, and drew arguments from it in favour of his messiahship.*

With this strange book opens an entire literature which lasted about four hundred years, and served for the expression of Jewish and Christian thought during the period of its torment. What is called the Apocalypse of "John the Divine" is of the same pattern with that so-called of Daniel. It is the same with the apocalypses of Esdras and of Baruch. The essential feature of the class is the pseudonym, or, if you prefer, the quality of apocrypha. Apocalypse, as we have often said, is the prophecy of an age when it was not thought that new prophets could appear. The impassioned man, who had something to say, had in those days but one course to take, — to assume the mantle of some old prophet or sage; to make his contemporaries listen to what from his own mouth would have had no authority. Criticism was so completely wanting that the book was readily accepted; and, as it answered the needs of the time, it made more impression and was more eagerly read than the ancient writings, which are far

---

* Matthew xxiv. 15, 22. The chapter about the weeks of years became one of the bases of Christian Apology, after the appearance of the epistle attributed to Saint Barnabas.

nobler in form but more difficult to understand, and often out of range with interests of the moment.

Compared to the old Biblical books, that of Daniel seems the expression of a new Judaism, much more like the earliest Christian writings than those of the ancient Hebrews. Old Judaism knows nothing of eternal life or of resurrection. The Kingdom of God, Messiahship, and the Last Judgment never take in it a concrete form. Here, all is fitly prepared for a world-wide faith. Eternity plays little part in the ideas of the old Jews; and even in this we must not be misled by the strongest expressions.* In later times writers of apocalyptic visions will put limits to the reign of the Messiah, — a thousand years in the Apocalypse of Saint John, four hundred in that of Esdras. The author of Daniel did not think of this. He stops short at the victory of the saints, and considers the condition of our race reached at that moment as fixed.

From Daniel to the Gospels and Saint Paul the doctrine of the Messiah went on completing itself by several necessary additions. The word "Messiah" is not in Daniel.† The singular expression "Son of Man" ‡ has not yet received its mystic sense. What is exclusively the property of the book is the Man

---

* לְעוֹלָם וָעֶד &c. ["for ever and ever" (Dan. xii. 3), rendered by the Vulgate *in perpetuas æternitates*].

† The word מָשִׁיחַ (ix. 26) does not refer to the Messiah. It alludes to the authority, probably sacerdotal, of Judea. יכרת does not mean "will be slain" (*occidetur*), but "will be suppressed."

‡ See previous pages 303, 304.

clothed in linen,* the great revealing Angel of the last three chapters. This angel resembles the supreme genius among the Elkesaites † of Hermas, or the venerable angel of the Gnostics,—who is not God, but who acts as an intermediary between God and the world, and is always imagined under the human form. Monotheism was growing pliant, and was losing its former rigidity. A sort of polytheism, or mythology composed of angels and divine impersonations, was making its way; supernatural personages, who were not God, were taking shape. Later, they will be called Son, Word, Christ; but centuries were yet to pass before any would dare to make them equal with the Father. The "Ancient of Days" ‡ was long to sit alone upon his throne. The Son would not supplant him till after the complete victory of Jesus.

The Book of Daniel is in truth the egg containing Christianity, the yolk by which it was first nourished. It marks the line between the Old and New Testaments; in it invincible hope becomes resurrection; the ideal of the future is Messiahship; the "Day of the Lord" is eschatology. Here, too, the doctrine of angels has remarkable development. The ancient prophets made very little use of the

---

* Cf. Ezekiel ix. 2.

† Jewish Christians of the second century, of Gnostic tendency.

‡ יָתִיק יוֹמִין. Daniel vii. 9. It is possible that this expression may have in Daniel a sacramental sense; and if so, it should not be translated simply "an aged man." The Book of Enoch takes it in a sacramental sense, through Christian influence.

machinery of angels to bring their visions to pass. Every apocalypse, on the contrary, makes them its chief wheelwork. Daniel is possessed with them; his book is a prelude to the superabundant talk of angels and demons in the Gospels, a displeasing blot upon their pages to every cultivated mind.

Human nature is so made that the different elements composing it are hostile one to the other. When one part rises, another sinks. A very moral people is almost always opposed to science; and, on the other hand, I have grave fears that what we scientists are doing will not conduce much to the moral advancement of the masses. The popular morality demands enormous sacrifices on the part of reason; the advance of reason harms the moral sense of the masses, who are governed by their instincts. The Jewish people were toiling not on an intellectual but a moral task. We must not judge their literature by the rules of good sense and literary taste. Absurdity in details should not blind us to the greatness of the work: that is as if, in the history of the Revolution, we should see nothing but follies, puerilities, and horrors. What is singular is that Daniel's near predictions almost came to pass sooner than he seems to have expected. Before the three years and a half, or the twelve hundred and ninety-two days,* were spent, the Temple was captured by pious men, and the idol — "the abomination of desolation" — was swept away to the dung-heap

---

* Possibly these figures were retouched after the event.

outside the walls of Jerusalem. The author of the Book of Daniel was no doubt in the band of those who made the assault. One likes to think of him as living in the immediate companionship of the Maccabees.

CHAPTER XV.

VICTORIES OF JUDAS MACCABEUS. — THE JEWISH WORSHIP RESTORED.

LYSIAS, having been invested by Antiochus with the duty of suppressing the Jewish revolt, made great preparations, and charged Ptolemy son of Dorymenes, governor of Cœle-Syria, to direct the campaign. Military operations were confided to two generals of distinction, Nicanor and Gorgias.* Victory appeared so certain that the Syrian camp was crowded with slave-merchants come to traffic in the prisoners that were to be taken. Judas massed his forces at Mizpah.† They were no longer bands of fanatics looking only to die for their Law; they were a small army, well organized in regiments and battalions. Their piety was fervent; they made ready for the unequal fight with prayer and fasting.‡

The military manœuvres of Judas § were those of a true captain; they are admired to this day

* 1 Maccabees iii. 38–41; 2 Maccabees viii. 8–11.

† Neby Samouil, about a league northeast of Jerusalem.

‡ Jewish historians probably exaggerate the strength of the Syrian army. When in front of the entire Syrian force Judas Maccabeus is always defeated. See below, end of the chapter.

§ 1 Maccabees iv. 1–25; 2 Maccabees viii. 12, &c.; Josephus, *Antiquities*, xii. vii. 3, 4.

by military men. When he learned that the Syrian army had reached Emmaus,* at the entrance of the narrow passes which lead up to the plateau of Jerusalem, he brought his army close to the enemy on the south. The Jews were terrified at the multitude they were to encounter. Judas sent home those lately married,† and those who had recently acquired landed property, fearing lest they should prove faint-hearted in the fight; then he announced that the next morning at day-break he should attack the enemy.

Nicanor was informed of all this by his spies. He thought he could carry the Jewish camp by a surprise at night. Gorgias was to make the bold attempt. Judas, having heard of it, made his men take food; then ordering them to light large fires, he silently decamped, and gained the mountains,— thus approaching the main body of the Syrian army on the flank.

Gorgias fell upon the Jewish camp, which he found empty. Thinking that the Jews had fled into the mountains, he followed them in hot pursuit. But Judas, who knew the country, had by dawn come in sight of the Syrian camp. His trumpets sounded a charge; his Jews rushed on with fury. Small as were their numbers, the complete surprise

---

* The Emmaus here spoken of = *Amwas* (not the Emmaus of the Gospels) was after A. D. 223 called Nicopolis, in memory of the victory of Judas Maccabeus. (*Chron. pasch.*) Year 223; Saint Jerome, *Onomast.* Julius Africanus.

† The law in Deuteronomy, xx. 7.

of their enemy enabled them, after a fight of a few hours, to gain a complete victory. All was over, and the Syrian camp in flames, when Gorgias, who had scoured the hills without finding a man, came up. His soldiers, filled with terror and discouragement, dispersed. The booty was immense.

The effect of this victory at Emmaus (in the spring of 165 B.C.) might seem to be the recapture of Jerusalem, which the Jewish hero must have had so much at heart. But Judas saw that the war in the country was not yet ended. Lysias indeed was not far off,* and he at once hastened in person to avenge the check given to his generals (autumn of 165).† He was completely routed at Bethsura near Hebron, and returned to Antioch to a revenge which was never to come about.

Nothing now prevented Judas Maccabeus from entering Jerusalem, and purging it of the "abomination of desolation." ‡ The position of Akra was so strong that he did not expect to dislodge the Syrians from it; but the two hills on which Jerusalem was built, being separated by a valley,

---

* 1 Maccabees iv. 29. This is hard to understand if he came from Antioch. Whether we read 'Ιδουμαίαν (Fritzsche) or the old reading 'Ιουδαίαν (cf. Josephus), we cannot conceive why, if there was a long interval between the battle of Emmaus and the arrival of Lysias in Judea, Judas Maccabeus did not sooner take Jerusalem. One cannot, indeed, but have some doubts concerning this battle with Lysias.

† 1 Maccabees iv. 26-35; 2 Maccabees xi. 1-15; Josephus, *Antiquities* xii. vii. 5.

‡ 1 Maccabees iv. 36-50; 2 Maccabees x. 1-8.

were so far independent of each other that the garrison stationed upon one of the heights could not greatly interfere with the religious services going on upon the other. The city walls having been destroyed by order of Antiochus, Judas could without striking a blow penetrate into the Temple court. The renegades fled to the protection of the Syrians in Akra.

The spectacle offered in the Temple court must have been hideous to a Jew. Everything told of uncleanness and desolation; the buildings were dilapidated, and weeds were growing everywhere. Not an hour did they delay to put such horrors out of sight. The soldiers of Judas kept the garrison of Akra in check, to prevent their interfering with what was going on in the other part of the city. The statue of the Olympian Zeus and the pedestal which held it were broken to pieces, and the accursed stones were flung into a loathsome place. As to the ancient altar, which had been once the altar of Iahveh but had been defiled by abominable sacrifices, they laid aside its stones in a certain spot until a prophet should appear, who might decide what should be done with them.* They chose priests unblemished, according to the levitical rule, and left everything in their charge. Things were put back to what they had been three years before. The holy vases, the candlestick, the altar of incense, the table of shewbread, and the hangings were all made new.

---

* 1 Maccabees iv. 43-46. Cf. Mishna, *Middoth*, 1, 6; Derenbourg, *Palest.*, pp. 60, 61.

On the 25th of the month Kislev, in the year 165 B. C., three years exactly to a day since the great profanation,* they offered a solemn morning sacrifice on the new altar. The Temple front was adorned with crowns of gold and with shields. The ceremony was accompanied by chants,† to the music of lyres, harps, and cymbals. The Psalm *Iakoum Elohim*,‡ was brought out, retouched, and completed for the second or third time. The piety of the people was at its height. The feast lasted eight days, and it was ordered by a decree of the community that it should be yearly celebrated in perpetual remembrance of that great day.§ The rite almost corresponded with the Feast of Tabernacles.‖ The Feast of Tabernacles was in commemoration of the wanderings in the Wilderness; the new Feast, they said, would call to mind a time when the true Israel dwelt in mountains and in caverns, leading the life of wild beasts. They brought garlands, branches of trees, and boughs of palms; they sang hymns, and in later times they added lamps, which were carried in procession, and illuminations.¶

---

* 1 Maccabees iv. 52. Cf. *Megillath Taanith*, § 23. Cf. Derenbourg, p. 62.

† Psalm xxx. has for its title שיר חנכת הבית. This means that they sang it at the Feast of *Hanouka*. Cf. *Soferim*, xviii. 2.

‡ Psalm lxviii.

§ It was the feast of *Hanouka*, in Greek ἐγκαίνια. Cf. the two letters placed at the beginning of the Second Book of Maccabees. See *Vie de Jésus*, p. 370.

‖ 2 Maccabees i. 9; x. 6, &c. Cf. John x. 22.

¶ Josephus, *Antiquities*, xii. vii. 7. *Baba Kama*, vi. 6.

The day, in truth, was one of the most remarkable in the history of Israel. A band of levites and of men not bred as soldiers had succeeded in wresting their Temple from a power which, though not the foremost in the world, had a large force at its disposal. The Syrian *dominium* was not driven out of Jerusalem; but Jewish autonomy had been that day established. Rome two hundred and thirty-five years later had better success; yet she too was powerless against the spirit. Rome was something other than Antiochus; and, besides, circumstances were very different. Similar movements of independence were taking place throughout Syria. The bond of the Seleucidæ was growing weaker. Republics and independent dynasties were set up on every side. To the period of Antioch, which dates from the complete establishment of Seleucus Nicanor, succeeds a period of numerous separate cities.[*] What founds dynasties is military power; and military power now shows itself in Judea as elsewhere. There is about to be a Jewish dynasty, drawn not from the House of David (which was now forgotten), but from levitical fanaticism. Jerusalem and Judea will have no new era; but the crisis has brought forth new dogmas, which will soon be the dogmas of the world. A new Israel has sprung from the Maccabean struggle. That poor little district is more than ever to labour for the good of all mankind. Now, more than ever,

[*] *Mission de Phénicie*, pp. 615, 616.

she can say like Rachel at the birth of Naphtali,* "I have wrestled the wrestlings of God."

It will be of far greater interest to study this interior wrestling than to follow the political ups and downs of the little dynasty about to be founded. Eager to hope for something to console its sorrowful destiny, our poor humanity will soon cling to the hopes that came so late to Israel. The people that was latest to attain faith in immortality will give that faith to nations that might seem to have received it from their ancestors. This is far better worth our knowing than the wretched little intrigues that had Jerusalem for their centre. The new dynasty displayed all the faults common to other Oriental dynasties, with all the faults of degenerate Jews. Forgetful of its origin, fanatic without piety, it soon became a mere worldly dynasty. It thwarted the true destiny of the people; it prepared the way for Herod; and strove against Jesus even before his birth. It is not from this that the true glory of Israel will proceed.

* *Naphtoule Elohim niphtalti* (Gen. xxx. 8).

CHAPTER XVI.

PRINCELY RULE OF JUDAS MACCABEUS.

For a year and a half after the recapture of the Temple, Judas Maccabeus was almost the sovereign of Judea.* Akra alone, from the height of its impregnable ramparts, maintained the power of the kings of Syria. The Hellenist Jews, or renegades, led a wretched life there, — almost that of prisoners. Lysias, absorbed by other cares, could not return to the attack. Judas Maccabeus fortified the Temple court. Bethsura, a very important point, he caused also to be fortified, in case any unexpected reverse should force the *hasidim* to evacuate Jerusalem.

One of the great faults of the Jews began now to show itself. Full of a sense of their own superiority, harsh in temper, quarrelsome, brought by their Law to a separateness that seemed disdain, the Jews were held bad neighbours, and indeed were so. They were detested by the populations that lived about them. This has been the case in all ages, too constantly not to have its cause. Every neighbour of the Jews ill treats the Jew: this is a rule with very

---

* 1 Maccabees iv. 60, &c. Josephus, *Antiquities*, xii. vii., &c.

few exceptions. The nations on the frontiers of Palestine had seen with an evil eye the Jewish revolt, and had taken part with the Seleucidæ. The re-establishment of worship in Jerusalem brought on a relapse of active hostility. People were murdered or seized as slaves. Judas Maccabeus held it his duty to avenge his co-religionists, and he did it mercilessly. Idumea especially was cruelly chastised. Then came the turn of the Ammonites, who resisted with an army well commanded by a certain Timotheus. But Judas prevailed. The town of Jazar was taken and sacked;* and Judas after this campaign, which must have roused bitter hatred, returned into Judea.

We can see already, in the early days of this half-autonomy, how impossible was a Jewish State under a Jewish sovereign. A sovereign should be free to act. Now, a Jewish sovereign is too hard-pushed by religious fanaticism; he hears too many complaints. Whenever the Jew finds himself supported, he begins to complain and to denounce. Jerusalem was hardly in the hands of a Jewish chief before complaints came in from every side. They were probably well-founded in part, but no doubt exaggerated. Eastern Christians in our own day are always complaining of massacre, when it is only the following up of local quarrels, in which they are often the first at fault.

* See the instances of Bosora, Maspha, Carnaim, Ephron. 1 Maccabees, v. 28, 38, 44, 57.

Recriminations came especially from Gilead * and from Galilee, where the Jews were numerous, and asserted that the heathen held the knife always at their throats. A great Assembly † took place. Simon, brother of Judas, was sent into Galilee with three thousand men. Judas and Jonathan, with eight thousand, were to act beyond the Jordan. Joseph, son of Zechariah, and Azarias were to protect Judea with the rest of the troops. The campaigns in Gilead and in Galilee were fortunate, — if we may say so of a succession of slaughters and conflagrations.‡

Timotheus, whom we again find measuring himself against Judas, was completely defeated. Simon pushed his arms as far as Acre. The object of these expeditions was not merely to punish the pagans. The apparent aim was to draw in the scattered Jews upon Jerusalem, so as to strengthen Judea, and not leave its too feeble population exposed to the vindictive raids of the enemy.§

Joseph and Azarias, who had been left in charge at Jerusalem, exposed their position to extreme risk. They imprudently made an attack upon a place called Jabne, where Gorgias chanced to be, who

---

* This name was given to all the country beyond Jordan.

† Ἐκκλησία μεγάλη.

‡ Echo in Baruch iv. 32.

§ This appears to have happened in Galilee, from 1 Maccabees v. 23 (the explanation of Josephus xii. viii. 2, is not admissible). It is clear as to Gilead, 1 Maccabees v. 45, &c. Compare 1 Maccabees vi. 53.

slaughtered many of their host, and forced the rest to return to Jerusalem.

Judas had now become a true soldier, a secular chief. He enjoyed his fame among the Gentiles, and liked to receive felicitations at Jerusalem.* He was not willing that priests should go out to battle: it was remarked that when such persons meddled with what did not concern them they got killed immediately.† A true military spirit was forming. A raid that Judas made towards the south was completely successful. Hebron and Maresa, which had for a long time belonged to the Idumeans, were conquered and dismantled. Azotus and towns in its neighbourhood were pillaged, their altars destroyed, and their carved images hammered to pieces.‡ The band returned to Jerusalem with immense booty; but thus far they never dreamed of lasting conquests, nor had they indeed soldiers enough to leave garrisons in conquered towns.

About this time they learned the death of Antiochus, who had long been engaged in his disastrous wars against the Parthians.§ Like his father, he

---

* 1 Maccabees v. 63, 64.

† 1 Maccabees v. 67. A passage composed of two readings, one placed over the other: ἔπεσεν ἱερεὺς ἐν τῷ αὐτὸν ἐξελθεῖν εἰς πόλεμον ἀβουλεύτως; ἔπεσον ἱερεῖς ἐν πολέμῳ βουλόμενοι αὐτοῦ ἀνδραγαθῆναι,— "certain priests desirous to show their valour were slain in battle, for that they went out to fight unadvisedly."

‡ 1 Maccabees v. 65, &c.; Josephus, *Antiquities*, xii. viii. 6.

§ 1 Maccabees vi. 1, &c.; 2 Maccabees i. 10, &c.; Josephus, *Antiquities*, xii. ix. 7; Polybius, xxxi. 11; Porphyry (*Fragm. hist. Græc.*, iv. 711); Appianus, *Syr.* c. 66. The narrative in 2 Maccabees ix. is wholly fabulous.

tried to repair the void in his treasury by seizing the wealth laid up in the great temples of the East. In so doing, his father had met his death; and his own fate was not much better. Obliged to retire from a temple of Artemis, or Anaïtis, in the Elymaïd, he endeavoured to get back to Babylon, when death overtook him at Tabæ in Persia (163 B. C.). His son, nine years old, succeeded him, not under the guardianship of Philip, as his dying father had intended, but under that of Lysias.

Judas, as was natural, made it his chief aim to capture Akra. He furiously attacked the citadel, in which not only the Syrians, but apostate or moderate Jews who dreaded the fanaticism of the *hasidim*, had taken refuge. The besieged, knowing the fate that awaited them, sent pressing appeals for help to Antioch. Many Jews of the Hellenist party, whom the victories of Judas Maccabeus had reduced to silence but not to exile, joined them. Lysias, accompanied by the young king, his ward, made a vigorous effort. At Beth-zechariah, half way between Bethsura and Bethlehem, was fought a terrible battle, where it was clearly seen how incompetent were the bands of Judas Maccabeus to stand against the mass of Syrian forces. The victory of Lysias was complete (163 B. C.), despite the heroism of the Jews. Extraordinary feats of daring are related of them, — among the rest, of Eleazer, brother of Judas Maccabeus, who, seeing an elephant larger than the rest and royally caparisoned, fancied he was bearing the young king. He then resolved upon a glorious death. Creeping under the belly of the enormous beast, he plunged in his sword as far as it would go. The great creature fell, and crushed him.

All that had been gained by the heroic efforts of the sons of Mattathiah and their party was brought to nothing. Judas fled with the remains of the army in the direction of Gophna,* and for several years seems to have remained in hiding.† There was evidently a strong reaction against him; and although he entered into many intrigues, and gained a victory over the Syrians, it is probable that he never again saw Jerusalem after the battle of Beth-zechariah.

The people, however, still hoped and prayed. A people never despairs, because it does not know what it is to doubt. For the people there is no such thing as utter failure, because for them there is no experience. Ten times beaten back, they still say, "It was only a blunder; we must begin again."

* This place is now Jifneh, near Beitin, north of Jerusalem.
† 1 Maccabees, chap. vii., seems to infer so. Josephus says so positively, *B. J.* i. i. 5. He contradicts himself, *Antiquities*, xii. ix. 5, 7.

CHAPTER XVII.

THE HELLENIST REACTION. — LIBERTY OF CONSCIENCE.

PROFITING by their victory at Beth-zechariah, the Syrians stormed the important post of Bethsura, and laid siege to the Temple, and to such parts of the city near it as the Israelites a few years before had surrounded with a wall. No provision had been made to stand a siege; the crowd of Jews brought from Gilead and Galilee fast consumed the food. To make the matter worse, the year 163 B. C. was, it is said, à Sabbatical year,* so that famine was soon felt everywhere.

If Antiochus Epiphanes had been still on the throne, the Temple would no doubt have been taken and destroyed in his rage. But it was beginning to be perceived that his system of policy was deplorable. People charged him with having resolved to force the Jews to change their worship; and those who had provoked this interminable war were severely blamed. Lysias was one of those who professed this opinion, and promptly carried it out. He even advised the king to put to death Menelaus, the high-priest, who

---

* See Schürer, i. 166, note 2.

had given his father such evil counsels.* Ptolemy, the son of Dorymenus (surnamed Macron), who had been always equitable in his conduct towards the Jews, and who thought they had been greatly wronged, gave his advice that this sad quarrel should be peaceably settled.† The Syrian generals saw no reason for pushing matters to extremity for the sake of a small party, which was now only a drag upon them. With the followers of Judas Maccabeus there was no way to come to an understanding; but this party was for the moment scattered, and its chief had lost his military repute at the battle of Bethzechariah. There remained a party of sincere Jews who had never apostatized, or at most had only shown some weakness; these did not share the extreme views of Judas Maccabeus, who sought the complete independence of Judea and the total expulsion of the Syrians. The moderate Jews limited their demands to abandonment of the disastrous policy of Antiochus Epiphanes, and permission for the Jews to live under their own religious laws. As enlightened Syrians held just the same opinion, a good understanding became possible; and while the siege of the *haram* still continued, conferences were held between moderate men on both sides. All this, of course, took place without any reference to Judas Maccabeus.

Another reason also inclined the Syrians to make

---

* Josephus, *Antiquities*, xii. ix. 7.
† 2 Maccabees, x. 12, &c.

easy terms of capitulation. Philip, whom Antiochus Epiphanes on his deathbed had named guardian of his son, was asserting his rights and marching upon Antioch. Lysias was extremely desirous to get back to the north. He urged the necessity of not exasperating a nation whom it would be wise to convert into an ally. The Hellenist Jews, the moderate Jews, and the renegades who ventured out from Akra, all surrounded him, and expressed their satisfaction. Peace was concluded on the basis of religious liberty. The Temple worship should be exactly conformed to the ancient rites; the Jews should be its guardians. They should also be entirely free to observe their Law according to their ancient customs. A truly just man, distinguishing religion from politics, could not desire more. The end for which a five years' war had been carried on was gained; every one was satisfied except the partisans of Judas, who wanted to have all things radically settled, and who may have had an eye to some dynastic settlement or personal advantage.*

The king ordered the fortifications of the Temple court to be destroyed. Only one citadel remained in Jerusalem, and that was Akra. This caused discontent; it was reported that the king, or those who governed for him, had sworn before he entered

---

* Of course, to arrive at the truth in these matters we have to rectify the extreme views taken by the Jewish historians. It is very much as if we had no knowledge of the wars in La Vendée except what we find in Vendean narratives.

the Temple precincts that he would not touch its walls.

The question who should be high-priest was especially difficult to settle. The hateful Menelaus, ready like Gobel* for any abjuration, was still living, and held the official title. He was equally detested by the Jews and by the Syrians; and Lysias said openly that he would have to get rid of him. During the dictatorship of Judas Maccabeus, who had actually performed the service of high-priest in the Temple? It is not easy to know. The son of the devout Onias III. never was high-priest at Jerusalem.† Judas Maccabeus, in spite of what Josephus says, was never himself high-priest. The official title of Menelaus was probably respected, though he was never suffered to exercise its functions. Antiochus V. had him taken to Aleppo, where he was put to death with great cruelty. Antiochus nominated in his place a certain Iakim,‡ who, according to the fashion of those times, called himself Alcimus § (162 B. C.). He was a member of the sacerdotal family,‖ a Philhellenic Jew, a man, it would seem, of moderate views. He did all he could to promote peace at a time when party animosity was at its height.

---

* A constitutional bishop, who was guillotined as an atheist in 1794.
† See below, p. 350.
‡ Eliakim probably, or Jehoiakim.
§ Josephus, *Antiquities*, xii. ix. 7. 2 Maccabees, xiv. 3, &c. According to another account, Alkimus was not nominated till the time of Demetrius I. (1 Maccabees, vii. 9.)
‖ 1 Maccabees vii. 14, in spite of what Josephus says.

What a fanatic most detests is liberty. He would far rather be persecuted than tolerated; what he wants is the right to persecute others. Judas Maccabeus would have nothing to do with the new state of things. He was at a distance from the city, getting all the fanatics together, and re-forming his army. The Syrian government had evidently little hold upon the outlying districts. All it could do was to send expeditions, and strike sudden blows; then it disappeared, and the inhabitants of the country were left to their old ways. The political machinery was getting more and more deranged. Hardly a year after the religious peace had been concluded at Jerusalem, the landing at Tripoli of Demetrius, son of Seleucus Philopator, with a few hundred men, was sufficient to excite a revolution. Lysias and his ward were put to death by their soldiers.

The government of Alcimus under these circumstances was very weak. Both parties, Hellenist and moderate, or patriotic and fanatic, found themselves much as they had been before the war, face to face, each incessantly complaining of the other. There were no horrors that were not told of Alcimus. This infamous high-priest, according to the pietists, had about him only apostates and the ungodly. Alcimus, on his part, accused Judas of an attempt to murder him, and of hunting down the friends of the king like wild beasts. Early in the reign of Demetrius these complaints reached Antioch, and brought about the sending of a grand commissioner, — Bacchides, a man of very high rank, — whom the king charged to inquire into the facts, and support the authority of Alcimus with a body of soldiers. The only decided opposition Bacchides met was from Judas and his partisans. The *hasidim* and the scribes* were ready to enter into an amicable arrangement, and made no objection as to the legality of the high-priesthood of Alcimus. Who was in fault? The Jewish historians naturally charged it to Bacchides. He, they said, made arbitrary arrests of those who came to him with the best intentions, and put to death sixty men at once: even the well was shown which he had filled with their dead bodies. The situation was worse than ever. Bacchides went back into Syria, leaving a few soldiers with Alcimus, who thenceforth passed his time in perpetual quarrels. He was not strong enough to maintain order, and what he did to preserve it increased his unpopularity. His adversaries, however, admit that the means he employed were not those of an illiberal man. He tried to gain the good-will of the people; he spoke to all men with gentleness and affability. The people about him were moderates, whom the pietists called deserters and ungodly. It was said that his adherents made no scruple to kill the partisans of Judas when they could. What is certain (since Josephus says it, to his honour) is that Judas

---

* Γραμματεῖς.

went through the country slaying the partisans of Alcimus.*

It is also certain that Judas grew stronger day by day. He did not stir from the district of Gophna, where he was reorganizing his army. The only choice was between him and the Hellenists, who could not rally the bulk of the nation. It was found that he, after all, was right; that nothing good could ever be obtained from the Syrians; that he alone could bring back order in the land. If a battle had taken place, Alcimus and his soldiers would have been inevitably defeated. Alcimus went to Antioch and explained the state of affairs. Nicanor came with a fresh army. He proved both treacherous and cruel. Judas contrived to escape a snare that the Syrian general had laid for him, defeated him at Capharsalama,† and forced him to fall back on Akra.

Nicanor was not ill-received in Jerusalem. The priests of Alcimus and the chief men, leaving the sacred precincts, came and saluted him respectfully, showing him the sacrifice they were offering for the king, whose subjects they acknowledged themselves to be. Nicanor made no favourable response to these advances. He was rough and threatening, and declared that if Judas did not surrender he would set fire to the Temple. Alcimus and his priests were struck with terror.

* Josephus, *Antiquities*, xii. x. 3.
† Not far from Ramleh.

Nicanor pitched his camp at Beth-horon, where he was joined by another body of Syrians. Judas was encamped at Adasa, not far off, with three thousand men. It was the thirteenth day of the month Adar (nearly corresponding with March) in the year 161, B. C. Nicanor, whose army was probably not strong,* was defeated and killed. The neighbouring country, which was all in favour of Judas, at once rose; peasants intercepted the fugitives and slew them. Nicanor's head and his right hand — that hand with which he had threatened the Temple — were cut off, and hung up by the high-road to Jerusalem. This victory was celebrated by a feast, held yearly thenceforth in Israel under the name of the Day of Nicanor.†

This brilliant victory ought, it would seem, to have restored Jerusalem to Judas.‡ This was not the case. Some weeks later a fresh Syrian army, larger than that of Nicanor, appeared before Jerusalem. It was commanded by Bacchides, and ac-

---

* The numbers of the Syrian armies, as given in the books of the Maccabees, are always exaggerated. After the death of Antiochus Epiphanes, the Senate had made great reductions in the Syrian forces. Polybius, xxxi. 12; Appianus, *Syr.*, c. 46.

† *Megillath Taanith*, § 30 (Derenbourg, p. 63).

‡ It is now that what relates to the treaty of alliance between Judas and the Romans must have taken place. (1 Maccabees viii.; Josephus, *Antiquities*, xii. x. 6.) We think this story, and the treaty that accompanies it, false and apocryphal. What is true is that the dynasty that succeeded Judas Maccabeus always looked for support to the Romans; and this has led the official historian (author of the First Book of Maccabees) to suppose the aforesaid treaty renewed subsequently (1 Maccabees xii. 1–16; xiv. 16, &c., 40; xv. 15, &c.). See p. 354.

companied by Alcimus. Judas was at Eleasa,* with three thousand men. Discouragement fell upon the little troop. It melted away; only eight hundred men remained with Judas. He was advised to retire, and come back with larger forces. But he answered: "God forbid that I should do this thing, and flee away! Retreat before these men? Never! If our time be come, let us die manfully for our brethren, and let us not stain our honour!"† Judas, like a true hero, then tried to reconnoitre the wing commanded by Bacchides, and flung himself upon it with the bravest of his followers. He gained a partial victory over the right wing, but was then crushed by the left (April, 161 B. C.).

It is often said that he fell in the midst of his triumph. This is not true. He was beaten at Eleasa, and his party was suppressed for several years But his cause was to revive. His heroism was that of all founders of dynasties, which avails for their descendants. The dominion of the Seleucidæ in Palestine had in fact come to an end. Jewish fanaticism is ill-favoured in our eyes; but it represented the cause of the human race. Judas was right in opposing Hellenists, moderates, and the men of peace-at-any-price. His great, courageous soul was that of a man of the people, and it

---

* Site uncertain.

† 1 Maccabees ix. 10. These words are quoted, not probably as the actual words of Judas, but as a specimen of how a Jew of the old school still understood, about one hundred years before Christ, the death of a saint.

obeyed profound instincts. He died for the future. A brave man has his own revelation from Heaven. He reads it in the strong beating of his own heart.

The body of Judas was lifted from the field of battle, and buried at Modin beside his father's. Later, there was raised above those graves a splendid monument. "Now after the death of Judas the wicked sprang up like grass upon the mountains of Israel, and the workers of iniquity flourished on every side," says the passionate author of the first Book of the Maccabees, borrowing his expressions from a Psalm.* The country itself (he thinks) took sides with the enemy; there was a great famine in the land; Bacchides made choice of ungodly men to be governors over the country. The anguish was greater than anything that had been seen since the days of the last prophets. This bitterness on the part of the Jewish historian is the best proof of the strong reaction that took place against the fanatics after the death of Judas Maccabeus. The Hellenists and the moderates, those called "the lawless" ($\mathring{α}νομοι$),† made themselves masters all along the line. Bacchides and Alcimus governed with their help, and were very severe on all survivors of the party of Judas. They employed against them all possible means of persecution and mockery. The name of Bacchides was almost as much execrated as

---

* 1 Maccabees ix. 23. Cf. Psalm xcii. 7.

† This is the name the Judaising Christians gave in after days to the disciples of Saint Paul.

that of Antiochus. The fanatics forgot that if they had been in power they might have done even worse. It is always wrong to persecute fanatics; but, in general, things are going right when they are in a state of discontent. To our thinking it is a sign, when fanatics are furious, that the state machinery is working well; for the State and liberty can never succumb while fanatics have their rights respected.

Bacchides wished especially to stop the recurrence of such raids in the open country as Judas had shown himself a master in. He fortified many cities, — Jericho, Emmaus, Beth-horon, Bethel, Bethsura, and Gezer, — which were amply provisioned and garrisoned. The citadel of Akra was enlarged. Here were kept as hostages the children of leading Jews, of whose fidelity some security was needed. For the first time since the revolt, the country was reoccupied in force by the government of Syria.

Alcimus had a very good idea. It was to do materially what Jesus was in after years to do spiritually, — namely, to break down the wall of separation in the Temple which divided Jews from Gentiles. His act was considered dreadful, subversive alike of the Prophets and the Law. This traitor pontiff, because he was tolerant, was struck with palsy just as the work was going on (May, 160.)* It was the punishment divinely inflicted upon his deeds: enemies of the clerical order have

---

* 1 Maccabees ix. 54, &c. There is an error in Josephus, *Antiquities*, xii. x. 6. Compare xx. x. 1.

no right to die without some special heavenly intervention.

Alcimus, at any rate, had no successor;[*] for seven years, at least, the high-priesthood was vacant. Tolerant parties are apt to be timid in matters of religion. The Hellenist Jews, now masters of the situation, were not reluctant to miss their pontiffs, and probably had within reach no one duly qualified for the post. This was a mistake on their part. By this side-door the Asmonean family could make its way to a position which, according to Jewish ideas, was almost equivalent to sovereignty.

The best proof that the Maccabean revolt had deep roots and a response in the hearts of a large part of the nation, was that the band of Judas, far from falling to pieces after the disaster of Eleasa, recovered strength, activity, and decision. With one voice the partisans of Judas chose for their commander his brother Jonathan. He had the boldness and tenacity of Judas, but a fanaticism much more moderate. His plan of conduct was naturally very different. Bacchides was now really master of Judea. An open war against the Syrians was impossible. Jonathan, his brother Simon, and their whole band resolved to take refuge in the Wilderness, where the national movement had grown up eight years before. They fell back towards Tekoa, and encamped near a well called the Well of Asfar. There Jonathan and his comrades led for seven years the life of ban-

---

[*] Josephus, *Antiquities*, xx. x. 1.

dits, very like that led formerly by David on those wild moors. Religion appears with them to have held a secondary place. These saints, these saviours of the Law, became real Bedouin plunderers. They were on good terms with the Nabathæans south of the Dead Sea, and put into their charge their wives, children, and goods. During these seven years they lived by pillage. A complete epic of their adventures was told or sung, similar to those in the old Hebrew books (like ancient Arab tales) of the days of the Judges and the youth of David. Especially famous were their fights with the Beni-Jambri of Medaba.* John, surnamed Gaddis, one of the five sons of Mattathiah, had been carried off and killed by men of that clan while taking the *smala* to the Nabathæans. His brothers avenged him. The Beni-Jambri were just then celebrating an important marriage. The bride was to be brought from Nadabath. Jonathan and his troop, hiding in the hills, watch the marriage procession as it winds in great pomp through the desert, with drums and instruments of music, then fall on the joyous company, and kill all who do not escape to the hills. " Thus," says the chronicler, " was the marriage turned into mourning, and the noise of their melody into lamentation." † After this exploit they go and hide in the jungles of the Jordan. Bacchides, being informed of the whole affair, crosses the river with a strong force.

---

* Clermont-Ganneau, *Journ. As.*, May and June, 1891, p. 540, &c.
† 1 Maccabees ix. 39-41.

It is the Sabbath; but Jonathan has no scruples. "Come on," he cries, "and let us fight for our lives; for the battle is before us and behind us, neither is there place for us to turn aside." * Jonathan perceives Bacchides, and is about to strike him; but Bacchides steps back and avoids the blow. The Jewish band plunge into the Jordan and swim to the other side, whither their foes dare not follow them.

Thus, we see, all is not sad earnest in these struggles, where a gleam of youth shows under the icy surface of theology. The Arab race has a gift for mingling these incidents of drollery with more serious matters. The fanatical gravity of the "true believer" does not shut out the reckless song of the Bedouin or the daring stroke of the bandit. It was really through this dash of soldierly temper in the Asmonean blood that the family kept up the energy which asceticism frets away, which yet is needed to inspire society with that element of strength and hardihood essential to its lasting vigour. The levitical revolt of the Asmoneans seemed likely to produce only ascetics; but it was soldiers whom it really made.

* Verses 45, 46: The popular-ballad character of this adventure is represented by the following stanzas in the French:—

> "La fête, ce jour-là, finit en élégie;
> A la voix de chanteurs
> Succedèrent les pleurs.
>
> "Allons! debout, mes braves!
> Vendez votre âme cher!
> Les choses sont plus graves
> Qu' à la noce d'hier."

We should picture to ourselves the government of the Seleucidæ as we do all Oriental governments, that of Turkey in particular, which really exists only in the towns; it never penetrates into the mountains, never ventures into the desert. The mountain and the desert thus become the mustering-place of all bold spirits,—those who live together a life of entire freedom, holding themselves in reserve for what the future may bring to pass. The country meanwhile lives in peace, knowing its anarchic forces to be diked back, but ready to be drawn upon at need.

This singular period, in which religious fanaticism seemed to have gone to sleep, lasted in Judea eight or ten years. It was a time of peace, when every man reposed under his own vine and fig-tree, and was tranquil. It was really due to the Hellenists and moderates, who did not reject on principle the Syrian domination. We, who think less of abstruse morality than we do of liberty, and who look upon fanaticism as the worst of evils, can think of these years as very happy. There was much less bloodshed; mutual hatred, too, was not so bitter. We like what soothes the nerves of that poor humanity which so often starts and quivers at very slight alarms. The fanaticism of the band that collected round the Asmonean brotherhood greatly fell off. The troop of saints (as we imagine them) about Judas Maccabeus had become a band of adventurers, passing its days marauding in the desert with the

Nabathæans. But that, after all, was better than to be setting their blood aflame for the Torah. Looked at in one way, this brigand life had its uses, nay, its necessity. There was energy in it, and manliness, after the Arab fashion. If La Vendée had succeeded, the soldiers of La Rochejaquelin and Charette would very soon have been engaged together in maintaining law and order. We shall presently see Jonathan employing his band as an instrument of public force, resuming, as captain of an armed police,* the position we have seen him occupy as head of an army pledged to a holy work, and the organizer of fanaticism.

* The same thing may be seen frequently among Arab chiefs; for example, in Akil Aga, at the time of the events in Syria in 1860.

CHAPTER XVIII.

THE ASMONEAN FAMILY: JONATHAN.

DURING this period of peace and prosperity, Bacchides was not always resident at Jerusalem; yet he was the real governor of Judea, and all its affairs passed through his hands. The situation grew daily more distinct. Jonathan and his band took more and more the character of a free company, ready to take service with any who chose to employ it. Religious dissensions were dying out. The government of Syria, renouncing the false notions which had misled Antiochus Epiphanes, became indifferent to the parties in Judea, and leaned first on one, then on the other, according to circumstances. Jonathan had one great advantage: he had a troop in his own service, brave, and it would seem under something like discipline. Attacks upon him had ceased.*
He lived as he pleased, quite quietly, in a part of the country remote from government authority, called the "Wilderness," or else in the marshes of the Jordan,†
which then as now made a jungle unapproachable

---

* Ἐν ἡσυχίᾳ πεποιθότι. 1 Maccabees ix. 68.
† τὰ ἕλη τοῦ ποταμοῦ.

to any regular police. An event, whose details we know very obscurely,* threw daylight on the situation. Jonathan and his comrades had discovered in the Wilderness a ruined stronghold, called "Beth-Basi," which they repaired as best they could, fortified in the manner of the time, and occupied. They were on bad terms with the Arabs of that neighbourhood, the Beni-Phasiron, also with a sheik Odomara,† and his brothers. Certain enemies of Jonathan (possibly these very Arabs) unhappily persuaded Bacchides that it would be easy to capture the Jewish rebels. A first attempt at a surprise turned out so ill that the rebels, having got wind of it, seized fifty men concerned in the plot, and slew them. Bacchides then laid siege to Beth-Basi.‡ Leaving the little fort in charge of his brother Simon, Jonathan went out with a few determined men, attacked Odomara and the Beni-Phasiron in their tents, defeated them, carried off many prisoners, and returned without loss; while Simon assaulted and burnt the siege engines. Joining their forces, the two brothers now attacked Bacchides, and got the better of him; and he, in rage against those who had drawn him into this unlucky venture, caused several of them, it is said, to be put to death.

These stories are told us in a way at once so partial and so incomplete that we have no means of

* 1 Maccabees ix. 68.
† עָרְבִּרָא (See Fritzsche, *Handb.*, 1 Maccabees, p. 144).
‡ The site is uncertain. Josephus substitutes Beth-Hogla.

knowing what was taking place behind the scenes. What we do know is that the affair, beginning with a battle, ended with a reconciliation. Jonathan sent agents to Jerusalem who negotiated the *aman*. Complete amnesty was granted him, with the promise that no inquiry should be made into any act of his life, past or future. All the Jewish prisoners held by Bacchides were set at liberty; and the most curious part of the affair is (though it was quite in accordance with the customs of the East) that the criminal hunted with an armed force passed without any interval to the exercise of officially recognized power. Enlisted thus into the service of the Syrian government, Jonathan established himself at Michmash, about two leagues north of Jerusalem, armed with all the powers of the government.* The first use he made of his authority was to carry out the ideas of an incorrigible theocracy, and to make the ungodly disappear out of Israel.† This probably he effected by a few executions, which terrorized the rest, and made them hasten to leave the country.

It is however certain that, for reasons mostly unknown to us, Bacchides at this time quarrelled with the Hellenists to whom he had hitherto looked for support. In Jonathan's band he found exactly what he needed, — soldiers trained to war through long experience in the Wilderness, — and in their chief a love of order, and a personal record which

---

* Ἤρξατο κρίνειν τὸν λαόν. (1 Maccabees ix. 73.)
† Καὶ ἠφάνισε τοὺς ἀσεβεῖς ἐξ Ἰσραήλ.

insured the pacification of the country. It is a matter of daily occurrence in the East for the ruling powers to form an alliance with some rebel they have taken arms against. Party hatred in these countries quickly yields to the shifting exigencies of policy and interest.

In 152 B.C. the tottering condition of the kingdom of Syria was shown by a new revolution, which added to the strength of those who desired to declare themselves independent. An adventurer named Bala, said to be the son of Antiochus Epiphanes, caused himself to be proclaimed king by the garrison at Acre. Jonathan skilfully profited by the long war that ensued to obtain from both sides an increase of power. Demetrius gave him permission to raise troops, and to take back the hostages that Bacchides had shut up in Akra. Jonathan entered Jerusalem, where the authority of his family had ceased to exist for about ten years, raised troops, and compelled the surrender of the hostages. Terror came with him. All who had opposed his revolt had to flee for their lives. The citadel of Akra and the fortified town of Bethsura alone remained in the hands of the Syrians. Here there was energetic resistance. The apostate deserters to Hellenism, shut up behind those thick walls, trembled for their lives should they fall into the hands of Jonathan.

Bala on his part tried to outbid his rival. He sent Jonathan a letter, in which he called him brother, offered him friendship, asked for his in return, appointed him high-priest, and promised the gift of a robe of purple and a golden crown. On receiving this letter, Jonathan assumed the pontifical dress to officiate at the Feast of Tabernacles, now near at hand, and made haste to raise an army, and order the forging of weapons. The great end was accomplished. What the courage of Judas Maccabeus had failed to bring about was done by dissensions in the kingdom of Syria. Towards the close of the year 152 B. C., Jonathan, under very few restrictions, was sovereign of Judea.*

The dignity of high-priest was, indeed, the very thing that might unite against him all shades of opinion among the Jews, who had grown indifferent to the idea of royalty. The result proved that it was an enormous evil. The Asmonean dynasty was destroyed by its unnatural union of military and priestly power. It was, besides, a formal defiance of the Law, which required that the high-priest should be of the family of Aaron. But at the point where we are now arrived, no other solution was possible. Since the death of Alcimus there had been no highpriest. It is doubtful if Alcimus had been of the house of Zadok; at any rate, no man of that family was high-priest after him : the position fell to the race founded by the heroism of Mattathiah. The son of Onias III. had never been recognized in Judea. This last of the family of Zadok conceived

---

* 1 Maccabees x. 1, &c. ; Josephus, *Antiquities*, xiii. 1, &c. The titles which are given him are those of στρατηγός and μεριδάρχης.

at this time a singular idea (150 B. C.): it was to get permission of the king of Egypt to build a Temple, like that of Jerusalem,* at Leontopolis in the nome of Heliopolis,† — in accordance with a passage in Isaiah,‡ which he interpreted to suit his purposes. This childish project had but little success. Jerusalem could not be dethroned. The little Egyptian counterfeit survived, however, as all religious establishments on a money basis will do, till the first century of our era.

Demetrius made Jonathan still higher offers than Bala; but not long after he was defeated and killed. Jonathan figured in great splendour at Acre, at the marriage of Bala with the daughter of Ptolemy Philometor (in the spring of 150). Thus all the courage of Maccabeus, and of so many Jewish heroes, had served only to give one showy figure the more to an ignoble world. The life led by Bala in Phœnicia was the most shameful ever seen up to that day. Meanwhile rivalries and treasons conflict on every side: men quarrel for the rags and tatters of a world not worth their pains to win. In 148 Demetrius II., son of Demetrius I., proclaimed himself king of Syria, assisted by an army of Cretan mercenaries. Jonathan, faithful to Bala, made on his behalf a successful campaign against Joppa, and gave himself the great pleasure, as a Jew, of de-

---

* Josephus, *Antiquities*, xiii. iii. 1-3; *B. J.*, i. i. 1; vii. x. 2-4; Mishna, *Menahoth*, xiii. 10.

† Concerning the site see Schürer, ii. 545, note.

‡ Chap. xix. 18, &c.

stroying the Temple of Dagon.* He gained for Judea, among all these bargainings, the old Philistine town of Ekron. Profiting by the troubles of the times, he kept to his fixed idea, which was to make Jewish independence slide safe through the clefts in a disjointed world.

The citadel at Jerusalem, still in the hands of the Syrians, was the thorn that pierced his heart. He thought that the existing state of anarchy would justify him in anything, and he undertook to storm the citadel with all the siege enginery of the time.† The apostates, or moderates, who had taken refuge there, saw that they were lost, and forewarned Demetrius. The boldness of Jonathan on this occasion had nearly been his ruin. Demetrius, very angry, hastened to Acre, ordered Jonathan to raise the siege, and sent for him at once into his presence. Jonathan suspended operations ‡ and went, with a large attendance of priests and elders, to face the peril. He brought with him great quantities of gold and silver, besides other superb presents. This gold and these gifts had their full effect. Jonathan gained the good graces of Demetrius, who confirmed him in his pontificate, and granted all he asked, except the evacuation of Akra. Three districts of Samaria — Apherema,§ Lydda, and Ramathaïm —

* Beit-Dedjan, between Joppa and Ramleh (1 Maccabees x. 84).

† 1 Maccabees xi. 20, &c.

‡ 1 Maccabees xi. 23; no doubt we should read ἐκέλευσε [μὴ] περικαθῆσθαι.

§ Probably the Ephraim mentioned in John xi. 54.

were annexed to Judea, and the tribute of those countries was capitalized for three hundred talents. These miserable latter-day Seleucid sovereigns were only kept in power by the aid of mercenaries. They were in continual need of money. It is curious that fifteen years after all kinds of disasters money was already abundant in Jerusalem.

It now appears that Jonathan, though nominally the vassal of the Seleucidæ, had really become (145 B. C.) a national sovereign, an ethnarch, making treaties for his nation, acting in her name, and watching for her aggrandisement. The Syrian monarchy was going from bad to worse. No national sentiment lay hid in that miserable empire, where all turned on subsidising foreign armies, always ready to desert. Up to the time of Demetrius II., claimants of the throne had had to wrap themselves in a Seleucid title, more or less authentic. This was now no longer necessary. A certain Deodotus, surnamed Tryphon, born at Apamea on the Orontes, — a man capable of any crime, — aspired to the sovereignty. He at first gave himself out as a Seleucid, real or pretended. Profiting by discontents among some disbanded soldiers, he raised up as rival to Demetrius II. a young son of Bala (Antiochus VI.). Then ensued a cross-fire of undecipherable intrigues. At this very time Jonathan was renewing his persuasions to Demetrius II. to relieve him of the Syrian garrisons at Akra and Bethsura. Demetrius agreed to all he asked, provided Jonathan would send him the reinforcements he needed. Military life had by this time made such headway among the Jews, that Jonathan sent at once to Antioch three thousand " strong men." These three thousand Jews arrived in the very midst of the disorder. The population of Antioch was on the point of overthrowing Demetrius II. The Jews arrested the revolution. Demetrius was saved for the time. The Jewish soldiers returned to Jerusalem laden with booty. But Demetrius, it seems, abominably broke his word. Far from showing gratitude to those who had saved his throne, he went back on all his promises, and behaved very ill to Jonathan, who accordingly considered himself released from his engagements. He formed an alliance with Antiochus VI., and received from him a confirmation of all his titles and privileges. His brother Simon was made military governor of all the country from the " Ladder of the Tyrians " * to the coast of Egypt.

The great ardour of Jonathan made him indifferent to all personal mortifications: never had he shown more activity than now, when age was stealing upon him. Ascalon, Gaza, and Damascus saw him always victorious. At Cades in Galilee he fell upon a body of soldiers belonging to Demetrius, and came near losing in one hour all he had gained during his laborious life. The adventure, however, was no new thing to him. He got back safe to Jerusalem; but no man in the East was certain in those troubled

* Cape Blanco [Ras el Abiad].

days of having one hour of repose. Again we find him warring in the direction of Hamath and Eleutherus, and afterwards making a raid among the Zabdean* Arabs, after which he went to Damascus to sell the booty he had taken. Simon, during this time, profiting by the general anarchy, captured the stronghold of Bethsura. The Hellenist Jews who harboured there were forced to leave the country. The place was purified and colonized with Jews strict in the Law.† Simon next made an expedition to Ascalon and Joppa, under pretence of taking those places from the soldiers of Demetrius, but in reality to get possession of them. He put Jewish garrisons into both places, and fortified Adida, a place near Modin.

Judea, though still nominally a vassal state, was rapidly becoming of importance. Jonathan might now turn his eyes on the Romans, who were at this time making so much noise in the world; it seems, however, that the relations of the Asmoneans with Rome (relations which gave them but an imperfect knowledge of that people) did not begin until a later period.‡ On all important questions Jonathan consulted his elders.§ He deliberated with

---

* The *Nahr Zebdani*.   † Cf. 1 Maccabees xiv. 7, 33.

‡ 1 Maccabees xii. 1, &c. See p. 334, note. They fancied that there was but one consul at Rome! The correspondence of the Jews with the Spartans (1 Maccabees xii. 6-18; 19-23; 2 Maccabees v. 9; Josephus, *Antiquities*, xii. iv. 10; xiii. v. 8. Steph. Byz., at the word Ἰουδαία) is certainly a fabrication about the time of the First Book of the Maccabees. Cf. 1 Maccabees xiv. 16, &c.

§ Γερουσία ; ἐκκλησία πρεσβυτέρων.

them especially on the construction of strongholds in Judea, on a project of heightening the walls that surrounded Jerusalem, and especially on building a great wall which should separate the city entirely from Akra, and prevent all intercourse between them. Not being able to take Akra, he resolved to isolate it, and to cut off its supplies of provisions. When his people attempted to meddle with the old wall, at least on the side of the ravine, it was found in bad condition, and crumbled down.

We do not know why, but it is certain that there came a time when Tryphon regarded Jonathan as his most dangerous foe. He prepared a trap for him. He invited him to an interview at Bethsan or Scythopolis. Jonathan came with a strong force. By various pretexts Tryphon succeeded in separating him from his army, drew him towards Acre, and promised to give him that city. Jonathan fell into the snare. He entered Acre with a thousand men; these thousand were easily dealt with, and the old chief of Israel fell into a captivity from which he never escaped (143 B. C.).

Thus ended the career of one of the bravest and most skilful warriors of the second century before our era. In Jonathan we see, not the believer or the patriot, but the successful chief of a band of warriors trained after the Arab fashion. By taking sides in every quarrel, by adroitly shifting to the side that was bent on shamelessly sacrificing the interests of the State to private ends, he attained his object, which was (it is true) patriotic, but would never have been effected unless the Syrian monarchy had been rotten at heart. The Jewish State was created by the internal quarrels that beset the State of Syria. But Jonathan fairly earned his title as founder of a dynasty. He exposed his life on all occasions; he had ever a single eye to the good of his party, and when his party had become a nation, the good of his nation, whose glory and success he sought through every kind of venture. His morality was the average morality of his time, which is not saying much. Naturally his loss was deeply felt. His people mourned for him as truly as they had mourned for Judas Maccabeus.

END OF VOL. IV.

Messrs. Roberts Brothers' Publications.

HISTORY OF THE PEOPLE OF ISRAEL.

By ERNEST RENAN,

AUTHOR OF "LIFE OF JESUS."

VOL. I. — TILL THE TIME OF KING DAVID.
VOL. II. — FROM THE REIGN OF DAVID UP TO THE CAPTURE OF SAMARIA.
VOL. III. — FROM THE TIME OF HEZEKIAH TILL THE RETURN FROM BABYLON.

8vo. Cloth. Price, $2.50 per volume.

It may safely be predicted that Renan's latest production will take rank as his most important since the "Life of Jesus." There is the same charming style, the same brilliancy of treatment, the same clear judgment and delicate touches, the deep thoughts and thorough mastery of his subject, which have made Renan one of the most fascinating of modern writers. — *New York Times.*

To all who know anything of M. Renan's "Life of Jesus" it will be no surprise that the same writer has told the "History of the People of Israel till the Time of King David" as it was never told before nor is ever like to be told again. For but once in centuries does a Renan arise, and to any other hand this work were impossible. Throughout it is the perfection of paradox, for, dealing wholly with what we are all taught to lisp at the mother's knee, it is more original than the wildest romance; more heterodox than heterodoxy, it is yet full of large and tender reverence for that supreme religion that brightens all time as it transcends all creeds. — *The Commercial Advertiser.*

Many are the histories of Israel. Among them M. Renan's is absolutely unique, though it has traits in common with the most diverse of them, — methods and results in common with Ewald and Kuenen and Wellhausen and Stade, beauty of style in common with Milman and Stanley. But the beauty of his style is not the beauty of theirs. It is something far more exquisite. More perfect in its delicate grace it could not be. . . . M. Renan is much more than a critic, much more than a historian. He is a creative literary artist. . . . It is hardly necessary to say that, incidental to the principal contention of his book, M. Renan has many just and admirable observations on the Old Testament literature, and on particular events. Moreover, his general reflections, though often cynical, are always bright and keen, and have frequently a serious and penetrative excellence. — *Am. Unitarian Review.*

Sold by all booksellers. Mailed, post-paid, on receipt of price, by the publishers,

ROBERTS BROTHERS, BOSTON.

Messrs. Roberts Brothers' Publications.

THE FUTURE OF SCIENCE.

By ERNEST RENAN.

One Volume. 8vo. 515 pages. Cloth. Price, $2.50.

"It would be difficult to name a man of literary genius comparable in breadth and depth of learning, or fertility and charm of expression, to M. Ernest Renan. Certainly in all France there is none like him. The fact is just as plain as that both in and out of France he has been persistently misunderstood by certain of his readers, and misrepresented by those who have not and will not read him. He has, for instance, been called a man without a religion, and now, as though in answer to this statement, and by way of refuting the commoner charge that levity is the characteristic and habitual frame of mind in which he lives, he has published a volume entitled 'The Future of Science' (Boston: Roberts Brothers), wherein he sums up the new faith which with him has replaced 'shattered Catholicism.' . . .

"It should not be supposed that M. Renan is here seriously attempting to found a new religion, or even to formulate a new system of philosophy. We have read the volume rather as a personal statement of the delights of learning and of productive scholarship, and as such it has a distinct and rare value. Nowhere does it open itself to a profitable criticism that would refuse to challenge the veracity of the author." — *Philadelphia Press.*

"Although Ernest Renan wrote much of this book many years ago (shortly after he left the Catholic Church) it is to-day an epitome of the most advanced modern thought. In a style so exquisitely simple that we think not of the words nor of the writer but only of the thought, he sums up what science has done for us already. We are brought into full view of the idols it has knocked down With clear vision we can look back and see the long road up which the human race has toiled ; our eyes, thanks to science, unclouded by superstition, can study it And how much man's position has altered ! He was not especially created. He was not foreordained to everlasting punishment, nor elected to eternal bliss. And this great change of thought, affecting the foundations of our social, political, and religious being, we owe to science. . . .

"Will science ever clear away the rubbish and show us a broader, fairer land than that which has encouraged the toilers before? Renan's book gives great hope of this. It is written in a tone of courage and cheerfulness that is very inspiring. He admits the danger of the transition period, the relaxation of moral strength with the stimulus removed. ''Chimeras have succeeded in obtaining from the good gorilla an astonishing moral effort ; do away with the chimeras and part of the factitious energy they aroused will disappear.'' But when between the lines of this book we can detect, as we do, a spirit devout, tender, upright, cheerful, and serene, it seems that the future state of pure rationalism which science aims to bring about would not be incompatible with human goodness and happiness." — *Chicago Tribune.*

Sold by all Booksellers. Mailed, postpaid, by the publishers.

ROBERTS BROTHERS, BOSTON.

www.ingramcontent.com/pod-product-compliance
Lightning Source LLC
Chambersburg PA
CBHW020232240426
43672CB00006B/496